120-123

Yale Studies on White-Collar Crime

Defending White-Collar Crime
A Portrait of Attorneys at Work

Kenneth Mann

Yale University Press: New Haven and London

KF 27847
9350
.M28

Published with the assistance of the
Samuel W. Meek Publication Fund.

Copyright © 1985 by Yale University. All rights reserved. This book may not be reproduced, in whole or in part, in any form (beyond that copying permitted by Sections 107 and 108 of the U.S. Copyright Law and except by reviewers for the public press), without written permission from the publishers.

Designed by Sally Harris and set in Times Roman type by Universal Printing Services, Inc. Printed in the United States of America by Vail-Ballou Press, Binghamton, New York.

Library of Congress Cataloging in Publication Data

Mann, Kenneth, 1947–
Defending white-collar crime.
(Yale studies on white-collar crime)
Bibliography: p.
Includes index.
1. White collar crimes—United States. 2. Defense (Criminal procedure)—United States. 3. Attorney and client—United States. I. Title. II. Series.
KF9350.M32 1985 345.73′0268 84-17357
ISBN 0-300-03254-4 (alk. paper) 347.305268

The paper in this book meets the guidelines for permanence and durability of the Committee on Production Guidelines for Book Longevity of the Council on Library Resources.

10 9 8 7 6 5 4 3 2 1

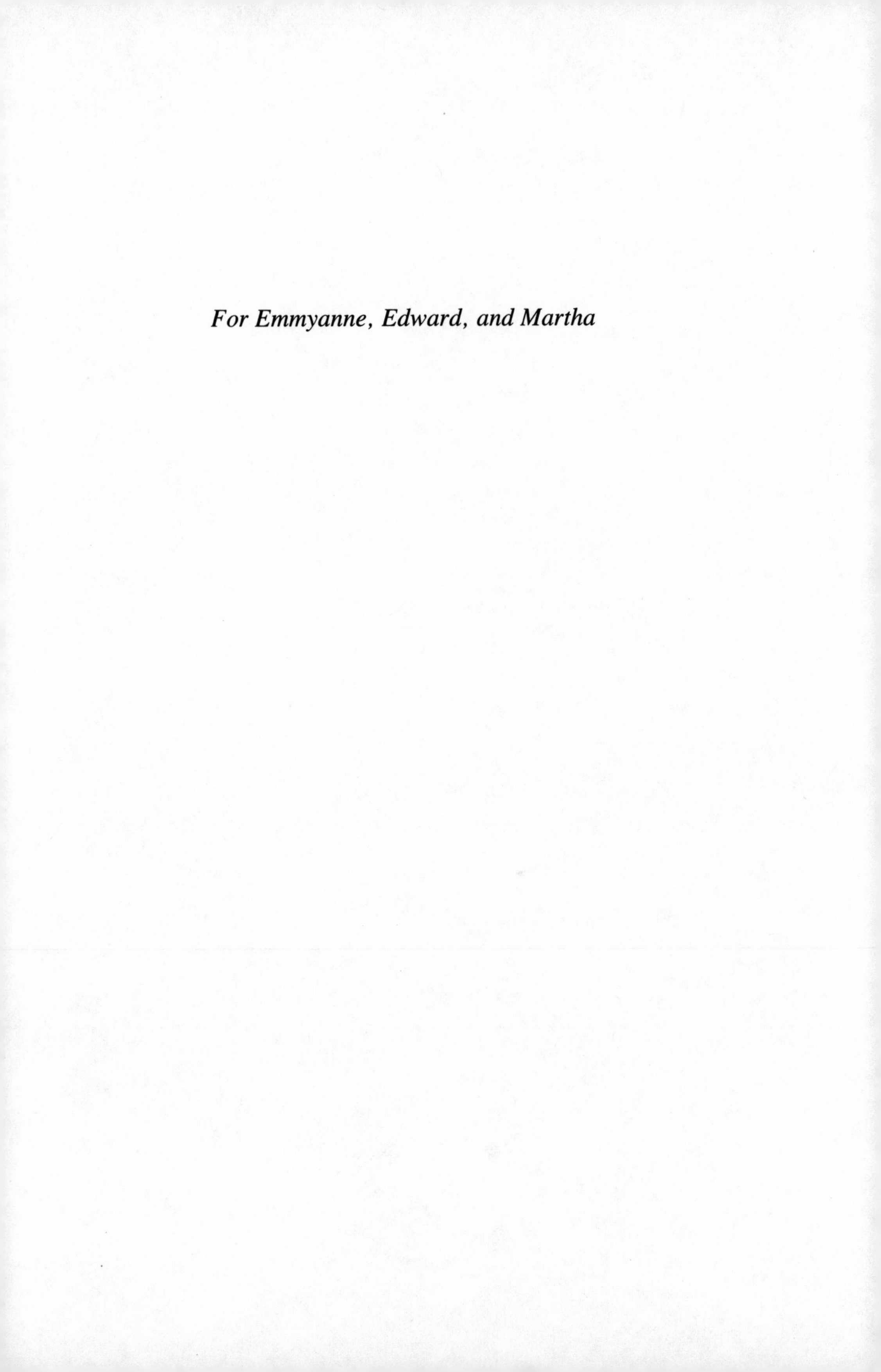

For Emmyanne, Edward, and Martha

Contents

Foreword

Despite the attention heaped upon the legal profession in American society, it is uncommon to find a detailed study of what lawyers actually do. Like other professionals, attorneys have a body of knowledge and craft known to insiders, though seldom shared with the outside world. Occasional highly publicized trials give a glimpse of lawyers at work in that most visible of public settings, the courtroom. But the vast amount of lawyering in our society occurs over telephones and in private offices. Save for occasional self-portraits by prominent attorneys, such behind-the-scenes encounters tend to be zealously protected from public view both by the attorney's promise of confidentiality to the client and by a set of norms that encase lawyers' activities in a shroud of silence.

Kenneth Mann's fascinating study of the white-collar crime defense bar provides a rare extended look inside that private world. Mann describes in rich detail the strategies and tactics of lawyers as they work to keep their clients from being indicted or convicted or, failing that, to negotiate the lowest possible sentence. He provides an ethnographic account of how lawyers use legal rules and argument in behalf of their clients and especially how they work to control the flow of information about their clients' activities. Indeed, the single most impressive achievement of *Defending White-Collar Crime* is its development of the beginnings of a theory of information control that helps explain why some cases are won and others lost.

Unlike common crime defense work, which typically begins only after an arrest has been made, the white-collar crime attorney is intimately involved in the case from the first stages of official investigation, when there may be only the whisper of a suspicion of wrongdoing and rarely a smoking gun. Instead of being on the receiving end of a set of largely pre-established facts, the attorney is in a position to influence and shape the very pool of facts that becomes the focus of legal argument. It is this shaping, through the careful counseling of client and indirectly other parties, that lies at the heart of successful defense work.

It is in the intimate description of the lawyers' meetings with clients and with government agents that we see how central information control is. Mann shows us how the client can be his own worst enemy, sometimes by revealing too much and sometimes by concealing too much from his attorney. And he shows how carefully the attorney works both to find out what facts are known to the prosecution and to keep harmful evidence from being revealed. We also see how valuable the attorney's own ignorance may be to a successful defense and how attorneys structure their meetings with clients so as to learn *only* what they need to know to best defend the client.

By highlighting the lawyer's role in information control, Mann helps us see that some of the most difficult ethical questions in the practice of law are a routine part of defense counsels' world. For if information is the key, crucial questions will concern which facts, under what circumstances, can be concealed, and we see the attorney walking the thin line between legitimate protection of client interests and fabrication or obstruction of justice. In our efforts to protect the lawyer-client relationship, have we made concealment of illegality an all-too-likely outcome? The Mann book provides both raw material and constructive thinking about the possible redefinition of the rules governing lawyers' conduct.

Mann's portrait is in stark contrast to the usual image of routine criminal defense work: a public defender, underpaid, faced with masses of cases, who comes into the case late and with few resources and works on behalf of a poor client. The attorneys Mann studied come largely from elite law schools. Their offices in the Wall Street or mid-Manhattan areas of New York City are like those of the most successful corporate law firms. They have the time and the resources to do high-quality, creative lawyering. Most important, they are in on the case at a time when their lawyering skills can really be used. Prosecutors in such cases are often in a weaker position, for it takes far more prosecutorial time and resources to develop a successful case than in most common crime prosecutions. Questions of equality of representation for differently situated defendants can hardly be avoided after exposure to these realities of legal practice.

That Mann is able to accomplish so much in an arena typically hidden from view is a tribute to his own very special talents as well as to the fruits of his genuinely interdisciplinary training. Mann came to Yale's Ph.D. program in sociology after completing a law degree at Boalt Law School of the University of California, Berkeley, and a master's degree through Berkeley's Center for the Study of Law and Society. His training as a lawyer was essential to his participation in white-collar crime defense work, a role that enabled him to observe the lawyering process up close, as a participant. His social science training led him to develop an interview and observation strategy that assures, in a way experience in one legal office could not, that his account holds for the white-collar crime defense bar as a whole, at least as it is practiced in America's capital of white-collar illegality, New York City. The result of this combination of training and social research methods is a lasting contribution to the enterprise of understanding law, not as a lifeless body of rules, but as an ongoing human process.

I take pride and pleasure in being able to introduce this valuable work as the second in a series of original books reporting fresh scholarship on white-collar crime. The first book in the series was Susan Shapiro's *Wayward Capitalists: Target of the Securities and Exchange Commission* (New Haven, 1984). The books are the product of a major inquiry into white-collar crime conducted over several years at Yale Law School, under support from the National Institute of Justice. Forthcoming books will examine, among other topics, federal judges and the sentencing of white-collar offenders. The entire series is being published by Yale University Press.

Stanton Wheeler
Ford Foundation Professor of Law
and the Social Sciences
Director, Yale Studies on White-Collar Crime
Yale University

Acknowledgments

I want to thank members of the faculty of Yale Law School who provided advice, encouragement, and criticism at each stage in my research and writing. Above all, I am grateful to Stanton Wheeler, project director of Yale Studies on White-Collar Crime, who spent many hours assuring that the right conditions existed for effective pursuit of research, who read and criticized several versions of the manuscript, and who was always available for friendly consultation. I am also greatly indebted to Daniel J. Freed, whose enthusiasm and prodding kept me going when I might otherwise have settled for less, to Abraham S. Goldstein, who introduced me to the white-collar crime project when I was a newcomer at Yale and took special interest in my research throughout, and to Burke Marshall, who gave generously of his time in reading and criticizing research plans, progress reports, and drafts of the manuscript.

I also owe an incalculable debt of gratitude to Boris Kostelanetz, who generously shared with me from his tremendous wealth of experience in the New York Bar, and who has been for me an inspiration throughout. In addition I want to express my appreciation to Jack Katz, whose urging about the potential in a study of defense attorneys and whose ideas about white-collar crime were formative in the development of the book.

The richness of the environment in which I worked is also evidenced by the persons who provided valuable comments. For this I want to thank Nancy Bode, Joseph Goldstein, Rosabeth Moss Kanter, Albert J. Reiss, Jr., William Schwartz, Edward B. Segel, Susan Shapiro, and David Weisburd.

The institutional support I had was of course an essential ingredient. During the initial stages of the research, I was supported by a grant from the National Institute of Mental Health. The main body of the research and first report of findings were done under a grant to Yale Law School from the Law Enforcement Assistance Administration.* And when the initial presentation of findings had to be reworked into a manuscript for publication, I enjoyed support from the Daniel and Florence Guggenheim Program in Criminal Justice at Yale Law School, both individually and through participation in the seminar on white-collar crime sponsored by the program.

At various stages I was aided by conscientious research and administrative as-

*Grant number 78-NI-AX-0017 from the National Institute of Justice, U.S. Department of Justice. Points of view or opinions stated in this document are those of the author and do not necessarily represent the official position or policies of the U.S. Department of Justice.

sistants. The former were Sandra Clark, Joseph Giovaniello, and Kevin McMahon; the latter Betsy Collins and Jill Zarnetske.

One other group of persons was indispensable, but must remain anonymous. These are the attorneys who participated in the field research. I thank them sincerely for the many hours they spent with me and for their tolerance of my sometimes prying questions.

Finally, I want to thank my editors at Yale University Press, Marian Neal Ash and Maura D. Shaw Tantillo, for their invaluable contributions in the publication process.

PART I
Major Themes of White-Collar Crime Defense

1 *Strategic Issues*

Imagine that three years ago you cheated on your income tax. Today you are being subjected to a routine civil audit by the Internal Revenue Service, and you are asking yourself, "How am I going to explain that cash bonus I left off my tax return?" This audit, you learn later, has turned into a criminal investigation. You are like many other persons investigated for white-collar crimes each year: you now need a defense attorney. And you need that attorney to achieve results such as these:

- In October 1980, the U.S. Attorney in a major city (the chief prosecutor in the federal district) closed a fraud investigation of an industrial equipment manufacturer that had falsified records to inflate losses and obtain tax benefits. This large company was also making illegal payments to congressional representatives to obtain influence over pending legislation. After many months of work, the defense attorneys had been successful in convincing the U.S. Attorney that his office could not carry out a successful prosecution of the officers of the company or of the company itself.
- In July 1979, defense attorneys traveled to Dallas, Texas, to meet with IRS criminal investigators investigating one of the largest oil producers in the world. Their objective was to prove that certain questionable tax writeoffs did not constitute a fraud on the U.S. Treasury. They failed to convince the investigators not to send the case to the Department of Justice with a recommendation for prosecution. But later they were successful in meetings with officials in the tax fraud division of the department. The case was closed without public knowledge.
- In the spring of 1978, defense attorneys in another firm accompanied subpoenaed corporate officers to an interview at the Securities and Exchange Commission (SEC). The officers had conducted an international scheme for hiding income in foreign banks. After careful coaching by their defense attorneys, the officers were able to talk their way around the questions asked by the SEC officials. And after opposing and quashing subpoenas for documents, the defense attorneys succeeded in putting an end to the investigation.
- In the same week, the attorneys who appeared before the SEC also handled the case of a used car salesman under investigation for turning back odometers to reduce the mileage of cars sold. No appearance was made by these attorneys before any investigator or court in this matter, but advice they gave to the client was critical to the case being closed at the field investigation stage.

These four investigations are representative of a broad range of cases in the United States that we have come to call white-collar crimes. The cases are prosecuted under such statutes as tax fraud, securities fraud, bribery, false statements, mail fraud, wire fraud, and conspiracy to defraud the United States. In the late sixties and the decade of the seventies these crimes came to be identified as a major social problem. It is now conventional wisdom that they cause the loss of billions of dollars a year to the public, which is victimized by individual swindlers and by corporations and corporate officers carrying out complex schemes of deception.[1]

But the cases exemplified in these paragraphs are not only typical instances of white-collar crime. They are also distinctive because defense attorneys intervened early in the criminal process—while the investigation was taking place—and stopped governmental action before an official criminal charge was made. The attorneys used one or a number of defense strategies that are distinctive to white-collar crime. And they were able to provide clients whom they knew to be guilty with protection from what could have been the most damaging event of their careers and family lives—the public revelation of a criminal accusation through the issuance of an indictment. They represent a special characteristic of the adversarial criminal process: the potential for early action by a defense attorney to prevent the issuance of a formal criminal charge.[2]

At its very foundation, an essential objective of the defense function in the Anglo-American system of criminal justice is to prevent imposition of criminal sanctions against a person accused of crime. But this objective has been masked in recent years by the overwhelming predominance of street crime in the criminal courts.* Defense attorneys handling street crime are usually restricted to helping their clients arrange a plea of guilty, and they bargain over facts already known to the government when they enter the case. Not only does the defense attorney typically assume that his client is guilty, but he usually assumes when he takes the case that the government has sufficient evidence to convict his client. Plea bargaining has become the norm, and, most observers agree, this has led to a system of assembly-line justice where compromise is the rule.[3] Legal rights are

*The term *street crime* will be used throughout to encompass the large mass of cases prosecuted in both misdemeanor and felony courts that have relatively low defense resources and do not fall within any of the many definitions of white-collar crime. These cases include primarily all crimes involving threat and use of physical violence against persons, drug violations, theft involving use of physical force, and other related crimes. Combining all these cases into one category overlooks significant differences in the way the cases are handled in misdemeanor and felony courts. But my assumption, which will be specified in detail in chapter 11, is that the similarity in how those cases are handled is more important than the difference when the comparison group is white-collar crimes, with the possible exception of a select group of felonies and misdemeanors of the street-crime variety that are handled with high resources and have other special characteristics. Throughout the discussion that follows, I have set up a dichotomy between street crime and white-collar crime that is to some extent artificial. I believe, however, that it reflects general differences and that it serves the goal of illuminating important themes in the criminal justice system.

not fully exploited in the interest of protecting the defendant. Norms of efficiency outweigh norms of due process. The defense function is weakened and distorted because attorneys do not have the opportunity to do more than negotiate a compromise.

In this book, I present a picture of a very different system of criminal defense work. It is a picture highlighted by the increasing investigation and prosecution of white-collar crime and by a group of attorneys who have become specialists in white-collar crime defense. It brings to light in a new way fundamental qualities of the defense function: its commitment to helping the guilty go free, its adversarial character, its tendency to operate on the margin of ethical, moral, and legal standards, and its reliance on the manipulation of people and organizations.

The white-collar crime defense attorney, like his counterpart handling street crime, typically assumes that his client is guilty. Certainly that assumption held in every case I describe in this book. But unlike the street-crime defense attorney—and this is a critical difference—the white-collar defense attorney does not assume that the government has the evidence to convict his client. Instead, he starts with the assumption that, though his client is guilty, he may be able to keep the government from knowing this or from concluding that it has a strong enough case to prove it. Though in the end he may have to advise his client to plead guilty and bargain, he often starts his case with the expectation of avoiding compromise.

The white-collar crime defense attorney is zealous in his advocacy of his client's interest, often rejecting government overtures to negotiate and compromise. In contrast to the attorney handling street crime, his time is not a scarce resource, and each case is individually cultivated with great care. In white-collar cases, the defense attorney is usually called in by the client to conduct a defense before the government investigation is completed and in some cases even before it begins. The defense attorney employs his own investigators, who are experts in accounting and finance, as well as a staff of legal researchers. He learns thoroughly the details of the case, usually having a greater ability to do this than the government investigator and prosecutor. This attorney, in distinct contrast to the attorney handling street crime, has a number of opportunities to argue the innocence of his client before the government makes a decision to issue an indictment. A plea agreement may be an important element in the final disposition of the white-collar case, but the compromise that leads to a plea agreement is the result of a carefully managed process of adversary interaction in which cooperation with the government plays little or no part. And in many cases the guilty plea is followed by a second period of intensive advocacy—at the time of sentencing—where compromise and negotiation again remain conspicuously absent. But above all, and this is the central theme of the white-collar crime defense function, the defense attorney works to keep potential evidence out of government reach by controlling access to information.

The Information Control Defense and the Substantive Defense

The defense attorney's adversaries are the government agents who decide whether a criminal charge should be made—government investigators and, eventually, prosecutors. To prevent issuance of an indictment, the attorney must keep these persons from concluding that the client has done something that warrants criminal prosecution. The central strategy question for the attorney is how to accomplish this end, and this applies in all cases, irrespective of whether the attorney's client has in fact committed a crime, or whether it is a white-collar or a street crime.

This question might seem to lead to a straightforward answer. If an attorney does in the white-collar case what is done in the street-crime case, he takes the evidence presented against his client, and other evidence known to him that is exculpatory of the client, and makes the appropriate legal argument. This evidence, so the attorney argues, fails to show adequately, that is, beyond a reasonable doubt, that the client committed a crime. The defense attorney's task is to draw on conventional sources of law—statutory and case law—to show his adversary that the client's behavior falls on the ''not guilty'' side of that line created by the substantive standard of criminal responsibility. This task is conventional legal argument and takes place at all stages of the criminal process. I will call this defense strategy substantive defense.

In making a substantive defense, the defense attorneys studied had a distinctive role because they were handling white-collar cases. Rather than waiting until trial or until the immediate pretrial period when plea negotiations usually take place, these defense attorneys had an opportunity to make a substantive defense before a charge was made. While attorneys in other types of cases also make opportunities for adversary argument before charging, in white-collar cases there is typically a series of institutionalized settings for conducting precharge adversarial proceedings on questions of substantive criminal responsibility. Substantive legal argument before the charge decision is a routinized pattern of defense advocacy in white-collar cases.

The substantive defense is not, however, the initial defense strategy for a competent attorney. The defense attorney's first objective is to prevent the government from obtaining evidence that could be inculpatory of his client and used by the investigator or prosecutor to justify issuance of a formal criminal charge. Instead of preparing legal argument, the defense attorney first devotes himself to keeping evidence out of any prospective adversary forum in which legal argument about the client's criminal responsibility might take place. This action is crucial to prevent issuance of a criminal charge. I call this task information control and the defense strategy built on these actions an information control defense.[4]

Information control entails keeping documents away from and preventing clients and witnesses from talking to government investigators, prosecutors, and judges. It will become evident as I describe defense attorneys handling actual cases of white-collar crime that information control is not the conventional advocacy task of substantive argument in which the defense attorney analyzes a set of facts and argues that a crime is not proved. It occurs before the substantive defense and is in some ways a more important defense. If successful, it keeps the raw material of legal argument out of the hands of the government, it obviates argument about the substantive legal implications of facts about crime, and it keeps the government ignorant of evidence it needs in deciding whether to make a formal charge against a person suspected of committing a crime. And, even if a formal charge is made, it keeps facts about a crime out of the arena of plea negotiations and out of the courtroom if a trial takes place. For these reasons, information control lies at the very heart of the defense function, preventing the imposition of a criminal sanction on an accused person who has committed a crime, as well as on the rare one who has not.

Attorneys act in two different ways to control information. First, they oppose their adversaries in quasi-judicial and court settings. In one situation, the attorney argues to a judge in court or to an investigator in an office that a subpoena for documents is improper because, for instance, it is overburdensome or vague. In another situation, the attorney argues that information already seized by the government should not be admissible evidence because of government misbehavior in making the seizure. The essential feature of these information control arguments is their focus on the behavior of the opposing party, directly by convincing that party not to press the request or indirectly through the sanction of a judge or other decisionmaker. The legal rules used to support these attempts to control information are communicated to the opposing party. For instance, the defense attorney argues that the law of search and seizure prohibits the government from taking the documents. The prosecutor argues that the law permits him to do so. In these contexts, the government has the opportunity to rebut the defense position with its own arguments about what the applicable legal rules require. I will call this adversarial information control.[5]

Second, the defense attorney uses an information control strategy that focuses on the potential source of inculpatory information, rather than on the behavior of the adversary seeking to gain access to the source. The defense attorney's aim is to instruct the client or third party holding inculpatory information how to refrain from disclosing it to the government and, if necessary, to persuade or force him to refrain. The legal justification supporting such information control actions is usually not communicated to the adversary. The setting of this action is typically concealed, behind the attorney-client confidentiality privilege or in private attorney-witness meetings, and concealment is often essential to success of the information control action. When this kind of information control is undertaken, the opposing party has no or little opportunity to rebut it using legal argument. I will call this managerial information control.[6]

When an attorney in a meeting in his office advises a client about to be questioned by a government agent to "avoid answering that question, and if pushed, tell him that you have to examine your books before responding," the target of control is the client and the aim is information control. The attorney has acted on the client and the information in the client's possession, in a setting concealed from the adversary. If the client handles the situation well, he may successfully avoid prosecution or avoid or delay raising of an issue where this result may be important to other defense efforts.* Managerial information control focuses on what the attorney does to manage the disposition of information sources.

Information control as a defense strategy is not exclusive to white-collar cases. In many kinds of criminal cases, defense attorneys move to exclude illegally seized evidence, an adversarial control device, and they engage in pretrial coaching of witnesses, a managerial control device. What is distinctive in white-collar cases is the centrality of information control strategies to defense work: they are fundamental modus operandi constituting a basic defense plan, rather than merely tactics in a broader strategy.

While adversarial information control is well recognized—particularly the law of search and seizure—characteristics of managerial information control are not well identified in the literature on law. In the past decade and earlier, attorneys and scholars raised issues bearing on the propriety of information control in the intensely debated question of whether a defense attorney can put a defendant on the witness stand when he suspects that false testimony will be given. But the broader range of information control strategies that will be examined here has not been brought together and considered as a systematic method of action. In large part, this is a result of the difficulty of obtaining research access to the setting in which managerial information control occurs: the attorney-client relationship.[7] But it is also a result of the fact that managerial information control is in the criminal process distinctive to cases of white-collar crime, and white-collar crime has not drawn until recently a substantial research concern.[8] As I will argue in more detail in the concluding chapter, the opportunities for attorney-assisted information control are more limited in cases of street and violent crime. In cases of white-collar crime, particularly when attorneys are brought into the case early, there are many opportunities for information control, and experienced attorneys have developed special skills for exploiting them.

*Some information control actions may be taken in plain view, for example, when in the middle of an interview with an investigative agent the attorney tells his client to stop talking. Information control will be achieved by affecting the client's behavior, but its effectiveness is diminished because it communicates to the opposition that a sensitive point has been reached. In this situation, the government agent—his interest stimulated—is more likely to be able to force the defense attorney into substantive adversary argument about the legitimacy of nonresponse in the particular context.

Stages of the Criminal Process

Defense attorneys handling white-collar cases rarely try cases. Occasionally a trial occupies an attorney for an extended period of time, but this is regarded as an exceptional event in most of the offices I studied. In this important respect, the work of the white-collar crime specialist is similar to that of the defense attorney handling street crime.[9] But there are many differences between the practices of these two attorneys. These will emerge in looking at the typical, patterned ways that white-collar and street-crime cases go through the criminal process.

Precharge. In the street-crime practice, defense attorneys are brought into cases by clients after a charge has been made. Before the charging decision, there is little or nothing that the defense attorney can do to control information or argue that the facts available do not prove a crime. This period is therefore generally unimportant for bringing defense resources to bear on the question of the guilt of the client for the crime that is likely to be charged. To the extent that defense attorneys do intervene actively before a charging decision, their work is concentrated on arrest, arraignment and bail processes. Some impact on the fundamental question of guilt may be had here, but substantive argument and information control will rarely reach the high intensity achieved by attorneys in white-collar cases.

The white-collar crime defense attorney more often gets into his case at this stage. Clients typically recruit their attorneys before an official charge is made and are sometimes able to do this simultaneously with or even before the beginning of a long investigative period leading up to the consideration of charges by an investigative agency or prosecutor. It is during the period before the government makes its charging decision that white-collar defense attorneys spend by far the largest portion of their work hours. They discuss their cases with their clients, evaluate documents held by clients, interview third parties, take affidavits from third parties, examine documents held by third parties, meet with investigators to argue their case, and return to clients, third parties, and documents to refine their knowledge of the case and their strategy.

The two main defense strategies—information control and substantive legal argument—are already being used at this period and with more intensity than at any subsequent point in the criminal process. The defense attorney is using all available resources at this stage because his primary objective is to prevent the government from discovering the guilt of the client or from coming to the conclusion that it can prove the guilt of the client. In the white-collar crime defense practice, issuance of a criminal charge is already a significant failure for the defense attorney and is for the client often the most severe sanction that can be meted out, even if at the end of the process a short prison term is given by the sentencing judge.

The centrality of this period to white-collar practice is indicated also by the attoney's desire to enter into plea negotiations at this time if he is forced to give up the preferred strategy of demonstrating the client's innocence. Before charging, the defense's bargaining position is stronger: the government has made less of an institutional commitment to the case, the investigation is at an earlier stage, and the defendant can earn credits for early cooperation. The defense attorney who gets in early wants to take advantage of this potentially better bargaining position. Whether and when to enter into plea negotiations (discussed separately below) is the major strategic choice for a defense attorney during the precharge period of the criminal defense in white-collar cases.

Pretrial. The street-crime defense attorney concentrates his work in the pretrial stage of the criminal process, that is, from the time his client has been charged up to the formal disposition made by guilty plea. In the vast majority of cases processed in lower criminal courts in the United States, this stage is short and the services provided by the attorney to the client are minimal, often negligible.[10] The negotiated deal is the almost exclusive method of disposition. Milton Heumann aptly describes this defense process:

> Typically . . . a line forms outside the prosecutor's office the morning before the court is convened. Defense attorneys shuffle into the prosecutor's office and, in a matter of two or three minutes, dispose of the one or more cases "set down" that day. Generally, only a few words have to be exchanged before agreement is reached. The defense attorney mutters something about the defendant, the prosecutor reads the police report, and concurrence on "what to do" generally, but not always, emerges.
>
> [In court] . . . the defense attorney embellishes the defendant's perfunctory plea of guilty with a brief statement about how repentant the defendant is, and/or how trivial an offense this actually was, and/or what a wonderful person the defendant really is. As the defense attorney drones on, the judge joins the prosecutor in directing his attention to matters other than the words being spoken in the court.[11]

This is a description of defense work in a misdemeanor court; in felony jurisdiction courts, the process may be longer and more formal, but the essence of the defense function remains constant. The defense attorney takes the prosecution's evidence, evaluates it, and makes an agreement about what the case is worth.

Thus, the street-crime defense attorney devotes most of his time to his cases during the pretrial period. That period may be longer or shorter or more or less adversarial depending on the resources of the client and the amount of time available to the attorney. But only in a very small number of cases does the attorney decide to argue that his client is innocent, which means going to trial. In presenting an overall analytic picture of the criminal process, Malcolm Feeley assigns most of what is significant that occurs to a defendant in a lower criminal court into what he calls the pretrial period.[12] Chronologically, some of this—

arrest, bail, and arraignment—occurs in what I have called the precharge period, but the processes for determining outcome—plea bargaining, adjudication, and sentencing—occur after charging and without trial. The pretrial period is the most significant phase in the defense and prosecution of street crime, not at all because a trial is planned for, but because this is where the prosecutor and defense attorney apply whatever resources they have in coming to a resolution about outcome.

The pretrial period may also be important for the white-collar defense attorney, but only where there has been some prior defense failure. This occurs when the defendant fails to recruit an attorney before the government charges or when the attorney fails in an attempt to prevent charging and fails to make a plea bargain before the charge is issued. Though it may seem inappropriate, white-collar defense attorneys tend to regard the case that extends past the precharge stage as a failure. This expresses the defense attorney's perception that a large proportion of guilty clients in white-collar cases are not charged, because they work their way out of the system before the government collects sufficient evidence.

Where the white-collar case moves past the precharge stage into pretrial, strong forces push the defense attorney to have his client plead guilty. But this is not due to the defense attorney's heavy caseload or lack of client resources, factors that make plea bargaining attractive in cases of street crime. It results from the perceived low possibility of winning after indictment, particularly when the defense attorney has already argued his main defense with the investigator or prosecutor in the precharge period.

Trial. The third stage of the criminal process presents very similar problems for the white-collar and street-crime defense attorneys. The defense attorney handling the white-collar case may find it easier to meet his client, and the client may be better at grasping legal principles he needs to know to testify, if he so chooses. But these factors are likely to be insignificant in the overall case. Both attorneys face the well-known problem of keeping witnesses willing to testify and keeping themselves apprised of potential changes in the content of witnesses' testimony. And both attorneys face the problem of picking a jury that will not be biased against either the client's class and place in life or the particular crime he is charged with committing.

One distinguishing feature—so some attorneys contend—is that the white-collar case gives the defense attorney more room to create doubt in the jurors' minds, due to the high level of ambiguity in many white-collar statutes, such as fraud statutes, compared to street-crime statutes, such as assault. These attorneys argue that the average juror has a less well-formed idea of what fraud is than of what assault is, and that this difference makes it easier to raise doubt about the prosecution's case.

This observation about statutes appears true, but a major problem in determining how it affects the trial stage is that white-collar cases are more often subjected to intensive adversarial argument prior to trial. It follows that the case that gets to trial is more likely to be a strong case (from the perspective of the prosecution). The weak cases that get to trial are more likely to be the street-crime cases because investigators and prosecutors are tested by defense attorneys less often and less resolutely. Thus, an alternative view of how ambiguity in statutes affects the criminal process would assert that it creates opportunities for legal argument but that in white-collar crime this effect is vitiated by the time a case gets to trial. Then, the defense attorney has fewer opportunities to create doubt.

It is thus difficult to determine whether there is any difference between white-collar and street-crime cases at trial, other than the amount of resources put into the cases by the defendants. What emerges as persuasive is that there are fewer differences between white-collar and street-crime cases at the trial stage than at other stages of the criminal process.

Sentencing. Much of the sentencing process in cases of street crime takes place in the pretrial stage, during and as a result of plea bargaining.[13] The defendant wants to extricate himself from the criminal process as soon as possible, but not at the cost of a prison sentence or other heavy sanction. The defense attorney aims at getting the client out of the system quickly, a goal that coincides with his own need to handle a large number of cases efficiently, while negotiating to obtain the lowest possible sentence. In most lower criminal courts the range of expected sentences for typical street crimes is familiar to defense attorneys and prosecutors. The bargaining process is then focused on reaching agreement about how to present the case to the judge in order to achieve an agreed-upon sentence. Though the judge is probably not bound by this presentation, the sentence decision is usually predictable within a small margin of error. By the time the formal sentencing stage arrives, the defense attorney expects to have a fairly limited role. The attorney makes a routine plea for leniency and routine recitations of the defendant's good and repentant characteristics. As Heumann states, he "drones on" while the judge and prosecutor direct their attention to other matters.

In the white-collar case, the sentencing hearing is the most important stage in the process, after precharge. The plea bargain reached by the defense attorney at an earlier stage will have been constructed, as in the case of street crime, with the intent of reducing the seriousness of the sanction. But in white-collar cases the role of the defense attorney in setting sentence continues to be important after the completion of the plea bargain. Defense attorneys use the sentencing stage as an opportunity to repeat one of the major tasks of earlier stages: substantive legal argument.

Traditional models of the criminal process place legal argument about substantive responsibility in the stages before sentencing. Distinctive to white-collar cases is the persistence of ambiguity about the true nature of the crime committed and the true extent of the defendant's blameworthiness. The persistence of ambiguity, coupled with the high level of client resources in white-collar cases, extends the salience of substantive legal argument beyond the formal determination of guilt into the formal sentencing stage. The interaction of this factor with the absence of adequate decisional guidelines in a discretionary system of judicial sentencing has given defense attorneys a central role in determining type and length of sentence in white-collar cases.

Caseload

The white-collar crime defense practice is also distinguished by the attorney's caseload, a characteristic directly related to the stages at which defense work is concentrated and to the resources the client has for funding the defense. The white-collar specialist handles a small number of cases, investing a large number of hours into most of them. The street-crime defense attorney has a large number of cases but spends a shorter time on each case. Therefore the workloads of white collar practitioners and street-crime practitioners cannot be compared merely by counting the number of cases each attorney has at any given time.

One distinctive factor reduces the workload represented by any particular white-collar case. The attorney handling a case in the investigative period—characteristic of the white-collar practice—works in fits and starts. At the outset, the attorney will make an overall evaluation, a task that often demands a substantial investment of time and concentrated work. But subsequently (because the attorney's work is keyed to the work of government investigators) a case may be in limbo for long periods of time. Investigators often take many weeks to locate witnesses; investigative obstacles typically forestall progress; the government may intermittently give priority to other cases; and internal reviews in the investigative agency may be required over long periods of time. All these events delay government investigation and consequently the defense activities that parallel the investigation. The defense attorney is likely to postpone certain of his activities to see if his client is subpoenaed or interviewed. He may also have to wait to meet with an agent until the agent is willing to discuss the case and wait to see who, other than his client, is interviewed by the government. When the attorney begins handling the case, he will examine the facts of the situation being investigated and he will take initial defense steps, but many months may pass before he knows whether the government is seriously investigating his client and what he is defending his client against. During this period, the case is on his calendar but occupies his attention only intermittently. In contrast, the attorney handling street crime handles mainly cases for which a charge has already been issued. His work, therefore, is generally channeled into a shorter time span, during which few or no significant changes occur in the prosecutor's case.

Plea Bargaining and the Major Strategic Decision

Striking a plea bargain for clients is no less important in cases of white-collar crime than it is in street crime. The statutory charges in a charging instrument, the number of counts alleged, the description of the crime, and the sentencing plea made by the government can all be influenced by a plea bargain. Whether the defense attorney enters into serious negotiations before or after charging, what has occurred before those negotiations may determine the nature of the deal that can be struck with the prosecution. There are important differences in the way that plea negotiations are prepared in cases of white-collar crime and street-crime.

In a street-crime case, the defense attorney has limited opportunities to control the facts that reach the government and determine its readiness to make a deal. The defense attorney will have to find substantive weaknesses in the government's case and play on the government's need to resolve cases quickly and efficiently.[14] In addition to making conventional legal arguments about what the available evidence proves, the defense attorney emphasizes the amount of resources that the government will need to take the case to trial.

Because the white-collar crime defense attorney gets into his case earlier, he prepares for plea bargaining by attempting to limit the government's access to facts inculpatory of his client. The strength of his position at the bargaining table vis-à-vis the government is often the result of steps he takes early in an investigation to protect documents from discovery and to influence the content of witnesses' statements. When negotiations are begun, the defense attorney will already have done a substantial amount of fieldwork.

The decision to start plea negotiations is a critical point in white-collar cases. An attorney who starts negotiations is communicating to the government that the client he represents is guilty of something and that the attorney thinks that the government will be able to prove it. When the attorney is conducting an information control defense aimed at preventing the criminal charge, he will not want to communicate this message to the government. The converse is true. The attorney wants to communicate a message of not guilty as long as there remains some possibility of preventing the government from coming to the conclusion that it has a chargeable case. If the defense attorney forgoes negotiations, he increases the possibility of persuading the government not to indict in the marginal case.

The decision not to enter into negotiations in order to maintain the facade of innocence is a difficult one because there are countervailing reasons to negotiate early. If at the end of an investigation the government is likely to decide that it has a strong enough case to charge, the defense attorney has an advantage if he negotiates early. The government will be more ready to grant concessions before it completes its investigation. At an early point in the investigation the government may falsely assume that necessary evidence is inaccessible. If the attorney gets to the investigator or prosecutor when the going is tough, he will be able to obtain a good plea bargain with substantial advantages for his client. The longer the defense attorney waits to start negotiations, the harder it will be to find flexibility in the government's position.

Not only is the government likely to have a stronger case as the investigation advances, but its readiness to compromise in the interest of efficiency becomes progessively weaker.[15] Investigators and prosecutors often work on cases for many months, during which they develop a substantial personal commitment to seeing the results of their investigation bear fruit. When this happens, there is a tendency to be overcommitted to prosecution, rather than, as in the street-crime case, overcommitted to disposing of cases through a plea bargain. Street-crime defense attorneys depend on backlog pressure to facilitate a deal. White-collar defense attorneys lose this advantage, particularly when they wait too long to negotiate.

Because of the importance of the decision to negotiate, one of the main tasks of the defense attorney at the precharge stage is to evaluate the probability of the government's finding enough evidence to charge. To accomplish this goal, the defense attorney must obtain access to the potential pool of information about his client's crime. First, he wants to know, with certain important exceptions that will be explained later, what might be discovered if the government were to be completely successful in its investigation. "What is the objective seriousness of the crime committed by my client?" asks the attorney. "What penalties might the client be exposed to if the government were to discover all the evidence?" Second, and here there is no exception, the attorney wants to know what information has already been found by the government and what information is likely to be found given its present location.

Essential to defense planning is knowing whether the government will be able to prove a crime against the client and, if so, whether it knows the true extent of the crime. Without this information, the attorney cannot properly determine his own position. The defense claim of innocence or limited culpability must be correlated to what the government knows and is likely to learn during the course of its investigation. The attorney conducts his own defense investigation to learn the facts and evaluate what the government knows.

On completion of the defense investigation, the attorney must make the major strategic decision of the precharge stage and what may turn out to be the most important decision in the entire defense: either to go ahead with the information control strategy—essentially a strategy of noncooperation—or to negotiate with the prosecution. As the defense attorney receives new information about what the government is likely to discover, he will have to reconsider this decision throughout the precharge period.

One example of the importance of the defense investigation for deciding when to start negotiations is the problem presented by crimes involving multiple perpetrators. In such cases, the defense attorney has to be concerned about a co-perpetrator making an agreement with the government to supply information against his client in exchange for a charging concession or immunity from prosecution. The attorney may conclude that if none of the perpetrators cooperates with the government there is a high probability of the government not getting the information it needs to indict his client. Working on that assumption, he will hold out, hoping and expecting that no indictment will be issued, as long as he knows that other perpetrators are not cooperating. If, on the other hand, the attorney concludes that there is a high probability of one of the perpetrators cooperating with the government, he may decide that the best strategy is to have his client cooperate first.

The skill of the attorney in making a plea bargain is first tested by his ability to know when to advise the client to go ahead with a deal—probably destroying the client's professional reputation in the process, even if immunity is obtained. Here again, there is a distinctive element in the white-collar crime defense attorney's preparation for negotiations. This attorney has lead time to influence who cooperates and has more opportunities to test the true strength of the government's legal case. This attorney is continually weighing the advantages in holding out against the advantages in conducting early negotiations. The decision requires that he judge carefully the facts, the law, and what he knows about the customs and policies of the prosecutors and investigator in similar cases. A mistake here can undermine the case completely.

Information Control and Ethical Problems

What I describe in the following chapters is principally what attorneys do to investigate their cases and control information. Other distinctive features of white-collar crime defenses will be described also to present a complete picture of the main tasks of these defense attorneys. But the information control defense will occupy center stage. This means examining, first, procedures of defense investigation and, second, procedures of defense control. These procedures have not been adequately described in previous descriptions of legal work; and they raise ethical questions about the character of the legal profession in the United States.

When an attorney decides that his main defense strategy will be to keep information out of the forum of legal argument, a fundamental ethical question emerges: "How far," he must ask himself, "can I go in my effort to keep facts from being revealed to my opponent?" This problem is a common one for attorneys who handle cases early in an investigation and are presented with opportunities to influence clients, witnesses, and the disposition of documents. The attorney must determine the proper standard of conduct when faced with two goals that may conflict with each other, one compelling him to create maximum control over information, the other to avoid committing an offense himself while attempting to help his client.

The attorney is mandated by the principles of the adversary system to be zealous in pursuing the interest of his client[16] and to resolve doubt in his client's favor.[17] A critical question then is how close to the margin of legitimate action he can go before violating ethical proscriptions. He must decide, for instance, how much he can help clients to understand which documents not to turn over to the government, when the relevant ethical rule states that an attorney shall not "conceal or knowingly fail to disclose that which he is required by law to reveal,"[18] or "knowingly make a false statement of law or fact,"[19] or "counsel or assist his client in conduct that [he] knows to be illegal or fraudulent";[20] and he must decide how far to go in secreting information he receives about a client's ongoing crimes or new crimes committed to cover up past crimes, when the relevant ethical rules state that the attorney shall "not knowingly reveal a confidence or secret of his client,"[21] but that he "*may* reveal the intention of his client to commit a crime and the information necessary to prevent the crime"[22] (emphasis added). He must decide whether he can influence a client to persuade his employees, associates, or other persons to keep silent, when the relevant ethical rule states that an attorney "shall not give advice to a person who is not represented by a lawyer other than the advice to secure counsel, if the interests of such persons are or have a reasonable possibility of being in conflict with the interest of his client."[23]

The defense attorneys studied here demonstrate particular behaviors when faced with these questions. How they act is significant for understanding the nature of criminal defense practice. But many opportunities for information control found in these criminal cases are also found in cases of civil litigation, where attorneys often represent clients whose objective of winning is dependent on concealing information from an adversary. A civil case for damages caused by fraud or misrepresentation brought by a stockholder against corporate executives requires that the attorney ask himself the same question: How far do I go in facilitating compliance with a discovery request made by the plaintiff against my client? How actively do I seek out the real facts and reveal them to my adversary? Or how far can I go in influencing my client not to cooperate or in bringing pressure to bear against witnesses who otherwise might weaken or destroy my case? While certain elementary rules about how the litigation is carried out are different in the civil cases, the ethical and moral dilemmas faced by attorneys handling criminal and civil litigation are fundamentally similar.[24] The advocate must weigh his commitment to the client against his commitment to the court, to the public, and to truth and justice. Providing the best available defense to a client—in a criminal case as well as a civil case—requires an acute sense of how to approach as close as possible to the margin of legitimate action, without going over it. I assess how these issues are resolved in the context of white-collar crime defense practice. But it would not be reaching too far to say that this assessment is applicable to any litigating attorney facing difficult issues of information control.

2 The White-Collar Crime Defense Bar

Growth in White-Collar Crime Prosecutions

Neither the term *white-collar crime* nor the phenomenon it describes
The sociologist Edwin Sutherland first used the term in 1940 in studyin
ties of major corporations.[1] The phenomenon itself drew the attention
rakers at the turn of the century, and the federal government in differen
during the 1930s and 1940s put special emphasis on prosecuting tax eva
entrepreneurs defrauding the public.[2] But it was not until the decade of t
that the law enforcement offices of the federal government made soph
white-collar crimes a top priority in their prosecution policy.[3] And it wa
til then that the public in the United States became keenly aware of the
cial and economic cost of corruption in business and government.[4]

The Watergate scandal in 1972–73 and the prosecutions that followe
marked a new high point in public awareness and concern for the crime
affluent and the powerful. But Watergate is now only a symbol of what h
to be a significantly more enduring concern: the illegalities of individu
businesses that make unwary victims of the public through the use of co
deception, violation of trust, and the power to mislead provided by ev
complicated business organizations. Computers, other high-technology
keeping, and the massive proliferation of documents as a form of entitle
wealth have made white-collar crime a major public problem.

This heightened awareness of the cost to society of white-collar crime
incided with a major new emphasis on white-collar crime prosecutions th
out the nation. Independent federal agencies and local federal prosecutor
began to give white-collar crime priority even before a general policy w
nounced by the Department of Justice.[5] From 1974 to 1981 Stanley Spor
chief of enforcement at the SEC, conducted an aggressive campaign
fraud by corporations and corporate managers. And the IRS during the sa
riod used the tax laws in a broad program of investigations of large corpo
for illegal payments to domestic and foreign authorities. By 1978, the D
ment of Justice had reevaluated its law enforcement programs and el
white-collar crime to the top of its priority list.[6] Though the Reagan admi
tion appears to be moving law enforcement efforts in other directions, as i
ted by the creation in August 1983 of a presidential commission to study
ized crime,[7] white-collar crime continues to be one of the major areas of f
investigation and prosecution. In 1982, crimes classified as fraud and emb

ment by the Administrative Office of the Court comprised between 25 and 30 percent of the total criminal caseload in many federal district court jurisdictions, including New York City, Chicago, Philadelphia, and Los Angeles.[8]

One of the earliest and most concerted efforts at prosecuting white-collar crime occurred in the federal district covering Manhattan, known as the Southern District of New York. The hub of the nation's financial markets and the headquarters of many of the nation's largest corporations, New York City is an obvious jurisdiction for concentrating resources on white-collar crime investigations. Many crimes of nationwide impact are planned in New York, and many others planned and executed in other places have significant impact there. This is the main reason why I made New York City the field site for studying attorneys who defend persons charged with white-collar crimes.

An outgrowth of New York's centrality in the business world and an independent factor in putting that jurisdiction into the very center of the prosecution effort against white-collar crime is the special character of its federal prosecutor's office. The office of the U.S. Attorney for the Southern District of New York has for a long time been the leader in giving white-collar crime high priority in resource allocation. It has also enjoyed the premier reputation among U.S. Attorneys' offices for the competence of its personnel and the quality of its work. Historically, it recruited top students from elite law schools and later became the object of intense job competition among graduates from the same schools. The office of assistant U.S. Attorney in the Southern District of New York carries high prestige; many of its incumbents have come from and returned to the nation's largest corporate law firms.

The prestige is in part built on its reputation for proscecuting white-collar crime. Robert Morgenthau, former U.S. Attorney in the Southern District of New York, is regarded by many New York attorneys as the father of white-collar crime prosecutions. He is credited with building the first U.S. Attorney's office with a capacity for investigation and successful prosecution of complex fraud cases, a policy that was considered to represent a new direction for U.S. Attorneys' offices when he sponsored it in the 1960s. In the 1970s, the high priority given to white-collar crime prosecutions already had become institutionalized in the Southern District of New York. Whitney North Seymour, U.S. Attorney there from 1970 to 1973, wrote in his 1971 Annual Report to the Department of Justice:

> This office has led the nation for many years in its investigation and prosecution of securities frauds and other violations involving the financial market. We have continued this tradition during the past year and have attempted to build upon it. . . . While we have committed major resources to the investigation and prosecution of securities violations and related white-collar crime, we have also given parallel attention to cases involving official corruption.[9]

His successor, Paul J. Curran, also reporting to the Attorney General about prosecution policy in the Southern District, wrote in 1975, "The net of this is that federal law enforcement must be directed toward what may be broadly labelled commercial crime in contradistinction to 'street crime,' which is the responsibility of local enforcement."[10] And Curran's successor, Robert B. Fiske, Jr., in his 1976 Annual Report, reported that the office had "devoted a major portion of its resources to combat business crime," increasing the number of experienced assistants in the business fraud unit in the criminal division.[11]

Growth of the White-Collar Crime Defense Bar

New Career Paths of Former Federal Prosecutors

As federal agencies and federal prosecutor offices increased their investigations into white-collar crime, more persons found themselves in need of legal counsel to help them. Particularly because government investigators focused on corporations, officers in corporations, and major political figures, a larger and more influential pool of clients was created. Reflecting on these changes, Paul R. Conolly, then chairman of the Section on Litigation of the American Bar Association, said in 1977, "White-collar crime is the fastest growing legal specialty in the United States."[12]

Conolly's statement was not based on an empirical study, but it expresses the widespread belief among the bar of the nation that defense work in white-collar crime has taken on significant new dimensions in recent years. Nowhere is this truer than in New York City. The priority given to white-collar crime investigations and prosecutions in the Southern District of New York and the high standard of practice maintained in that office created a cadre of skilled young attorneys who could become defense practitioners after training in handling white-collar cases from the prosecution side. The prosecution policy of the district created not only a pool of clients but also a pool of attorneys who could meet the new demand for legal services in the private sector. The recognized competency of these attorneys has led to a demand for them in jurisdictions outside New York. They travel to major metropolitan areas to represent clients in white-collar investigations and prosecutions, and they appear in these same cities to give courses and lectures on the prosecution and defense of white-collar crime.[13]

This new movement of attorneys into white-collar crime defense practice started in the mid 1960s in New York City, when some graduates from the U.S. Attorney's office went into small law offices where they might have an opportunity to specialize in criminal work or started their own offices where they could specialize in that area. This was a break with tradition. Typically, new recruits to the U.S. Attorney's office in the Southern District of New York served four to five years and then went into private practice in large corporate law firms, where they would do primarily civil litigation. The decision to seek criminal work marked a significant deviation from the normal pattern for these attorneys.

As the demand for white-collar defense work grew, other attorneys also found that they were able to develop practices in this area. Attorneys trained in state district attorneys' offices who previously had expected to limit private criminal practice to street crime now took on clients in the white-collar cases. So did a number of attorneys without prosecutorial experience who had worked with leading litigators and received their basic training on the defense side. But the most identifiable group of new white-collar crime defense attorneys in New York City is comprised of the former federal prosecutors, most of them from the Southern District of New York but some from the Eastern District of New York in Brooklyn. Labeled by some attorneys as the "white-collar crime defense bar of New York City," it has been described as a small group of attorneys in New York who specialize in handling the matters of targets and witnesses in criminal investigations conducted by the Department of Justice, the U.S. Attorneys' offices, the IRS, the SEC, and state special prosecutors' offices.

The increased number of former assistant U.S. Attorneys now in defense practice marks not only an important change in career pattern for these individuals, but an important change in the character of the criminal defense bar. Criminal defense practice was traditionally regarded as a second-class practice. It had a bad public image and a bad image among attorneys in other fields of practice. As one of the attorneys I interviewed describes the situation,

> Criminal law, now going back thirty years, had a very low image. Those who couldn't make it in civil law went to criminal law. The criminal lawyer at that time was the guy who hung around the courthouse. I am eliminating the top dogs because even then there were top dogs. But the basic practice was five and ten dollars or twenty-five dollars, and hanging around the local criminal court.

The image began to change when the public defender systems were set up in the states and by the federal government. It was then that significant numbers of top law graduates began to go into the practice of criminal law. But criminal law still suffered from the fact that the criminal defense attorney typically worked with an unsavory client, for low wages, and in an overcrowded and demoralizing court system.

Now, however, the image of the criminal defense attorney is being upgraded as former assistant U.S. Attorneys move into the practice of criminal law, defending persons accused of white-collar crimes. Although the principal reason for this change is the new demand for legal services created by the high priority given to white-collar crime by law enforcement agencies, there are other reasons, stemming from the differences between white-collar crime and street crime. First, of course, there is a great deal of money to be made. Many of the clients are affluent, and because they are in deep trouble when they approach a defense attorney, high fees can be collected (usually between $150 and $300 per hour). But the new market and high fees are only part of the story. The former assistant U.S. Attorney who chooses a position as a white-collar crime defense attorney is making, in terms of his own career alternatives, a substantial monetary sacrifice. He will never have the consistent high income of a partner in a major Wall Street or midtown firm, and he is unlikely to approach, even in his good years, the income of a senior partner in a major firm. As one of these defense attorneys stated, "I have cases, not clients." By this he meant that his clients bring him one large problem but retain their regular attorneys for treatment of routine personal and business matters. The defense attorney is constantly in the market for new cases and inevitably suffers periodic drops in income.

Another reason for the move by attorneys to white-collar defense practice applies to those going into the small firm and solo practice—an antipathy toward the large organization as a work setting. Many of the attorneys going into defense practice are independent types, shunning the large firms where they would be only another cog in the wheel. In fact, some large firms avoid criminal cases, even for affluent corporate clients, either because of a lack of expertise or through a desire to remain disassociated from clients who are accused of crimes. While a few large firms certainly do white-collar defense work, more do not. It is therefore more difficult to find a comfortable position in a large firm when handling criminal defenses is one's objective.

Even more important in explaining the attraction that a new class of attorneys has for criminal practice—and this applies to attorneys in large and small firms—is the tremendous fascination that many of them have for dealing with the problems of affluent and powerful people on the verge of ruin. Here the attorney enjoys a special prestige and confidence, and he is put in the unique position of moral superiority over individuals who otherwise represent established, if not elitist, values. He is deferred to as an expert who can help the high-and-mighty out of trouble. If defense attorneys possess a high level of social conscience, then these particular defense attorneys are different only in that they help the rich instead of the poor. Additionally, many cases of white-collar crime, as distinct from street crime, present complex problems of legal interpretation, which many attorneys who think of the street-crime practice as removed from the challenge of complex substantive legal problems find attractive.

The Idea of Specialization

In interviewing attorneys who began practicing prior to 1950, I was told repeatedly that the idea of specialization in white-collar crime defense is a new feature of the bar. Thirty years ago, the attorneys who handled the few big cases that would be called white-collar crime today were trial attorneys with predominantly civil cases. The important cases of litigation, criminal as well as civil, were in the federal courts, and these cases were out of reach for the criminal defense attorney. As one seasoned criminal practitioner explained,

> The only ones to do federal practice were Wall Street firms. The average guy, forget it. There was no way you were going to get in there. It was a closed fraternity. It was a whole big thing to get admitted to the federal district court and the circuit court of appeal. I had a state license for all courts in the state, but the federal was separate. They were older men and generally quite more experienced and better lawyers. So I think that instilled in the young lawyer thirty years ago was the idea that the big white-collar case was a Wall Street law firm's case and you'd better stay out of there. Defense attorneys wouldn't be doing many important white-collar cases.

The attorneys who handled the white-collar cases in the 1930s and 1940s did not think of themselves as having a specialty in white-collar crime defense work. They were trial attorneys. And today they do not understand why the younger attorneys persist in calling white-collar crime defense a specialty. An experienced trial attorney, now a senior partner in a major corporate firm, describes the situation this way:

> In the thirties and forties you had advocates of the old style. These were real swordsmen. You could hire them for a criminal case or civil case. It didn't matter. As long as it involved court they would do it: Stever, Gainsburg, Kaufman, lawyers like that. Lloyd Paul Striker was one of them. A lot of what we did was defense of federal criminal cases. They were like what you call today white-collar cases. These were violations of the immigration and naturalization laws. They [the federal prosecutors] didn't go after the aliens themselves. They went after the guys who supported them—the crooked employers, the guys who changed the records, the racketeers, you see fellows like that. Then there were all those cases that we used to call mail fraud cases—before the '33 and '34 Acts.[14] They prosecuted securities fraud under the mail fraud statute. And perjury and bankruptcy and so on. All criminal cases. I did lots of these cases, but I wasn't a defense attorney. I was what I am today—a trial attorney and a litigator.

There is a clear division in the attitude about specialization among the attorneys in New York City who do white-collar crime defense work. The younger attorneys, who started practicing in the 1960s and 1970s, share a strong consensus that white-collar defense work is a specializaton. Some have begun to proclaim openly that they are specialists, expressing a real professional identity, although such statements are also something of an advertising strategy. It has now become accepted to call oneself an attorney who does white-collar crime. One highly reputed attorney in New York, again among the younger group, not a former assistant U.S. attorney but one who tutelaged under a well-known Wall Street trial lawyer, explains as follows:

> For some time, I've sold myself this way. I will be frank when people ask me what I do; I say I specialize in white-collar crime and I explain what that is and if they say, "Do you do anything else?" I leave the door open, never knowing when I might have to fill my larder, but white-collar crime is essentially what I do and I say that up front.

I then asked the attorney how he explains what constitutes white-collar defense work.

> Well, I say that it has to do with stock fraud, or tax fraud, or cases which involve alleged sophisticated stealing; I think a better definition would be sophisticated crime or economic crime, nonviolent or nonstreet crime. I also say that I make great efforts to point myself toward the federal courts. If asked, I'm willing to tell people that, yes, sometimes I do deal with a real criminal, but I don't volunteer it. I prefer to be known as a white-collar defense attorney.

Another corroborating statement came from a former chief of the fraud unit in the U.S. Attorney's office of the Southern District of New York, now a partner in a small defense firm.

> We specialize, and it means following white-collar cases on a day-to-day basis, like you would in any other area. I read the cases that come down which are specifically pertinent to that area. You pick up the paper this morning, for instance, and you see that General Motors case out in Detroit. It is a very significant white-collar criminal case because it holds substantial implications for how an investigation is going to be conducted in tax cases from this point on. The average Wall Street law firm is not going to pay particular attention to that case. I will, however. I will make it a point to get the opinion and read it and follow it with regard to the text. I follow court trends and legislation. There is obviously lots of reform legislation going on with regard to the Grand Jury now. If I am making a set of pretrial motions attacking some problem in the Grand Jury, one of the things that I may want to point out to the court is that the very same thing I am attacking is in the process of being reformed. So there is that. There is having the contacts. You are Joe Shmoe if you are at a big law firm. Take for instance if a guy comes in and says I got a problem down at the U.S. Attorney's office, you're not going to have the advantages that we do because we work in the U.S. Attorney's office on a daily basis. We know everybody down there. They know us.

The idea that you are Joe Shmoe if you work in a large law firm sharply emphasizes an important aspect of specialization in defense work. These defense attorneys believe that if you have not been on the prosecution side and made yourself a reputation for knowing how to prosecute big white-collar cases, then you are not going to get very far in defending them. Being bright and talented, like most attorneys in large firms, is not enough. You have to be savvy, and that's a quality achieved through experience.

The difference in thinking between the younger and the senior attorneys extends to this idea of competency as well. The senior attorneys think that the new graduates from the U.S. Attorney's office are overvalued and that the best person to have in a white-collar case is an experienced trial lawyer. One such attorney said the following:

> Now, first of all you must understand that these young guys who got their experience as prosecutors got very little experience. They might have handled one or two big cases. I don't want to denigrate any of these hotshots, but if they tried three securities fraud cases and three income tax evasion cases, that's a lot. On the other hand, you talk to a guy like Boris Kostelanetz, who is an old cock like me. He knows more about handling criminal tax fraud cases than any six assistant U.S. Attorneys you could put together because he has handled more of them. I know more about the defense of a securities fraud case than any ten of those guys.

Practices of White-Collar Crime Defense Specialists

Whatever view one holds on specialization, it is clear that in the last decade a new group of attorneys has been identified by the bar at large as particularly competent in defense work in cases of white-collar crime. These attorneys can be divided roughly into two groups based on the setting and composition of their practices: attorneys practicing in small firms and single practitioners constitute one subgroup, attorneys practicing in large firms the other.

Small firms have become prominent in New York in spite of their being few in number (certainly not more than ten) because of the presence in a single firm of a number of former assistant U.S. Attorneys or other attorneys who have otherwise received recognition for skilled defense work in white-collar cases. These attorneys have good connections in the prosecutor's offices of the Southern District and are experienced with white-collar cases, thought to be advantages over other attorneys without this background. It is not uncommon to find attorneys from several of these firms representing different persons in the same investigation. And in many instances they receive referrals from large firms, many of which refuse criminal work. They also receive referrals from large firms who cannot handle a particular client because of a potential conflict of interest, for instance, between a company and the company's chief executive. Rather than refer the chief executive to another large firm where he might be wooed as a permanent client, the large firm refers to smaller firms who have no pretensions to handling the regular civil matters of clients of large firms.

In small firms and single practitioner offices the attorneys spend the largest percentage of their total work hours on criminal cases, with civil matters being a smaller part. Many of the civil matters handled by these attorneys are connected to criminal matters, such as litigation about civil sanctions in the same matter or private civil suits involving the same issues underlying the criminal cases.

One example of the small firm is the partnership of Obermaier, Morvillo, and Abramowitz (formerly Obermaier, Martin, and Morvillo). Robert Morvillo, former chief of the fraud unit and former chief of the criminal division of the U.S. Attorney's office of the Southern District of New York, joined in the mid-1970s John S. Martin, Jr., and Otto Obermaier, both of whom had also been assistant U.S. Attorneys in the Southern District of New York. Elkan Abramowitz, chief of the criminal division in the Southern District from 1976 to 1977, joined the firm in 1978 after five years as an assistant U.S. Attorney. Martin was later appointed U.S. Attorney in the Southern District in 1980. In 1982 there were seven attorneys in this firm; most of its cases were white-collar crime investigations and prosecutions. For instance, when the Amerada Hess Corporation, a large oil producer, was investigated in 1978 for criminal tax violations in connection with operations in Abu Dhabi and Iran, Morvillo, along with the corporate firm of Millbank, Tweed, Hadley, and McCloy, represented it. He also represented Arthur Young and Company when it was asked to turn over Amerada documents to the IRS. In 1977, Morvillo represented Anthony M. Natelli, charged with producing false and misleading documents in a proxy statement of the National Student Market Corporation. In 1982, Elkan Abramowitz of this firm represented Mordecai Weissman, president of OPM Leasing Services, in opposing disclosure of documents by its law firm to the trustee in bankruptcy of OPM in that multimillion dollar fraud investigation.

Another small firm specializing in white-collar crime is the partnership of Kostelanetz and Ritholz. This firm had been working in the white-collar crime area before 1970 and grew rapidly in the mid-1970s as it took on several former assistant U.S. Attorneys as partners. Boris Kostelanetz and Jules Ritholz specialized in tax work, criminal and civil, prior to the new growth in white-collar prosecutions. And Kostelanetz, also a former assistant in the Southern District of New York, had earned a substantial reputation when representing the only defendant to be acquitted in the famous electrical industry criminal antitrust case in 1961. In the mid-1970s Jack Tigue, Lawrence Feld, and Gerald Feffer left the criminal division of the U.S. Attorney's office in the Southern District of New York and joined the firm. Subsequently, Feffer left the firm for the tax fraud division of the Department of Justice and Peter Zimroth, former chief assistant to the District Attorney of New York, joined it. Kostelanetz and Ritholz is now the largest firm in New York City specializing in defense of white-collar crime. Its clients—in criminal matters—have included Stirling Drug Company; Phillips Petroleum Company; Zale Corporation; Cargill Corporation; Kenneth W. Riland, Richard M. Nixon's personal physician; J. Anthony Conrad, former chief executive of RCA, and Marc Rich and Company, A.G., a Swiss corporation.

An example of a smaller office specializing in white-collar crime is that headed by Stanley Arkin, who has not worked with more than one or two other attorneys. Arkin is one of a minority of the specialists who is not a former government prosecutor, though in the past he has had former prosecutors work for him. He is known as a shrewd and aggressive advocate. He has represented chief executives of the Franklin National Bank, charged with bank fraud, and AMREP Corporation for the multimillion dollar land fraud prosecution growing out of the sale of property in New Mexico. He also defended Vincent Chiraella, charged by the SEC in a novel use of securities law for exploiting inside information to which he had access as an employee in a company printing prospectuses containing data about pending takeover bids.

Another specialist in a small firm setting, James LaRossa, typifies a special caseload mix. LaRossa, a former assistant U.S. Attorney in the Eastern District of New York, has a wide reputation in the bar for white-collar defense work. But most of his work has been with individuals outside the corporate setting, rather than with corporations and executives of corporations, and he has defended a large number of persons reputed to have organized crime connections. In this sense, his practice is representative of the overlap of white-collar crime and organized crime. As the tax laws and other fraud statutes have been used to prosecute organized crime figures, some attorneys have been drawn into a caseload mix of this type. Attorneys who regularly handle organized crime figures must handle cases charged under white-collar statutes, which leads to their being perceived as part of the white-collar defense bar. And other attorneys who specialize in white-collar cases find that they are sometimes heavily recruited by organized crime figures. Many of the attorneys who have white-collar practices refuse to take on these clients. Others take on an occasional "crime figure," probably causing strain among partners in their office, and still others have large numbers of clients of this type. Making a decision about whether to handle a fraud investigation of a person who is reputed to be connected with organized crime may be difficult for an attorney who wants an establishment reputation in order to attract corporate clients; in a practice that is not always financially healthy, there are pressures to take on any well-paying client. This, of course, is a problem not faced by the white-collar specialist who works in a large corporate firm.

In the large corporate law firm, the defense specialist's criminal caseload is likely to be more homogeneous, that is, he will handle mainly corporate matters and individuals in relation to their actions in a corporate setting. But the overall caseload of this attorney is more heterogeneous than his counterpart in the small firm. This attorney puts a smaller percentage of total work hours into criminal cases. A few of the white-collar crime defense attorneys working in large firms who are well known for their work on white-collar cases handle only one or two per year, devoting more of their time to civil litigation handled by their firms. Former assistant U.S. Attorneys who go to large firms may want to handle criminal work, but they are often dependent on decisions taken by senior partners about what work the firm will do. They may wait years for an important white-collar case, meanwhile not developing a reputation for defense work on criminal matters and losing contact with personnel in the U.S. Attorney's office. The few attorneys in large firms who are recognized as specialists in white-collar defense work either have specifically negotiated agreements with senior partners in the firm that criminal work will be sought or at least not rejected or have joined a firm that is traditionally open to this kind of work.

One example of a firm that has accepted criminal work for a long time is Paul Weiss, Rifkind, Wharton, and Garrison. Arthur Liman of this firm was an assistant U.S. Attorney in the Southern District from 1961 to 1963 and returned in 1967 as special assistant to the U.S. Attorney to participate in the celebrated investigation and prosecution of Lowell M. Birrell, a Wall Street financier convicted of fraud in illegal sales of stock of American Leduc Petroleums (allegedly causing a $20 million loss to the public). Liman defended in 1981 Gulf and Western Industries and in 1977 Bausch and Lomb in criminal investigations. During this period, he also represented defendants in the Amrep land fraud prosecution. Jay Topkis, also a partner in this firm, represented Arnold Arnoff in another large fraud that was uncovered in the Penn Dixie Corporation investigation. The firm also represented Robert Vesco in 1972, when the SEC investigated International Controls Corporation, of which Vesco was a director and officer, for broad-ranging and highly sophisticated securities fraud schemes.

A second example of a large firm that has handled criminal matters is Curtis, Mallet-Prevost, Colt, and Mosle. This firm did criminal work mainly because of the presence of two former assistant U.S. Attorneys from the Southern District of New York, Peter Fleming, Jr., and John Sprizzo (now a federal judge in the Southern District of New York) and Barry Kingham. These attorneys have represented major corporate figures. Fleming defended Robert P. Beasley, executive vice-president of the Firestone Tire and Rubber Company, in an embezzlement prosecution. He also represented defendants in the Equity Funding Corporation investigation and in the AMREP prosecution.

A third large firm that has done criminal work is Proskauer, Rose, Goetz, and Mendelsohn. But it may be inaccurate to specify the *firm* in this instance, because it appears that only one former partner did this kind of work—former federal district Judge Marvin Frankel—and he left the firm in the spring of 1983. After resigning his judgeship, in 1980, while at Proskauer, he represented

Michele Sindona, an Italian financier who controlled an international group of banks and corporations. Sindona was charged with several counts of fraud, including misapplying $15 million in bank funds, and bribery of bank officials. In 1981, still at Proskauer, Frankel represented Marc Rich and Company International Limited, a subsidiary of Marc Rich and Company A.G. The former was charged with diverting at least $80 million of its taxable income from the United States in connection with its dealings in petroleum, metals, and minerals.

Research Method

The above examples are meant to illustrate some of the variation in practice type, but the names and the descriptions are in no way exhaustive. While the best descriptive data about the setting of law practices came from my interviews, I also wanted to obtain a broadly based and more representative picture of the attorneys who specialize in white-collar defense practice. To accomplish this, I conducted a survey of a large group of New York attorneys. Budget and time limitations required that it be a mail survey.

The sample population was the entire group of defense attorneys who handled white-collar cases in the district court of the Southern District of New York in the years 1974–78.[15] I defined white-collar as these major offenses: securities fraud, tax fraud, embezzlement, corruption, bribery, conspiracy to defraud, criminal regulatory violations, antitrust, and bankruptcy fraud. My assumption was that a significantly broad-based perception of specialization in white-collar defense work, if it existed, had to be expressed in the group of attorneys handling those cases. The questionnaire included inquiries about practice type and defense tasks in white-collar cases and concluded by asking attorneys to identify specialists in white-collar crime defense.

Questionnaires were mailed to 934 attorneys out of 1048 who were listed on the court docket, all those for whom addresses could be found. Of that number, 249 responded by returning the questionnaire with valid responses to a majority of the questions asked, representing a response rate of 26 percent. (Eventually the response rate was raised to 37 percent by a second mailing, but then the questionnaire was shortened, resulting in elimination of the specialization question.) Of the 249 attorneys who responded, 127, or about half, listed names of persons they considered to be specialists in white-collar crime defense. Altogether, 184 attorneys were named as specialists. Eighty-one attorneys were named as specialists by more than one respondent, 20 attorneys by more than 10 respondents, and 3 attorneys were named as specialists by more than 30 respondents.

The practice and career characteristics of this group of specialists confirm the picture of white-collar defense specialization already presented. This is demonstrated by a group of attorneys who received a high ranking as specialists—the 20 attorneys who were identified by 10 or more respondents.[16] Their career patterns confirm what was learned from interviews: 14 are former assistant U.S. Attorneys. Their work setting also confirms the findings: 2 are from large corporate-oriented law firms; 2 are from firms with between 15 and 20 attorneys; 4 are from firms with between 6 and 8 attorneys; 6 are from small firms of 2 or 3 attorneys; and 4 are solo practitioners. All the firms in which these attorneys work, except the large corporate firms, specialize in white-collar defense.

The results of the mail survey support the conclusion that the idea of specialization in white-collar defense work is current in the bar. But it is difficult to assess just how widespread that idea is. Some attorneys who did not provide names of specialists may not know attorneys who specialize, even though they are aware that there are such persons. And it can be assumed that other attorneys simply did not want to name names. Certainly the fact that three attorneys were named as specialists by more than thirty respondents confirms the existence of some consensus about attorneys who are most qualified to handle white-collar crime. Moreover, the survey responses probably underestimate the real level of perceived specialization, because some persons who specialize—namely, attorneys in large corporations—have little visibility. They handle few cases, and some of these are resolved at the precharge stage before there is any public knowledge about the case. Within their own reference group, among other attorneys practicing in large corporations, they are well known as white-collar crime specialists, but they are not known among the broader practicing bar. They are like doctors who specialize in rare diseases: they get few cases, and they are not widely known, but they occupy a distinctive place in their profession.

Most of the material which I report in the following chapters comes from observations of attorneys working on actual cases of white-collar crime. As stated earlier, I chose New York City as the site for research because of the high priority of white-collar crime prosecutions in that district and the high level of practice in the bar.[17] It was also geographically accessible to me.

At the outset of the research, the raw material for analysis was to be descriptions of how attorneys handle cases; I intended to use the interview as the main method of data collection. It was important to gain access to a population of attorneys who were highly knowledgeable about white-collar defense practice, rather than a population broadly representative of all the attorneys handling criminal cases, or even all the attorneys handling white-collar cases. I did not want to use the list of attorneys from the mail survey population as a basis for choosing the interview group; there was no necessary correlation between competence, expertise, and experience in white-collar practice, on the one hand, and high numbers of identifications as expert among the surveyed attorneys. Even if I was to start with the group of specialists identified by the survey, I needed to know whom to choose among the group.

To accomplish the objective of gaining immediate access to attorneys who had the most experience with white-collar cases and who would be most perceptive in their observations, I used a snowball reference procedure, a variant of what is called judgment sampling.[18] This is a method for selecting persons who would best qualify as subjects to be studied by using knowledgeable informants to guide the selection. First, I approached a small number of distinguished law professors in the field of criminal law who were also familiar with the practicing legal community and who could identify persons in New York City who would qualify as specialists in white-collar crime defense. The attorneys so identified were interviewed, and they too were used as informants to identify more attorneys who were specialists in white-collar crime defense. This procedure was followed with each new group of interviewees.

In this way a list of 60 specialists was compiled, each of whom had been identified as such by experts in the field of criminal law or by other specialists.[19] Their work settings were: 9 single practitioners, 28 in firms with 2–15 attorneys, 11 in firms with 20–50 attorneys, and 12 in firms with more than 80 attorneys (in each instance counting partners and associates). That this tends to be an elite group of attorneys is indicated by educational background. Over half of the attorneys attended Columbia (10), Harvard (10), NYU (9), or Yale (8). It is also a relatively young group of attorneys; 34 were admitted to practice in the 1960s or later.

Of this group of 60 specialists, 29 attorneys were interviewed. Preference was given to interviewing attorneys who were identified most often as specialists, although in some instances scheduling problems or resource limitations interfered.

I used a random sampling as a method for choosing a second group of interviewees. This was done to counteract the weaknesses in the snowball reference procedure for selecting a study population, a method that is efficient for getting to particularly knowledgeable informants but weak at testing a wide diversity of views available on the research subject. To diversify the research population, 25 attorneys were chosen randomly from the total list of attorneys who handled any white-collar criminal case in the district court of the Southern District of New York during the five-year period from 1974 to 1978. I was able to locate 15 of these attorneys, each of whom I interviewed about practice characteristics, the idea of specialization in white-collar crime defense, and the identity of specialists in New York City.

Each of the attorneys in this randomly sampled group was able to identify specialists in white-collar crime defense. All attorneys identified as specialists by this group had already been so identified through the snowball reference procedure, thus confirming the success of the snowball technique for reaching attorneys who are also known in the broader bar as specialists.

The total interview population included 44 attorneys, 29 chosen through the snowball reference procedure, 15 chosen through random sampling.[20] Most of these attorneys are members of the top strata of the nation's bar. They attended top-ranked law schools and many of them served as former assistant U.S. Attorneys or former assistant district attorneys. Of this total interview population, 5 attorneys were members of firms of more than 100 attorneys; 6 were in firms of 20 or more attorneys (but fewer than 100); 14 were in firms with 5–19 attorneys; 10 were in firms of 2–4 attorneys; and 9 were solo practitioners.

Irrespective of size, the offices of attorneys who were identified as specialists in white-collar crime defense were located exclusively in two small geographic areas. The first included a few-block radius around Wall Street; the second included the midtown area around Grand Central Station—Park, Madison, Fifth, and Third avenues. In every instance the specialist attorney had a high-rent, expensively decorated office with the latest high-technology support facilities. They were attorneys who follow the Wall Street pattern, typically dressed in the classic three-piece dark suit with light pinstripes.

In meetings with these attorneys, I used an open-ended interview procedure, with three main areas of inquiry. First, I asked attorneys about their practices: what kinds of cases they handle, how the cases come into their offices, what conversations they have with their clients, what decisions they make in conducting a defense, and how work is delegated to others. As part of this questioning, at the end of the interview, attorneys were asked to describe in detail their handling of an actual case of white-collar crime.

Second, I focused on the career history of the attorneys: where they received law training, what positions they held before their present positions, and why they were doing their present kind of work. Attorneys were also asked to describe characteristics of the caseload of other attorneys in the firms in which they practiced.

Third, I asked these attorneys about specialization in white-collar crime defense. In this context my respondents were asked to identify attorneys in New York City who could be said to be specialists in white-collar crime defense.

The most instructive findings came from conversation with attorneys about actual cases they were handling. As the number of meetings with attorneys grew, I tended to focus the interviews more and more on this objective. While I emphasized that clients' names or other details indicating the identity of the participants were irrelevant, attorneys were encouraged to describe actual conversations carried out with clients, investigators, prosecutors, and other attorneys and to assess strategy decisions made in the particular cases being discussed.

The interview method provided a general outline of defense functions and certain information about actual cases. Its success, however, revealed also its shortcomings. It was ineffective for obtaining essential detail about what attorneys actually do in meetings with their clients and in meetings with investigators and other attorneys. I received a picture of defense work that was often blurred or truncated when the attorney felt obligated not to violate his client's confidentiality privilege and, so it seemed, when he was reluctant to disclose the true nature of strategies because of sensitivity about his own role in the case. An occasional telephone conversation between an attorney and a client or an investigator, overheard by me during an interview, made it obvious that the attorneys' own description of what they do was not capturing all that occurs during a criminal investigation.

This problem was largely overcome when I began working in a firm in New York City that specializes in handling white-collar cases. Following a series of interviews with one of the partners in this firm, in which I asked my usual set of questions, I proposed that I come to work for the firm. Being an attorney, and interested in the criminal law, I felt that I could make a contribution to the work of the firm, while learning more, at close range, about the process of white-collar crime defense work. They agreed. This position allowed me to take part in meetings between attorneys and clients, attorneys and government investigators and prosecutors, and in strategy sessions conducted by groups of attorneys in the firm. I contributed to the work of the firm by doing legal research and writing memoranda.

My work in the firm lasted for a year and a half. During this period I took notes, not of names and places, but of the types of conversations carried out and the choices made in carrying out defense strategies. The majority of this firm's cases involved criminal investigations conducted by the IRS, the SEC, U.S. Attorneys in several federal districts, and state special prosecutors. The remainder of the firm's caseload was civil litigation, much but not all of it related to matters also handled during criminal proceedings.

All of the chapters reporting field data are based on interviews of the population described above and observations of the attorneys working in the firm where I was a participant observer. But the interview comments, observation scenes, and anecdotes have been altered or rephrased to preserve confidentiality. Names have been changed and identifiers removed. In addition, certain factual attributes of cases have been changed where the uniqueness of the situation would risk identification of a case from its particular characteristics. As a further measure to preserve confidentiality, there are a few instances where I present situations observed as if they were described to me in an interview, and in another few instances I present situations described in interviews as if I observed them. In all instances where changes were made, great care has been taken to preserve the structural features of the case and characteristics of the issues.

PART II
Obtaining Access to Information

3 The Client

If you are a target of a criminal investigation—imagine that the IRS audited your books, found some hint of concealed income, and sent your file to a criminal investigator—meeting the attorney whom you have chosen can produce tremendous personal tension. A first meeting with a defense attorney is something like a first meeting with a surgeon. Each one is going to look at symptoms and, perhaps, give a fateful opinion. And you are expected to trust this person's judgment in what may be the most delicate question of your life. Faced with the situation, some clients (and patients) give themselves over completely, that is, they share all relevant facts, and they rely completely on the expert whom they have chosen. But others have strong, overpowering resistance to telling everything that should be told and to letting the expert make the decision. This is true in the patient-doctor relationship, and it is all the more true in the attorney-client relationship, because in the latter case the client may know more about the setting of the problem—a company, a corporation, a particular business or occupation—than the attorney. A sharing of expertise occurs in the attorney-client relationship. This complicates the task of the defense attorney, who at the outset of his work must determine the nature of the problem that needs to be treated.

Clients in cases of white-collar crime can help an attorney accomplish this goal. They are typically viewed by their attorneys as intelligent, high in analytic skills, and verbally competent. These are individuals, so say defense attorneys, who quickly are able to understand the importance of documents for proving intent and the meaning of an attorney's instruction not to talk to business associates about events related to a particular legal question. Clients in white-collar cases have the ability in most instances to provide major assistance to an attorney who is trying to determine the correct factual picture of issues being investigated and control disclosure of inculpatory evidence. But there is a paradox in the behavior of these clients. They often resist giving the attorney all the information he needs, in spite of the attorney's urging and his explanation that complete cooperation is needed so that appropriate strategic decisions can be made and a defense plan successfully carried out.

When a prospective client prepares to meet an attorney for the first time, he asks himself a critical question: how much information should I give the attorney about myself and the situation for which I need legal counsel? With this question the client affirms to himself his ability to control the attorney's perception of him as a person and the situation that now constitutes a problem.[1] But this affirmation carries with it also a message of vulnerability and risk.

In order to obtain legal counsel, the client must reveal to the attorney information about his private life—facts perhaps secret from all but his intimate associates or known to none other than himself. And when a charge of grave wrongdoing looms, the question of how much the client will disclose is felt to have a determinative impact on the future. The resolution of this question may determine the client's moral stature in the community, his ability to protect his professional position or business success, and his standing in a family.[2]

Persons who go to attorneys for legal counsel are therefore concerned not only with the result, but with how the result is achieved. They are concerned with what people will think of them—how their families, close associates, persons in their community, and their attorney will judge them. These matters—seen by attorneys to be of secondary or tertiary importance—often constitute formidable obstacles to the successful execution of a defense strategy because they prevent the attorney from obtaining necessary information from the client.

This paradox is seen in another aspect of client behavior. Attorneys report that clients often come to them with their own defense plans. When this occurs, the client makes private decisions about what the attorney should know, and these decisions often do not become known to the client's attorney until late in the adversary process, if ever.

Client withholding of information may be consistent with the best defense strategy. Defense attorneys sometimes facilitate withholding of information, a subject discussed in chapter 6. Yet there is always a substantial portion of the facts that must be disclosed to the attorney in order to properly guide the defense. Ignorance of these facts can delay important defense decisions or undermine defense efforts completely. The defense attorney is thus always concerned with the question of whether his client is giving him all the information he needs to know.

Faced with a client who has many reasons to withhold information, the attorney must develop interview, teaching, and social skills that enable him to extract information. Attorneys have different styles. Some treat their clients gently and hope to move toward their goal slowly but surely. Others press the client hard at the outset, less concerned about the client's sensitivity to telling his story. But the bottom line for all attorneys is proper execution of the defense investigation: collection of facts so that he can evaluate the extent to which inculpatory information is accessible to the government and usable to frame an indictment. The client sits at the center of this process not because he is the potential defendant, but because he is the primary source of information and the primary vehicle through which additional sources can be located and used. This chapter describes the obstacles that attorneys face in obtaining access to information from clients who resist and the techniques attorneys use to overcome those obstacles.

Factors Facilitating Information Disclosure

Client Sophistication

When a defense attorney first meets a new client, his initial objective is to obtain information. He needs to know many details about the situation that now constitutes a legal problem for his client. And the more complex the situation, the more details the attorney will need to know. Attorneys said that, as a rule, their clients in white-collar cases are sophisticated in identifying significant information and in understanding its relationship to a potential criminal prosecution. One attorney described his clients this way:

> Most of the people whose cases I handle—criminal matters—are corporate types. They spend most of their days at work reading documents and writing memoranda. They also put a lot of time into meetings where program is discussed. They certainly know a lot more about their businesses than I do. They are capable of informing me of the entire structure of the company in which they work and the industry of which they are a part. These are people that know how to talk. If they are willing, they can educate me very fast.

Another attorney, who had been a public defender before becoming a major figure in white-collar crime defense work, compared his past clients with his present clients:

> I remember that when I was handling these cases on a regular basis [as a court-appointed defender in state court] I always had a hard time getting clients to give me facts straight. Invariably they would give me one version one day and another version the next day. And this is not because they were intentionally concealing facts. Often I felt that they just remembered the incident differently from one meeting to the next. For instance, one day he didn't know if anyone saw him buy the gun. The next day he remembered that there were other people in the store, or that he showed the store owner his license in order to prove his age. Now with many of these men I work with today [defendants in white-collar cases], they are truly obsessive about who was where when and what they wrote down and where pieces of paper are. They don't always recall *everything*, but they recall more.

Attorney-Client Meeting Place

Defense attorneys meet clients in different settings. Some settings facilitate support and encourage open communication. Others are obstacles to both. And when a client is particularly sensitive to being overheard, the place where the first attorney-client meeting occurs affects the manner in which the client talks about his problem. The fact that clients in certain cases are first met in an attorney's office—not in a courtroom, a jail, or a precinct office—means that discussion can start with ease and in an open-ended fashion. In the attorney's office, the client is more likely to feel that the critical nature of his situation will be appreciated and his disclosures kept in strictest confidence. A highly regarded attorney with more than twenty years' experience provided me with this illustrative comparison. He emphasized the manner in which the private setting facilitates communication and makes his debriefing task easier.

> If your client is in jail, you have got enormous problems. Where is he being detained? How often can you visit him? How much privacy can you have? There is an inhibiting factor about him being in jail. In the white-collar practice . . . [there is] a very big difference: your client can come up to your office, and you give him a cup of coffee and you sit him down comfortably. You can chit-chat, you can keep him waiting, you can see him in the evening, you can have a meal with him. There is a more civilized relationship. You can have longer, more frequent conferences with him. On the other hand, if you are in State Court practice, your client is out on Riker's Island and you have got problems. I had one case in which I had a client on Riker's Island. He was detained throughout a very lengthy period of time. In order to have one one-hour conference with him, it took me five hours. To get to Riker's Island, to get on the bus, to go out to the cellblock, to get admitted, to have the prisoner brought down, to sit in the counsel room, and they only have partitions, no booths. Having to whisper and then getting back to the office. The length of the enterprise was very discouraging to frequent contact.

The client who sits in his attorney's office over a cup of coffee and shares pictures of his kids enjoys a natural rapport-building environment.

It was evident throughout the research that affluent clients could feel comfortable in most of the offices of attorneys identified as white-collar crime defense specialists. The decor and tone-setting appointments follow closely the model of the large corporate firm: expensive Park Avenue, Fifth Avenue, and Wall Street office buildings, plush carpeting, expensive paintings and other artistic ornaments. And one finds an omnipresent feeling of confidentiality. In a typical firm each attorney's office is carefully separated from secretaries and other attorneys, and in some offices clients leave through a separate door so as not to be seen by another waiting client. The attorney makes a great effort to appear to be an integral part of the business establishment. In short, the physical surroundings are reassuring. During the period of a long-term investigation, attorney and client are likely to form a close relationship in which they share social occasions and confidences beyond the issues relevant to a prospective criminal charge.

Factors Preventing Information Disclosure

Lack of Trust and Embarrassment

In spite of the cultivated rapport they are often able to develop, attorneys emphasize the problems they have in getting clients to disclose necessary information. While one might expect that targets of investigations would give maximum cooperation to their attorneys out of self-interest, the research findings did not support this. Persuading clients to be straightforward and open about events that may constitute a crime is a complex and often lengthy process. Very few attorneys stated that they obtained all the relevant facts at their first meeting with clients. It is more often a gradual process of give and take, wherein the attorney dispels a client's fears and anxieties and educates him about the importance of disclosing facts that the attorney needs in order to make strategy decisions and carry out a particular defense plan. As described by a former assistant U.S. Attorney, now a defense attorney, it is more often a process of "truth by evolution."

ATTY: Sure, I had a meeting with the client, first of all because he wanted to decide whether or not he wanted to retain me. And secondly, after he made his decision, to discuss what he thought the investigation was about—what problems he had, what skeletons were in the closet; if the investigation went in certain directions, what was going to happen. As often happens, especially early in the criminal process, the client was either not willing to talk about any transgressions or was not familiar enough with the direction that the investigation was taking to define for us the extent of his problems. So we had to go and discuss the matter with the investigative agency, in order to determine what they were looking for.

MANN: Does it occur that when the defendant comes in, you really don't get much help, or do you generally get a lot of help?

ATTY: Very rarely do you get a lot of help. Nobody is going to—and for reasons, I think, of basic psychology—nobody is going to come in to a strange person, whom they have never met before, whom they don't know any way other than by recommendation—and is going to bare his soul and say, I am a bad person, I stole here, the documents are here, the witnesses are there, I did this wrong and I did that wrong, and so forth. It is simply not going to happen. At least it certainly doesn't happen with a high degree of frequency. What you generally get is sort of truth by evolution, over a long period of time as the client begins to develop confidence in the attorney, and the attorney is able to demonstrate his skill. And as the two develop a rapport more and more facts come out.

After years of experience, this attorney learned not to expect the whole story at the first meeting. He explained that as more information comes from the client, he is progressively better able to use the client as a resource in locating potential evidence, in getting access to people, and in forewarning himself of problems that may arise.

Attorneys experienced with client conduct in the context of litigation assume that if they are patient and if the investigation proceeds slowly, the client will soften up enough for timely decisionmaking and action. Another attorney called it an "accumulative process."

> MANN: How does the client approach you in the first meeting?
>
> ATTY: He usually comes in absolutely terrified, and it is important to establish a relationship in which you try and calm him down a bit. He has a serious problem. You have got to calm him down. You have got to give him confidence that you know what you are doing and you tell him, "Relax a little bit, let me be the doctor."
>
> MANN: Does this bear at all upon difficulties you have in learning about the client's situation?
>
> ATTY: Partly, sure. It is a perfectly natural reaction for a man who has never met you before to come into your office on a referral and be reluctant to tell you his life story on day one, or to tell you intimate details of something he may be ashamed of. You have to work to that slowly. You can't expect people in the first contact to tell you all. It is an accumulative process.

Several attorneys reported that they often conduct their own investigations for weeks or months without knowing whether the client has provided essential information. In order to avoid being misled, attorneys may watch for client behavior indicating that information is being held back. Choosing what he called an extremely obvious example, one attorney explained that a client virtually forced him to intensify questions to determine whether a truthful picture was being presented:

> I had a very uneasy feeling about this client. Every time I met him I seemed to get a bit of a different story. Last week when I was up at the headquarters of his company he told me that he had had his office checked by a professional company for wiretaps. And while we conversed he turned on the stereo—said that would garble our voices if there was any listening-in. This is a guy who has assured me that he has no problem at all. But I think that this case is likely to get hot somewhere down the line.

Lack of trust in an unfamiliar person is one obstacle to the attorney trying to get information from his client. Another is the client's insufficient understanding of the privilege of confidentiality that surrounds his relationship with his attorney. And when the client fails to grasp the importance of giving the attorney facts and access to facts, the investigation may move very slowly.

A closely related concern is the client's personal anxiety about moral criticism. For a new client, particularly one who never imagined himself involved with the criminal law, discussing a potential criminal problem with an attorney who shares one's high social status and who outwardly stands for conventional moral values can be extremely difficult. It requires that the client expose himself to personal embarrassment and brings up feelings of shame. The client is concerned not only about what kind of moral personal evaluation the attorney will make of him, but also about negative and critical responses from family, business associates, and friends, when and if the fact of the investigation is revealed. To be sure, some clients are less concerned than others. But sensitivity to this issue was common among clients of attorneys interviewed or observed. The following sketch of one client was provided by a defense attorney who handles mainly criminal investigations.

> Take, for example, the guy who was in here this morning. He is paying off people all over the city. Here's a crime, there's no question about it. There's a big ritual that comes along with the conversation I'm conducting in order to learn the facts of the case. [The client says] ''This is going on all over the industry, everybody does it, you can't survive without it. . . . I don't think anybody would do any different than me.'' And there's this bit about his wife doesn't know, and does he have to have her sign a power of attorney also. . . . ''It will destroy her, she's so fragile,'' etc., etc. The guy also wants to talk about his last vacation and I told him I was in Switzerland also last year, and that makes him feel good because then he's not so different from me.

The rationalizations presented to his attorney are of course used by the client to mollify himself as well. With others—friends and associates—he may start out by hiding his involvement, simply preventing them from knowing, in order to avoid the shame and the necessity to explain and justify himself. When it is only the attorney and himself that the client is concerned about, this phenomenon may have little impact on legal strategy. But when wrongdoing must be revealed outside that relationship, the client's resistance may severely complicate the carrying out of a defense program:

> My client was straightforward with me—right from the beginning—yes, he was. The problem he had, and it was something we had to work on for a while, was that he couldn't get himself to obtain documents from his company because then he would have to tell his business associates what was happening, and he knew they would speak about it at the golf course on Saturday and everyone in town would know.

Client Concern with Business Interest

The new client's reluctance or inability to be open with his attorney is also a reflection of his anxieties about other matters unrelated to defense strategy. Foremost among these is the client's concern about the impact of the criminal investigation and the defense attorney's action on his business. Here the client is not worried about moral indignation from business associates, but about financial loss to his business. In the following excerpt, an attorney describes the reactions of a distinguished New York entrepreneur targeted in an SEC investigation.

> One reason why I have to assume that clients are not always open with me is because of what I learn sometimes late in the game. In a recent case, as we got deep into the investigation, we found that many of our client's clients, if you will, had been interviewed by SEC officials. Our client had known this and didn't tell us, it turns out. And when we queried him about approaching these people—to debrief them and to find out what their roles in the matter were—our client told us not to do it, flat out not to do it. He said he was going to lose contracts and business, alienate potential business contacts, if he let it be known that a criminal defense attorney was working for him. We had a bit of an argument about this; I told him that for us to conduct a proper defense we had to do these kinds of interviews. But he had the final word and insisted. By the way, I put a memorandum in his file memorializing our discussion. One does that as a matter of course just in case an ineffective counsel or other similar claim were ever to arise. That's called covering your ass.

This client was intent upon keeping his attorney away from potential information sources and maintained his stance even after the attorney told him of the possible disadvantages to the case.

Government and private civil sanctions for the matter under criminal investigation also constitute a major threat to certain clients. They occupy the defense attorney's attention more than any other collateral concern of the client's. Protection against civil suit is a vital client interest that the attorney must attend to even if he does not or will not represent the client in parallel civil proceedings. In some instances, the best criminal defense and the best civil defense dictate different strategy decisions. An attorney will usually give priority to protecting the client from the criminal sanction, but not always. Some clients are more interested in preventing damage to their businesses than in preventing what they expect to be the criminal sanction, should they be prosecuted and convicted. Other clients simply do not believe that they could be the subject of a criminal conviction, in spite of what the attorney counsels.

One frequent manifestation of a client's withholding of information because of feared civil sanction is nondisclosure or actual hiding of assets. While some attorneys said that clients sometimes hide assets to discourage attorneys from charging high fees, more often it is a client's own strategy to discourage civil suits. Targets of criminal investigation believe that if they disclose assets to an attorney, they will also have to disclose them to an adversary party when a motion for discovery in a civil suit is made. Here is one attorney's comment on the adverse effects of this situation:

> We prepared our usual income and expenditure balance sheet and were able to

straighten his books out. This meant that if the *corporate* investigation became an *individual* one also we were prepared to show that all individual income was accounted for by legitimate sources. When the individual investigation actually did get underway, the client then showed us other accounts. We had to start over again with the balancing operation. He said he had wanted to protect himself from a stockholders' suit that might be brought against him in his individual capacity.

An attorney who handles both civil and criminal litigation described a client who prohibited him from taking certain defense actions in order to protect business interests.

When the SEC investigation started, we were brought in by the corporation law firm to represent the chief executive and other officers. [Another firm] represented the corporation. We handled all of the contacts with the agency—appearances of the officers and so on. One issue handled by the corporate counsel was a problem for us. They did a huge research job on the question of whether the fact of the investigation had to be reported in the company's annual report to investors. That was mainly legal research. The officers had decided that the company would not report the investigation in the annual report and wanted an opinion letter supporting that decision from [the corporate counsel] to put into their files. This caused me concern because I thought it might be used against the individual somewhere down the line in connection with proving intent. Our difference in view was resolved against my position.

The corporate officers' desire to withhold information took precedence over the defense attorney's strategic calculations, indicating the client's intense concern with impact of an investigation on business interests.

Another attorney explained that a client continually requested him to take actions to prevent the investigative agents from contacting his business associates.

What was happening was that the agent was going around to my client's customers asking to see their records of the amount of merchandise supplied to them by my client. His is a very competitive business and he was certain that this would cause him to lose contract renewals and work to exclude him from the bidding pool. His feeling was that we could be more active ourselves, supply the agents with copies of his company records of what was shipped to his customers, and try to meet with the agent more and explain things, handle the matter without this damage to his business. My opinion, all along in that matter, was that we should minimize our presence entirely. I told him that if he lost some business that was a small price to pay, smaller certainly than indictment and a *Wall Street Journal* article.

The client was keenly aware of the business loss that he would suffer even if the investigation was resolved in his favor. Another client, fearing the consequences of an investigation, made this remark: ''How do you think the chief executive of the corporation with whom I do business reacts when he gets a call from the 'criminal investigation' division of the IRS and is then subjected to a raft of questions about his and my business?''

Client's Legal Strategy

Another obstacle to the attorney trying to obtain information and use it in a manner most consistent with defense objectives is the fact that clients have their own concept of what kind of information and what use of information will most effectively achieve the desired results. A client asks himself, for instance, ''If I want to avoid being charged with violation X, is it not better that fact Y *not* be known to my attorney?'' Or a client concludes, ''If I say that fact Z does exist, then I am less likely to be charged with crime W.'' Other clients, while they reveal the essential factual information relevant to the potential criminal charge, also have strong opinions on how it should be used by the attorney. Still others prefer that the defense attorney take complete control. Where the client attempts to control the attorney by controlling what information is disclosed by him, their relationship may include a conflict over strategy. In dealing with clients who want to determine defense strategy, one attorney said that he makes a gross distinction between ''good clients'' and ''bad clients.''

> By bad client, I mean someone who doesn't help you in developing a coherent defense. I'll give you an example. In a criminal investigation of a large drug company for mislabeling and adulterating its product, I wanted to build my defense around the ''industry-wide practice'' concept.* I was prepared to have extensive research carried out in the industry to show the high frequency and prevalence of the practice that was being questioned. I had developed this idea with the house counsel. Now this is what I call a bad client: when I interviewed the chief of the quality control division, he had worked up this elaborate explanation of how this problem that his company was experiencing was an isolated event which, he said, was the result of mistake and that therefore there couldn't be any criminal intent. And he had prepared documents with statistics to prove his point. He said, ''It was an oversight . . . the technicians were not adequately informed . . . we are taking steps to remove the supervisor.'' He was as much as telling me that this is the way the defense should be handled, and he was really enthusiastic in his presentation. I needn't tell you

*The ''industry-wide'' concept is a defense based on the assumption that if the government can be convinced that the behavior being considered as a criminal offense is in fact widespread—a norm—then it will refrain from prosecuting. Attorneys reported that they were sometimes successful with this defense argument.

that that should never have occurred—and wouldn't have had the house counsel kept his lines of communication open with me.

Here, one of the clients (all the clients being the corporation and officers of the corporation who were responsible for production of the questioned drug) openly declared a position on the factual issue with the intention of facilitating a desired legal consequence. In so doing he foreclosed or made substantially more difficult the use of the preferred defense strategy. The chief of quality control limited the attorney to a particular interpretation of the facts by producing documentary evidence to prove his point. The attorney would thereafter not be able to contradict this position without appearing to influence the client illegally or unethically. If the chief of quality control had indeed fabricated the facts underlying his defensive posture and the attorney's interpretation of events more nearly reflected the actual state of facts, then the attorney faced the problem of persuading this man to repudiate his story. This would be a precondition to advancing the "industry-wide practice" defense, because of the possibility that government investigators eventually would determine, through interview or cross-examination, that this inconsistent position had earlier been taken by a managerial employee. Otherwise, the client would be seen as having concealed facts, which would frustrate the attorney in his attempt to build what he considered to be the most appropriate and best defense.

Another attorney described Mr. Cook, the target of a tax fraud investigation. When he came to the attorney for the first time, Cook brought a letter that he had received from the IRS requesting presentment of all bank books, cancelled checks, and brokerage records for the prior three years. At the first meeting, Cook haltingly admitted that he had not reported interest and dividend income from some of his many accounts. He sat silent for some minutes, then gushingly apologized to the attorney, "I'm sorry, I didn't know what I was doing . . . I didn't mean to do this."

In a discussion following this meeting, two attorneys from the office evaluated the case on the basis of their knowledge of IRS practices and decided that the extent of Cook's nonreporting would be fully discovered when the investigator checked bank and broker reports of dividends through Cook's social security number. They assumed this procedure would be used by the particular investigative unit. The attorneys then decided that it would be most effective to take a cooperative stance and enter into plea negotiations. There being no factual defense and no tax-law legal defense that would negate culpability, the attorneys would try to mitigate damage by portraying the client as psychologically disabled. They would attempt to litigate substantive responsibility at the pretrial stage, using an argument of reduced mental capacity. Their aim would be to resolve the case administratively through a civil penalty procedure or by affecting the portrayal of severity that a prosecutor eventually would put into an indictment or sentencing plea.

A cooperation strategy thus became the accepted defense program for Mr. Cook, which prevailed until another meeting with the attorneys. At that time Cook brought his own records of dividends and interest. The attorneys then discovered a very important fact, one that had not been revealed earlier. Cook had falsified social security numbers at his banks and brokerage houses. Income from these accounts was reported on social security numbers not associated on government records with his name. The lead attorney had the following to say:

> Cook's a weasel type. He made himself out to us to be stupid, to have sort of fallen into this thing. He said he couldn't organize himself because he was always depressed. Now we have determined that he systematically falsified social security numbers to cover up his nonreporting scheme. Didn't want to admit that to us. I don't think he could bear it. He thought he could put this thing over on the government by not telling us. What he didn't know is that this puts us in a different position. All along we were weighing whether we should cooperate and negotiate or stay tightly quiet. Now that we know that the social security numbers were falsified, we think that there is some likelihood the agent will not find all of the nonreported accounts and it is probably better for us not to cooperate—at least not until we get a clearer signal that the agent knows about, say, ten accounts rather than only one or two.

The disturbing aspect of Cook for the attorney was not his apparent crime, but his failure to disclose information that was essential to a proper defense. Before the attorney was informed about the false social security numbers, he had intended to advise cooperation with the agent. The client would have incriminated himself; instead, he benefited from a strategy of silence that eventually led to the closing of the criminal file without prosecution. The defense attorney did not question Cook about why he failed to disclose the information. He shared his critical feelings only with his associates.

In other instances, the client is helpful in that he provides the attorney with access to his associates and documents—to all the information that the attorney needs to draw his own picture of the ultimate vulnerability of the client. But he is not willing to tell the attorney what he should be looking for or what he should find. It is as if the client hopes that the attorney will not see the forest for the trees—and if the attorney does not, neither will the government investigator. The dynamic is captured by this short portrayal given by a defense attorney:

> MANN: After you've met the client, do you work alone essentially, or do you continue to talk with your client regularly?
>
> ATTY: Oh, of course you do. You always talk to your client. You talk to your client every step of the way. When we found out what the real allegations were going to be, we came in and discussed it with the client.

MANN: Was there a point during this interaction when the client's attitude turned and he began to help you?

ATTY: Well, he was always helpful in the same sense that he was always able to pinpoint for you where the documents were and where the witnesses were. He was never helpful in the sense of saying, "I did it, so there is no sense for you to proceed as if I didn't." Or, "Find a defense for me within the ambit of 'I did it,' and here's what I did." But he certainly was able to understand what the nature of the charges were as we proceeded with our investigation and as we came close to the day of indictment.

Another complication in the defense attorney's attempts to obtain information occurs when a client's civil attorney becomes involved in the case. The civil attorney is so accustomed to making decisions for the client that the defense attorney has a hard time taking the lead position on the criminal issues. Some of the large New York law firms that pride themselves on being able to handle any kind of case are often forced in criminal matters to bring in independent counsel to represent individuals with whom the regular firm would have a conflict of interest, for example, a vice-president of a company in which the regular firm is representing the president.

When a high prestige firm refers a high prestige client to a lower prestige firm or attorney (the defense attorney), a dissonance may result, which affects client disposition.[3] The client's corporate counsel—or his regular civil attorney—has not brought the defense attorney into the case because he reasons that the defense attorney will better handle the matter; he has brought the defense attorney in because he is required to by a court-enforced and ethical doctrine prohibiting multiple representation of parties whose interests may diverge significantly. The client's regular counsel may continue to feel that he is more competent to make strategy decisions than anyone else; he will therefore attempt to bring this competency to bear on the defense attorney. It is also not unusual that he coaches his client about what information to disclose to the defense attorney, in spite of the fact that this violates a conflict of interest prohibition, which creates an information retrieval problem for the defense attorney. Moreover, the referring attorney may continue to view himself as the client's counsel in other matters and thus attempt to create a cocounsel relationship with the defense attorney. This situation puts the defense attorney in an ethical bind. He is likely to be dependent on conflict-related referrals from corporate law firms and does not want to alienate the referring attorneys. On the other hand, the ethical obligation and his professional integrity require him to make independent strategy decisions. He thus finds himself in the awkward position of trying to make his own decisions while preserving the good will that got him his client in the first place.

Some clients have yet another view of strategy. They believe that the attorney can "fix" the matter, either directly by the offer of a cash bribe or indirectly by exercising influence in an "old boy" network. Though not frequently reported by attorneys, this notion of strategy particularly bothered two attorneys interviewed. One attorney from a medium-sized midtown firm described the following situation.

> Sometimes I get clients who hint that they expect I can exercise special influence for them. They know I have a reputation, that I'm experienced, that I've been in government and so on. Nobody's ever asked me straight out to "fix" something, but there are certainly those who intimate in different ways that they expect that I can mysteriously bring powers to be exercised over the government and their problem will go away. They assume that's the way things are handled—from the inside. Just the other day a client—a businessman whose company you would surely recognize—came in and complained that his case was taking too long. He had just heard about another case, of a prominent politician who had a similar problem and apparently got a good deal. In a nutshell, my client said to me, "You see, so and so got out quickly without any serious problem. He had the inside connections." The kicker was that I just finished putting over two years of hard labor into the case of that very politician. It certainly satisfied my client to find that I was the one who had represented the politician. But I don't think I convinced him that it had nothing to do with insider influence, even though I told him that in that case we had very little rapport with the prosecuting agencies—that it was a long bitter struggle.

At the other extreme of a continuum measuring client tendency to assert control over strategy is the client who turns his problem over to an attorney without any expectation that he should or could have any contribution on questions of strategy. If the client is able and willing to supply all the necessary factual information to the attorney, there is no client-created obstacle to a well considered defense strategy decision. However, contrary to the general rule that clients in cases of white-collar crime are sophisticated or at least competent in matters of information communication, there are some clients who are not capable of quickly providing the necessary information. Such a client is fortunate when he gets to an attorney early in an investigation; often, his very lack of sophistication delays his consulting an attorney until an indictment has been issued, a decision made to recommend prosecution, or damaging admissions already made. Early or late, this client is completely cooperative with the attorney—he listens and agrees and has very little of his own to add. He is an easy client to converse with, but, as one attorney explained, he is also a client who is less likely to be helpful in developing the factual side of the case. He is not attuned to what information is relevant for the attorney and is not as likely to respond quickly and effectively to an attorney's request that he document certain facts or have certain conversations with associates. In the context of comments about attorney-client relations, one attorney so described a client:

One I have now is a real depressive type. He's a businessman who has stumbled along for years. Hasn't kept passable records, doesn't really comprehend his own financial situation. He has no conception at all what's going on here. He certainly is not going to interfere with how I handle the case, but neither is he going to be much help. I think he's more involved now with depressing himself about his predicament. Can't seem to get on his feet.

Attorney Responses to Information Withholding

Attorneys often have to adopt special methods to encourage a client to be progressively open with confidential information and to forgo attempts to impose his own view of legal strategy. The following excerpts from interviews show some of the techniques attorneys use to maneuver clients into divulging the information necessary for the attorney to make proper strategy decisions and to effectively execute a defense plan.

The Therapeutic Approach

One attorney describes an approach akin to a therapeutic dynamic.[4] By controlling his impulse to take a hurried and matter-of-fact approach, he is able to gently break down the client's defenses.

> You have to indulge yourself in a lot of fictions. First you say yes, yes. Give the client a feeling that you believe in him, that you trust him. Then in later meetings you draw on information you have located independently, and you demonstrate to the client that his story has inadequacies. You continue with this process until finally it dawns on the client that his fabrications will no longer hold up. You attack him with gentleness, with compassionate understanding.

Moving slowly allows the client to save face, to come to accept the attorney, and to understand that it will be better for him in the long run if he is open. Where the defense attorney moves ahead too fast, he risks losing the client:

> The clients came in together and gave me what they said were "all the facts." The company had received a subpoena for documents. They also had an explanation cooked up, how the company had been deferring income. I questioned them as I usually do—about their personal finances. Have you had large deposits in your personal account? Do you have large expenditures for which there are no large withdrawals, etc.? My questions began to show them that it wasn't just the company that had a problem, but also they as individuals. They never came back. My assumption is that they were scared away—were not yet ready to recognize that they had their own problems. They wanted a lawyer who would keep it in the company.

This attorney concluded that his potential clients feared that his ''prying'' into personal finances somehow would make it more likely that they would have problems in that area, too. The clients had come to the attorney with a set idea of what they wanted to share with the attorney and were put off by his intrusions. Acknowledging this problem, one attorney proclaimed, ''In the beginning you have to hold the client in. Get your retainer before you let the guy know how bad his problem is.''

While attorneys are clearly aware of the dangers of pushing clients too hard at the onset of their relationship, several of the more highly reputed attorneys appear to be able to take more liberty with their clients. One such attorney stated his view in this way.

> MANN: In this particular case, did you tell the defendant that it is going to help you if you lay it out on the table?
>
> ATTY: I tell that to every defendant. Simply in every case when people come in, my own philosophy—some attorneys don't have this—but my own personal philosophy is I want to know all the facts immediately, because the way I view my role is that it is my obligation to come up with a strategy, a defense strategy, and if I don't know all the facts or if I am given an inaccurate fact, what is going to happen is that the strategy I develop may not be the strategy which is the correct strategy for the case. I generally explain it like a game plan: if you have Joe Namath playing quarterback, you have one game plan. If you have Al Woodall playing, you have a totally different game plan. The game plan that you produce for Al Woodall is not the game plan that you would produce for Joe Namath. The client needs me more than I need him. If he doesn't want to cooperate with me, he can see another attorney.

Upstaging the Client

If the client does not give adequate information at the outset, the attorney has to conduct his defense strategy for some time on the assumption that the client has not yet revealed all essential information. In the meantime, however, he can work independently to discover facts about the case. If he is successful in determining the outlines of the case, he may then approach the client and confront him with his own knowledge. Once the client believes that the attorney has discovered or is likely to discover basic facts about his involvement in a potentially criminal matter, the client is significantly more willing to cooperate by supplying his own information.

The following description of a return meeting gives a sense of the way in which the attorney moves the client into a position of cooperation, so that the client will disclose more information to the attorney and provide assistance in making the fundamental strategy decision: to what extent he should pursue a strategy of withholding of information from the government and to what extent he should pursue a strategy of cooperation. The attorney recounted how the client had come into the first meeting dumbfounded. He had received a subpoena but couldn't imagine what the investigation could be about. "The client wanted us to do something but had no idea where we should start." I asked the attorney, "What happened in later meetings with the client?" He responded:

> When we discovered what the areas of interest were, we sat down with the client again and said okay, we are now getting a pattern of what they are looking at. These seem to be the problems; what have you got to say about that? And then the client said, "Well, I think you have got to talk to X, Y, and Z with regard to problem A and you have to talk to D, E, and F with regard to problem B. There are some documents which relate to problem C which you have to dig out." And that is what we started to do. We went out and started to interview people who could have information, sometimes getting there before the investigative agency did. And also we got the client's version of the facts. Now that really went on for a considerable period of time.

The Pitfall of Nondisclosure

Nondisclosure can weaken a defense strategy because the attorney is led into an adversarial confrontation with a more limited picture of events than his opponent possesses. A sudden factual revelation will catch the attorney unready to make a convincing plea for his client. Or it may completely undercut the defense position, if a damaging fact not known to the defense attorney is an essential element in the investigator's or prosecutor's case against the client. One attorney gave this example of how nondisclosure of information sets the stage for bad defense strategy:

> ATTY: I had a client who was taking payoff money from local contractors, that is, he was alleged to be taking payoff money from local contractors.
>
> MANN: Did he come to you before indictment?
>
> ATTY: Oh, yes, he came to me before indictment. He told me that he was innocent and that it was a frame-up. While the great danger for a prosecutor is that his informant will turn on him, change his story, it is much the same for a defense attorney. The great dread is that a defendant will turn upon his defense counsel. You know, go to the prosecutor and say, my lawyer wants me to get up and lie. So my client told me that certainly he was in the places alleged and certainly he dealt with people but he never besmirched his office. And quite candidly I was all enthused. Basically, because it was an important case and I thought I was going to win. He had an excellent professional record, and I had never heard anything about his being corrupt. I just thought this was going to be a great case. The most important thing for any defense lawyer is not getting paid per se but winning and getting a win is absolutely—I mean, shall I say I was veritably ecstatic at the prospect? A few days before the trial two assistant U.S. Attorneys invited me into their office. They said, "We want you to listen

to some tapes.'' Now this was before the open discovery days. I said look, I'll listen but only on the condition that my client be present. Well, we listened. And it was inculpatory in every conceivable fashion. So he walked out and said, ''I'm going to cooperate. My fellow employees were supposed to help me, but they have not.''

MANN: How did it happen that the assistants called you in on this matter? They could have easily taken this case to trial and simply—

ATTY: They wanted my client to lead them to others.

MANN: Did he have information that they wanted?

ATTY: I should assume so, otherwise he never would have gotten this suspended sentence, being put on probation.

Here the client's withholding of information put the defense attorney in the untenable position of arguing facts that the prosecutor knew and could prove to be completely erroneous. The short-term effect would clearly be detrimental to the client. In the long term, misrepresentation by the client can hurt the defense attorney severely. In future cases this attorney may have difficulty convincing prosecutors and investigators of his trustworthiness in working out a deal for a client. For instance, in immunity agreement negotiations a prosecutor often has to rely on the defense attorney's representation that his client can supply inculpatory information against a third person and that the client is not as culpable as the person against whom the information will be supplied. This kind of deal requires trust. Trust relationships are difficult to build when an attorney acquires a reputation for being misled by his clients. Several respondents who were formerly assistant U.S. Attorneys said that there is a definite informal categorization of trustworthy and untrustworthy attorneys. One major difference relates to how much information the defense attorney will receive from the assistant about the facts of a case.

The strength of a defense attorney's inclination to press for disclosure of information and the degree of client willingness to volunteer disclosure are two factors that strongly affect defense tasks and strategic opportunities. While attorneys and clients handle themselves differently in communicating and reacting to information, the net result is that the ability of an attorney to achieve a successful attorney-client relationship, the satisfaction that client feels from his attorney's work, and the effectiveness of a defense program are significantly determined by how much and how quickly information is retrieved from a client. Because ultimately the question of whether an indictment is issued or a prosecution is successful depends on the ability of the government to obtain access to information, client use of information is a critical factor bearing on the final outcome of the case. The initial period in the defense investigation is then often concerned with putting the client in his proper role. As I have shown in this chapter, one part of that role is as a provider of information about the events being investigated. The second part of that role is as a concealer of information that would be detrimental to effective defense strategy. While the major problem for the defense attorney at the outset of his handling of a case is often the resistance of an apprehensive and fearful client, the attorney may also want to encourage the client not to share a certain portion of what he knows. That is part of the task of information control, as distinguished from information retrieval (to be discussed later, in Part III). The attorney must guide the client along the narrow path of proper disclosure so that he provides all necessary information but none that would be counter-productive.

4 Sources Subject to Client Control

During initial meetings in preparing a defense, some clients provide their attorneys with substantial information, yielding a list of sources to be examined. Other clients are not so helpful; they remain reluctant to share information, or they have truly forgotten, or they do not know what the government is investigating. The defense attorney is likely to find himself in one of two positions. Either he will conclude that he has received significant information from the client—and if this is true it will advance his work in important ways—or he will conclude that he is lacking significant information; this will lead him to feel insecure about decisions that must be made. In either instance, however, the attorney then sets out to make an independent examination of available information sources.*

Even when the client has been completely cooperative, it is the usual practice of the attorney to examine sources independently. And it is rare that a client alone possesses enough information to enable the attorney to make strategy decisions and carry out defense plans without additional investigation. In the following interview, an attorney was asked if he could recall the initial meeting with a client whose case was prosecuted after a year-and-a-half investigation conducted by the SEC.

> ATTY: Specifically, no. All I can tell you is that it was a difficult discussion, in which the client reported what he had been told by the investigative agencies, which was very vague and ambiguous. And he indicated that he was aware of no real problems, and that he certainly had an explanation for the questions that had been asked at that point and [that] there was no wrongdoing on his part.
>
> MANN: Could I ask you to specify the facts a bit more? What was he being charged with?
>
> ATTY: At that point, there were no facts. At that point it was simply an SEC investigation of embezzlement.
>
> MANN: But did you have anything of substance at all?
>
> ATTY: We didn't. I mean that is precisely my point. At that point in the in-

*I have used the term *information sources* throughout. These sources can be divided into two major groups: persons and documents. A person can be a source of information because he or she has created the fact by acting or has learned of facts by hearing or seeing. A document can be a source of information because a person has recorded in the document a piece of information.

vestigation we had no information one way or the other, and that is why we went to the investigative agency. And the investigative agency was unwilling at that point in the investigation to tell us what the charges were.

In the next statement, another attorney indicates that he was suffering from a similar problem of information scarcity after meeting his client. The client, an executive of a large trucking company, reported that he had been contacted by an FBI agent.

MANN: What was the crime?

ATTY: It is not the crime, it is what the allegations are. You never know what the crime is unless somebody tells you. Okay, the investigative agency would not tell us what the crime was, and the client would not tell us that he had committed a crime. So what we were doing in that situation is trying to find out what possible crime was being, one, investigated, or two, had been committed.

MANN: What was the agency after?

ATTY: It was basically a fishing expedition. They had some reason to believe that the integrity of the books and records of the company were not at [their] best. Consequently, what they wanted to do was determine whether or not the fact that the books and records didn't look right to them was symptomatic of the fact [that] there was an underlying crime that had been committed. Eventually they did in fact establish that. At the beginning, since all they were doing was kind of poking around and looking at airline trips, looking at petty cash, and looking here and there, there was no way for anybody to figure out exactly what it was that they were going to find without their telling us, and they would never tell us.

MANN: The defendant could have told you.

ATTY: If in fact he was guilty, he could have told us that.

Even after lengthy meetings with the client, the defense attorney is often faced with a vague and undefined set of circumstances that he will attempt to bring into progressively sharper focus. The attorney must push his investigation beyond what he learns from the client directly: to verify facts, to measure the potential seriousness of the problem as it is defined by all the facts potentially accessible to the government, to look for latent independent problems that might be uncovered in the course of the government investigation, and, most important, to evaluate the likelihood of the government's locating still undisclosed inculpatory information. Indeed, all these elements must be examined even when the client or the government has given the attorney a clearly defined picture of the scope of the investigation and its targets. The accumulated information is critical to making the fundamental strategy decisions—when to withhold information and when to cooperate with the government, when to negotiate and when to deny guilt and go to trial.

To advance the defense investigation, the attorney begins with the client's own records: personal receipts, diaries, logs of financial transactions, notes, and other similar documents held by him in his home, office, or comparable place. Next, the attorney turns to sources of information which, though not the client's property, are controlled by him or accessible to him by virtue of authority or influence he exercises over the person or entity who holds the information. These sources include persons and documents in the setting—usually an occupational or other organizational setting—where the events that are apparently the subject of the criminal investigation occurred.

The defense attorney thinks early in an investigation about persons within the client's own setting because he surmises that they possess relevant information and that it is more likely to be accessible to him than information held by persons who have no continuing relationship with the client. But a second and more important reason is that the attorney wants to get to these sources before the government does so. Defense attorneys and prosecutors alike know that he who arrives first has a distinct advantage in interpreting and using information. An important feature of information control is ''helping'' a person—a witness as well as a client—draw facts out of his or her recollection. The ''drawing-out'' process is creative. In other words, if your adversary gets to a source of information before you, what you learn from that source when you get there is likely to be different from what you would have learned had you arrived before your adversary. What the defense learns in its investigation of the facts is to some extent a function of who arrives at the sources first.

The Client's Personal Records

Identifying Weak Points

When the apparent subject of an investigation involves personal gain to the client—for example, in some embezzlement cases—or when the IRS is auditing the client's personal income tax return, the reason for examining the client's personal financial situation is clear. The attorney needs to know what the records show and how exposed they are to government access. The reason is less obvious to clients when the crime is independent of any personal financial gain. Crimes such as antitrust violations and securities fraud may focus on wrongs that are completely independent of financial gain to the individual. Investigations of business-entity tax violations may center solely on the tax liability of the entity. Bribery and other forms of corruption are defined independently of any wrongful financial gain to the briber.[1] Yet an investigation of any one of these crimes may well lead to, or be circumstantially proved by, unexplained transactions in an individual's finances. For example, in an illegal price-fixing agreement a client had been receiving personal profits from participating companies as compensation for influencing his company to cooperate. An audit of that individual's personal tax returns might have led to discovery of the price-fixing scheme. Similarly, an investigation of a price-fixing scheme might easily follow a path to a payoff, which could then be prosecuted as an independent crime (formulated in an indictment as tax fraud or commercial bribery charged under a mail fraud statute) or be used as evidence to prove a price-fixing agreement. Therefore an antitrust price-fixing investigation would lead the defense attorney to also raise questions about personal financial status with the client, if the client did not raise them himself. And after disclosure of any potential problem a complete accounting analysis would have to be made.

An attorney who first directed my attention to this issue made the following statement:

> One of my first concerns in any case is to get my own accountant working on an analysis of the client's books and records—his bank accounts, securities accounts, check stubs. We approach the client as if the government is going to attempt to make a net worth case against us. This means that somewhere down the line the government may be looking to see if there is evidence of large expenditures or large income or large transfers that can't be explained by regular sources or regular living expenses. Sometimes we have our own accountant go back over five years. We determine a baseline net worth and then compare it with the present net worth. If there are large unexplained differences we know we have a problem in this area.

In the analysis of a client's personal financial status, the attorney focuses first on income and expenditures. This requires complete access to the client's records, an objective which is not easy to meet if the client is reluctant to disclose concealed sources. Second, the attorney seeks disclosure of all assets, including deposits of capital and real and movable property accumulated during periods that may antedate the years under investigation. From this information the attorney is able to develop a picture of the income and assets that are reported in documents and records assumed to be directly accessible to government investigators. Moreover, where there are concealed or unreported sources—not directly accessible to government investigators—the attorney can develop a "worst case" profile. An accountant working for a defense attorney explained his financial analysis of a client under investigation.

> I have had my associates work on the period under investigation. The upshot of our work was three distinct accounting profiles. In the first, we compared the tax returns with the sources of income that were in the client's name and would be located by any superficial audit. These were all reported to the IRS

> and things looked good from that perspective. Second, it seems that the client had been drawing on a trust fund that received income from a stock portfolio; that would make the funds actually his, that is, he was treating the trust as if the principal were still under his control and the income his. That could be a problem. Third, the client has an account in Vaduz which has never been reported. That's not likely to show up anywhere. I think our worst-case profile is the second one.

In this case, the defense attorney's strategy was built on the assumption that the Vaduz account would not be discovered by investigators. On the other hand, the likelihood of the trust distribution being discovered by investigators appeared to the attorney to be high. Early identification of this potential problem allowed the client to recompense the trust before the investigator made an issue of it. The investigator did make an issue of it, but since he had corrected the situation earlier, the defense attorney was able to argue that the client had "taken a loan from the trust in exigent circumstances." "This was a violation of the fiduciary duty that the client had to the trust," said the attorney, "but the receipt of the funds did not constitute income and there could be no tax crime."

The "Net Worth" Case

An attorney's investigation of a client's records in some instances may constitute virtually the entire defense procedure. In the case described below, an IRS investigator was attempting to establish a net worth tax fraud prosecution. In a net worth prosecution the government tries to prove that the defendant's total assets indicate that he had more income than he reported. It is a case built on circumstantial evidence in which the inculpatory conclusion may be rebutted by the defendant who presents direct or circumstantial evidence showing legitimate sources of income accounting for total net worth and showing that the correct or nearly correct tax had been paid.

In this particular case, IRS investigators conducting a routine audit found that the client had deposited over $200,000 in cash in a bank account during the audit period. This led them to question whether the income had been derived from legitimate sources. The auditor's main task was to establish a net worth financial figure for the beginning of the period for which the underreporting of income would be alleged. Without a prior net worth statement, the present net worth could not be used to show a reporting discrepancy. The following excerpt is presented at length to give a detailed picture of how the attorney viewed the case, how he conducted his own investigation, and the difficulties of gaining client cooperation in restricting contact with the government.

> This is called the Beckwith case. It is one which didn't go to trial, an example which may illustrate some of the points that I have been making. The case started when my client, Beckwith, purchased from a bank, with cash,

$200,000 worth of bonds, and the bank, pursuant to routine procedure under the Bank Secrecy Act, reported the purchase to the IRS. Eventually the case was referred to the criminal investigation division and then I was called in by my client's attorney. I saw immediately that my client's only criminal problem could be a net worth case. So my job was to determine if the government would have a reasonable chance of success in trying to construct a net worth prosecution. If I determined that it would, then I probably would have decided to build my defense around a cooperation strategy. If I decided that they would not be able to establish a net worth prosecution, then I would keep silent, which is what I eventually decided on—to keep silent. The main burden for me in this case was to make an absolutely thorough investigation of my client's financial history to determine if the elements necessary to the net worth case could be established.

A very young client with no or negligible work history and without a potential family source might have a hard time escaping the allegations in this case. But my client, 50 years of age, had been working since he was 12. He was a musician and he had a great deal over $200,000 income during his work life. Making my case depended on two questions, both of which I had to put considerable time into clarifying: (1) were his expenses so extravagant over this period that he could not have saved, and was there evidence of those expenses, and (2) was there some point during my client's 38-year work history at which the government could draw a line and say at this year it was established officially or by the client himself that his net worth was such and such—for instance, a loan application—and since then he hasn't reported enough to account for his net worth and he can't account for it in any other way. To make a full clarification in regard to both questions, I had to interview my client very thoroughly and examine all the possible sources of documents that might be used to show extravagant living or a net worth beginning point, a prior net worth statement. I examined bank records, check stubs, record books that he had. I even got into some of the books of former employers. From the interview and the record search I was able to conclude to my satisfaction that our best strategy was to remain silent, that the government would not be able to prevail. For instance, I could show that during a long period when he first started performing he was receiving room and board from his employers as well as a wage. This meant that he had very few expenses and could have saved his wage income. He was not in a business where one is required to keep the kind of documents that are often used in the net worth cases. He was relatively removed from the intense record-keeping sector of the economy. I felt safe in relying on my assumption that a base net worth would not be established.

My investigation efforts were tremendous. On the other hand, the amount of actual litigation I did here was negligible. Because we decided not to cooperate, I knew that I couldn't get any information from the agent [IRS investigator]. You don't get any information unless you are cooperating. I did meet the agent, but I simply expressed belief in my client's innocence, and that was the end of the matter from my point of view. There is a psychological problem vis-à-vis the client in this situation, when you don't have a lot of meetings with the government. The client doesn't think that you are doing anything for him, when actually you have done a great deal. Keeping quiet and before that getting a comprehensive enough grasp on your client's position to confidently counsel noncooperation is a major task. You have to be confident that the whole thing won't blow up in your face. You have to trust that your client has given you everything that you need to know or leads that will get you to what you need. Clients like their attorneys to talk a lot. They think it is a good strategy because it shows the agent that you are a nice guy. Nice guys cooperate. Getting a client not to do this may leave him feeling that he is not getting his money's worth—and these cases are very expensive.

The Kovel Accountant

A client's personal financial status is one of the first elements examined when an attorney takes on a client. In some instances the attorney or an attorney's associate will undertake this task, but often it is accomplished by a professional accountant. Research findings show that there are accountants working regularly with defense attorneys. They have developed special skills for handling IRS cases and other investigations with complex financial aspects in which a defense attorney needs accounting analysis in order to evaluate the client's vulnerability to criminal prosecution. The professional accountant can bring to the client's material refined analytic skills that the attorney may not possess. And where the defense attorney can effectively delegate this responsibility, his own time can be concentrated on other tasks and other cases.

A key factor in this arrangement is that an accountant hired by and working for a defense attorney enjoys the protection of the attorney-client privilege. The work papers he holds and his analyses of client exposure are therefore not accessible to the government. Such accountants have come to be dubbed ''Kovel'' accountants by attorneys, after *Kovel v. United States*,[2] a decision holding that the attorney-client privilege applies to accountants employed by an attorney. The attorney-sponsored Kovel accountant can protect the financial records of a client from government access in a manner that the client's regular accountant cannot.

Because a client's personal or company accountant can be a rich source of information for the government investigator, frequently one of the first requests that an attorney makes of a client is that he retrieve all of the records from his regular accountant and deliver them to the Kovel accountant. There they will be less accessible to the prosecutor, and the Kovel accountant can examine them without stimulating the curiosity of business associates or the concern of family.

The defense attorney defines the nature of the investigation for the accountant and describes the kind of evaluation needed; the accountant executes these analyses and submits his report to the attorney.

Several attorneys stated that they often invite their Kovel accountant to the first meeting with a client when it appears from what the client has said—in an initial telephone conversation, for instance—that a net worth workup will be needed or that other specific tax items will have to be examined. The questions that the Kovel accountant asks the client as he prepares to do his evaluation indicate the expertise that the accountant can bring to a criminal case. This is evident in the following set of questions, posed after the client had explained that he had received kickbacks from a major electronics firm in exchange for preferential buying.

> Now I want to ask you about your bank and checking accounts. Do you have regular cash withdrawals? . . . You have to be able to show a legitimate source for your cash expenses. What is the size of your cash outlay? Do you purchase most items on a credit card or through some kind of billing system?
>
> Where does your wife get cash? . . . What is the amount of cash she uses per week, per month? . . . Do you give cash to your children? Have you had in the last couple of years purchases of large items—a diamond ring, mink coat, house, car? . . . Are there withdrawals from your accounts to cover the expense of these items? Do you have large stock purchases? . . . Do you have withdrawals from other sources to show that you have covered the purchase with legitimate income?
>
> Have you opened new bank accounts in the last few years? Where did you get funds for the new account? . . . Is there a legitimate transaction in your brokerage account that would have generated money for that deposit?

These questions are clearly directed at determining whether the government could ascertain from circumstantial evidence that the client had a source of income not reported. What is distinctive about the accountant's approach to the client is that he assumes the role of an adversarial interrogator. It is a different approach from that characteristic of an accountant meeting with a client for whom he is preparing reports such as a tax return or a financial statement. As one accountant explained:

> I don't probe for information when I'm working on tax returns and annual reports. If a client doesn't want to give me certain information, that is his business. I'd rather not be in the situation where I get things out of the client that he doesn't want reported. That puts me in an untenable ethical bind. It's also a way to lose clients. This can be avoided most discreetly simply by not asking too many questions. When I'm working on cases here [at the office of a defense attorney], on the other hand, I take a much more active role in getting things out of the client.

The Kovel accountant must be aggressive and probing; what he doesn't discover may be discovered by the government, thereby disrupting defense strategy and foreclosing protective actions that might otherwise have been taken. A good defense attorney's accountant over time will develop an understanding of the various ways that individuals hold and spend money secretly and the places that government investigators look for evidence of nonreported transactions. This expertise also is developed by the defense attorney, but the Kovel accountant is often the technician, coordinating the records analysis, allowing the attorney to concentrate on other matters.

Another example of the importance of an accounting analysis was reported by an attorney handling a securities fraud case. The focus of the investigation was a pattern of stock trading by individuals who were alleged to have received inside information from directors of a corporation. Persons under investigation included the corporate directors and the individuals who were alleged to have executed the trades. When the defense attorney first met his client, a corporate director and insider, the specific issue in the investigation was the timing of the purchases and their correlation with records of telephone conversations and board-of-director meetings in the client's corporation. At the first meeting with the defense attorney, the client explained his role in the transactions:

> We were in a period of merger negotiations that continued for over a year. During that time, the market price of the stock fluctuated radically. I would call [the brokerage firm] after most of our meetings and let them know what the public statement about the negotiations, which would be made the next day, would show. [Client looks at his records, leafs through them.] I think there were eight such occurrences. [He replies to questioning about how he received benefits from these transactions.] I had already been on the account of [the brokerage firm] as a consultant for some time. They increased my consulting fee for months, probably for as much as a year. I reported that as regular income.

At the time of this conversation, the client's defense attorney learned from the attorneys for the brokerage firm that a meeting with an assistant U.S. Attorney had already taken place. At that meeting the attorneys for the brokerage firm had produced documents showing that the brokerage firm had purchased and sold shares of the company whose stock was fluctuating for a long time before and after the merger consideration period, not just during the merger negotiations. The brokerage firm attorneys believed they had made a persuasive case demonstrating the absence of any pattern of purchases correlated with directors' conferences related to the merger. They also indicated that their own analysis of telephone records demonstrated conclusively that such records would not be a useful source of data for the government investigators, who might want those records to prove that calls had been made by the corporate officer to the brokerage firm after each merger negotiation. The government had been inactive for several months, but because no formal notice of investigation termination had been issued the attorneys could not assume that the potential problem had disappeared.

At this point in the investigation the client's defense attorney had enough favorable information to tell the client that the case might ''die on the vine.'' ''Nevertheless,'' he said, ''a full accounting analysis will have to be done of your personal income records.'' The attorney later explained what had been his early concern and the reason for undertaking the expensive auditing procedure even though there was a favorable outlook for the client.

> The question that we wanted to answer was whether the increase in the consulting fee bore a systematic relation to the profits that an insider taking advantage of his position could have received during the months that the merger was under consideration. The client said that he never kept track of the percentage he was receiving of the excessive profit. What we wanted to do was to see if the client's own records would reflect an increased income from consulting fees parallel to excess profits that [the brokerage firm] would have been receiving. If we found, for instance, that after each merger meeting there was some consistent time lag, and then [the brokerage firm] paid a larger consulting fee, we would certainly feel uneasy about an examination of his books. We also had to check out our client's diary. Was there any notation of hours spent consulting, and did they increase his fee over the period, was he getting higher consulting fees? ——— [an associate attorney] went into that issue.

This particular procedure was a preventive measure. In the event that the case went forward, the defense attorney would have already apprised himself and the client of the factual areas that might cause problems. He could therefore prepare explanations prior to possible additional government inquiries and take other measures to keep the inculpatory information from being discovered.

An attorney who has no corporations or corporate officers as clients but who has what he called an active white-collar crime practice described his work on a mail fraud investigation. The case involved a nationally publicized mail order sales gimmick in which the client had placed advertisements claiming that he had a large collection of stamps and coins and wished to sell it piece by piece. The advertisement offered the interested reader a catalog for a small fee. The catalog was designed professionally and made a good impression on the prospective buyer. The scheme was simple. The catalog stated that a 25 percent payment was required with an order. Upon receipt of the order the client would deposit the payment in a business bank account. He would then write a letter to the purchaser in which he explained that the particular selection was out of stock and that he was returning the deposit under separate cover. Simultaneously he would withdraw, in the form of a bearer bank check, the amount to be returned. This check was deposited in a personal account that he had opened under a pseudonym. He then carried on lengthy correspondence with purchasers who complained that they had not received back their deposits. He reassured them that he was investigating the lost correspondence through the post office.

Shortly after the FBI entered the case, the client appeared in the attorney's office and gave a full explanation of what he had done. In this instance, the attorney did not report any problem in obtaining information from the client. He believed that after their first meeting he had a complete understanding of the nature of the scheme. The central question for the attorney was this: did the FBI know the extent of the fraud, that the client had received deposits of between $35 and $65 from more than 250 persons? As the attorney stated, "From the questions that the FBI agent asked, all he knew was that one person had complained. And the client was very smart. He told the agent that he would have to examine his records, that he 'didn't remember the case.' " The attorney described his defense plan, the first part of which required extensive examination of the client's own files.

> My long-shot idea was to get the client to issue repayment checks immediately to all the persons whom he had defrauded. This was intended to put an immediate stop to additional complaints. My assumption was that nothing would be made of the case if there were only a few complaints; the FBI wouldn't get a sense of the systematic nature of this guy's work. After all, they really had no way of determining how many people were victimized without getting my client's records or waiting for more complaints. They were not going to put an advertisement in the paper asking for new complaints.
>
> I started then by examining all the purchase orders received from buyers and correspondence that my client had with these people. I examined their letters and his letters. I wanted to know how geographically spread the purchasers were and how long this had been going on. We figured that the purchasers who had been waiting longest were most likely to complain, so we wanted to get checks out to them first. Another question we had was whether there was more than one person from the same small town who had ordered and been defrauded. We were afraid these people might know each other—you know, stamp collectors in a small town know each other—and that would make them very suspicious. We thought we might send a personal letter of explanation in such a case, but we didn't find anything like that. With three or four letters exchanged in some cases, and with over 250 people, the total correspondence was gigantic. I also wanted to know if anyone was threatening to go to the police. I found that some of the purchasers had actually received their merchandise.

Access to the available information in this case led the attorney to a decision to allow the client to deny guilt, which is what the client had wanted to do. It was a decision that could be attributed to the early investigation and conclusion that the government was unlikely to determine the true dimension of the criminal behavior. The decision to allow the client to assert that he was not involved in a scheme to defraud his buyers—an assertion the attorney knew was a lie—would raise a difficult ethical question for one who believed that an attorney has an obligation not to allow a client to defraud officers of the court. Should he report the true facts to the government? Should he withdraw from representing the client, and if so, for what manifest reason? Would this not also communicate to the government that the client was guilty of something? This attorney felt that the formal ethical rules did not give him a straightforward answer to these questions. He would have to decide for himself, and he decided to allow his client to deny guilt, because "the attorney's job is to protect the client, not hurt him."

Information Sources in the Client's Organizational Setting

Examining a client's own records may be time-consuming and complex, depending on the quantity and organization of those records. When the client is cooperative there should be direct access. Evidence of the events and transactions constituting the potential criminal problem is also likely to be held by persons other than the client. That the scope of the questionable activity has led to the creation of evidence held by persons other than the client himself adds to the difficulty of a defense investigation and increases risk of exposure. But when such evidence lies within a setting in which the client exercises power, these matters are easier. While strong personal relationship can make a person accessible to the client and subject to his influence even in the absence of an organizational context, the structures of authority, constancy of interactions, and conformity aspirations of persons within organizations make them a setting in which information access is facilitated. The extent of access is related to the position the client has in the organization, with higher position correlated with more access. In many cases, however, even when the client has a low standing in the organization, access to someone in the organization will be easier than access to someone outside. Persons in high positions in organizations often cooperate with persons in lower positions in order to protect the integrity of the organization.[3]

As the number of persons, transactions, places, and documents related to a subject under investigation expands, the defense investigation must grow proportionately. Several factors operate here. One relates to how numerous and dispersed the sources of information are. Another relates to the question of how much influence the client has over the source—influence that can be translated into defense access to information. Here the attorney is examining potential inculpatory evidence over which the client has a significant measure of influence. The major variable factor is then the extent of dispersion and quantity of information that must be examined.

Multiplicity of Information Sources

An attorney who represented a client investigated for land fraud described his initial task in the following interview. His description makes it clear that a large portion of the total defense time was spent examining documents that the attorney obtained by virtue of his client's control over an extended organizational setting, and that the large number and geographic dispersal of information sources made his investigative job demanding and difficult.

> ATTY: My client was one of a number of persons being investigated for land fraud—for supposedly fraudulently selling residential housing in [a western state] to unsuspecting investors in all parts of the country. It was a very complex affair. First of all, I had to learn the land business from A to Z—selling, buying, and investing. I had to go there and see the land with my own eyes, study what they had been doing, what the geography was like, what representations were being made to people; was there really egregious misrepresentation or really nothing at all? I had to interview salesmen, buyers, talk to state and federal regulators. It was a tremendous operation. I started by documenting from day one how my client's company managed the project. I wanted to know what they had done and what understanding they had of how the operation was to work.
>
> MANN: What were the first things you did?
>
> ATTY: Like I said, I set about learning the business. I sent my associate to their main office with instructions that he be given access to all records—memoranda, drafts, plans, letters, interim reports . . . whatever. We needed to reconstruct how the officers of the company viewed the operation. Then I later had him interview salesmen; there were over 50 of them. I did a few of the interviews myself here.

The goal of reconstruction in this investigation was similar to that in the net worth evaluation made by the Kovel accountant: to develop the whole picture and to make a judgment about actual and potential exposure. From his meetings with the investigators, and from his own examination of the context of the potential criminal activity, the attorney needed to answer the questions "How much has the government learned?" and "How much can the government learn?"

At the early stage of an investigation the defense attorney's pool of information for answering these questions is not limited to the client. The client has access to additional sources. But in spite of this, examining available information may be a difficult task. Attorneys repeatedly stated that it was very hard to convey the complexity, length, and detailed nature of an examination of records in a case that involved substantial business transactions. Some attorneys described the physical quantity of records delivered to their offices by clients—"They had three large filing cabinets sent here" or "We had one room in the office devoted completely to housing the corporate records, and they were worked on in that room by us.'' Other attorneys detailed the number of people and hours used for examining the records—''Three associates worked on the accounts for over two months'' or ''We billed over 150 hours in three months on that case, all in the investigative stage.'' And still others searched for superlatives to emphasize the obstacles—''It was absolutely impossible to handle all the records in the sixty-day period we had to comply with the subpoena.'' In probing for a more concrete view of the nature of the defense investigation, I asked one attorney to go through his diary and provide a day-by-day picture of what he defined as defense investigative activities for a particular case that had been identified early in the interview. The case involved a bribery investigation; in addition to the substantive charge, alleged destruction of evidence was investigated.

ATTY: I've gone over my diary and looked at our billing sheets. I'm only going to give you an account of my diary for the first three months. . . . There's just too much time involved in my going through the whole period . . . over a year and a half. [He brought out a large ledger book marked ''Current Accounts.''] In the last year and a half, to March of this year, we have billed the corporation over $400,000. In the first of the six quarters we billed about $100,000. That represented approximately—and these are ballpark figures—840 hours of associate time and 200 hours of partner time. As I recall we did put together one brief on a subpoena, but most of the associate's time was devoted to studying our client's in-house memoranda, letters, and performance charts. Later, we had an accountant in on the analysis but that wasn't in the first quarter.

MANN: Can you give me any better sense of what an associate does when he looks at corporate memoranda?

ATTY: [He paused and thought about the question for some time.] They [the agents] were trying to show a pattern of cover-up, failing to keep normal corporate records. In an early conversation with the assistant U.S. Attorney [no indictment had yet been issued], he intimated that they were going to subpoena corporate records in order to demonstrate that the memoranda would show reference to documents that they were claiming had been illegally destroyed. The analyst's division chief [at the corporation] told us that they never existed. [The] vice-president for marketing told us that there might have been such records in existence at one time. What we knew was that none were there when we got into the case. We had to see whether the logs and so forth that might be subpoenaed would show reference to such documents.

MANN: But I don't understand, what did they [the associates] do, just read the documents?

ATTY: [A bit frustrated at being pushed] We—they—made a complete listing of all the in-house memoranda, without reading them completely, on the basis of their captions, for a three-year period, that is, my associates would read the title of the memo or other document, get a quick sense of the subject, and record that. Later they went over the listing with corporate counsel and flagged the ones that could have referred to such documents, had they existed. The corporate counsel was our resource in this straining process.

MANN: Then what?

ATTY: What do you think? They read the flagged ones, in detail.

MANN: Did you find any reference to those documents?

ATTY: You already know that our position is that there are no such references. [Attorney then suggests that we move on to another subject.]

The attorney in this matter was conducting a defense aimed at the potential bribery and obstruction of justice charges. His defense position on the bribery issues was dependent on what was found in the corporate memoranda; if those memoranda made reference to the corporate records allegedly destroyed, then his entire defense position would be seriously weakened. He would then need to ascertain whether there was a nonincriminating explanation and develop an appropriate posture for a meeting with an investigator or U.S. Attorney. Returning to the subject of the investigation, the attorney commented:

> If we had found that documents had once existed, our evidentiary burden would have changed substantially. All presumptions would have been against us. They would probably go ahead with an indictment unless we presented documented legitimate explanations on the bribery issue. As it is now, we have kept the burden on the government . . . they have to have proof on the issues rather than we.

Dispersal of Information Sources

Obtaining access to and information from a large number of widely dispersed sources was characteristic of defense work in many of the cases studied. A number of these were what are called ''questionable foreign payment cases,'' in which major American corporations were investigated for making illegal payments to government officials in foreign countries to obtain advantages in competition for contracts with foreign governments.[4] The payments were thought by U.S. government officials to be illegal because they constituted bribes—that is, payments to government officials in consideration for their not acting in a manner consistent with their public mandates. Prior to the Foreign Practices Act, there was no direct way in which these payments to government officials in foreign countries could be sanctioned.[5] In order to circumvent this, the SEC defined the payoff as a violation of corporate charters and therefore a fraud on the stockholder, and the IRS defined the same behavior as a tax fraud. The IRS did its investigation after the SEC's was completed, with the intent of recommending prosecution of company executives. The SEC's sanctions had been limited to obtaining corporate commitments to cease and prohibit continued violations. When the IRS entered a case of this type, the defense attorney often focused his initial investigation on detecting whom the real client would be: the president, a vice-president, treasurer, accountant, or subsidiary chief of the corporation.

One attorney discussed a case involving a field investigation of a Fortune 500 corporation that allegedly had contributed substantially to a foreign government official's political campaign fund. An IRS audit of the corporation's tax returns indicated that an accounting mechanism had been devised for characterizing the contribution as a company expense. A criminal investigator reported to his superiors that a corporate tax violation had occurred, and the IRS became interested in developing the case for reference to the Department of Justice tax fraud division for prosecution.

When the defense attorney was called into the matter, it was not certain which individuals at the corporation might be the focus of the investigation. To establish individual liability the government would have to show that the accounting mechanism was used with the intention of overcoming a legal prohibition and would need to identify the particular individuals who instigated or carried out the plan with such intention. Though the government had determined that there had been a violation, it was not evident that there was an intent to defraud, and if there was such intent, it was less clear which officers in the corporation possessed it. On the one hand, it was possible that all the officers believed that the accounting mechanism was legitimate. On the other hand, it was possible that some of the officers knew the plan was illegal but convinced others of its legitimacy and facilitated their carrying it out without an intent to defraud. The defense attorney described what actions he took when he entered the case.

> The most important thing I had to do first was to learn as much as possible about the case by speaking to my clients. Subpoenas were served on the corporation for corporate books and records. I had to start off with the assumption that it was possible that both the corporate officers and the corporation itself were targets of the criminal investigation. In fact, the corporate officers—obviously the corporation can only act through people—had retained me. They were referred to me by [a major midtown law firm]. In some investigations, one firm will represent the corporation and each of the officers will have a separate lawyer from a different firm to avoid any conflicts of interest. In some cases it may not be entirely necessary, it may not be necessary at all, and you can represent a corporation and its president. In any event, I was representing both. This gave me a great deal of leverage over most of the managerial staff in the company. They couldn't very well refuse to interview when their boss was telling them to cooperate. So what I did was I debriefed all the large number of vice-presidents and staff people about what they had been asked by government investigators. In addition, I tried to find out everything

> about the subject of the investigation. What is the business all about? What did they do in such and such a period of time? What are these books that are called for in the subpoena? How did you conduct your section of the business? Depending on how perceptive these people are, and how honest they are, you will begin to put together a picture of what behavior is being questioned. I never did come to know who the government was interested in prosecuting because the case was closed after about six months. But I knew exactly whose neck was sticking out and how far.

Determining "whose neck was sticking out" required a large investment of defense resources—interviews, document analysis, travel, transcription, and many hours of secretarial time. I asked the attorney to give me a more concrete sense of what was required.

> In that case, the consent decree had required that an audit committee and special counsel do an investigation of the company. By the time we got into the case, that investigation had been completed and a report issued. The report was bad for us. I'll never understand why the regular corporate counsel let all those people be interviewed without individual counsel present. Their responses, though certainly open to more than one interpretation, were not as they could or should have been.The special counsel spent over 500 hours doing the investigation for their report. We had to go back and reinterview each one of those persons. Then we had to compare the second interview with the first. Our interviews indeed raised doubt about the first interviews. It was a very long and arduous process. Several times we had to go back and reanalyze each pair of interviews to compare their positions on one question or another. That's the best I can do for you!

The Organizational Setting

The importance of an organizational setting and its authority structure can be seen in the next example. In this case a political official was being investigated for misuse of state funds in his office. This was an elected official connected with a government financed budget to conduct the affairs of his office connected with governmental activities. Over a period of several years he raised the wages of several employees on his staff in return for a partial rebate from them. In this way he was able to siphon off for personal use funds designated for governmental use without his books and records indicating improper use of funds. The scheme collapsed when one of the employees reported the payments to law enforcement agents after an argument with the official about job responsibilities. The official explained to his attorney that the employees had voluntarily given back part of their wage increase as a contribution to his upcoming election campaign. The client said to the attorney, "Isn't this a legitimate thing to do?" The attorney responded, "It all depends upon what the facts are . . . Can we prove that it was really voluntary?'' The attorney described his first step in preparing the defense:

> I needed to get good statements from the employees—seven of them. The eighth, the fink, was of course already a problem for us. The question was, what would the others say? Would they say they were involved in a fraudulent trick to get a pay raise for themselves? Or would they say they had been given pay raises and then voluntarily contributed to their employer's campaign without any prior agreements? No one else, outside of his office, so he said, had any knowledge of the affair. So he set meetings for me with each of his employees.

The structure of this arguably criminal scheme is similar to the commercial bribery cases that have been prosecuted in certain federal courts using wire and mail fraud statutes. In those cases, the typical transaction involves a special relationship between an individual buyer of supplies for one company and the seller of those supplies in another company. The buyer agrees to buy exclusively from that seller in exchange for a personal gratuity. Sometimes the buyer's company funds the gratuity by paying more, unknowingly, than the normal selling price. The seller then returns the extra income to the buyer in cash. In other instances, the seller's company pays out of its own funds.

What is relevant here is the basic difference in the situation faced by an attorney handling a commercial bribery case as compared to the above case of public official corruption. In the commercial bribery case, the coparticipants in the suspected crime are not part of the putative client's legitimate organizational structure. The attorney is less able to obtain access to these persons if and when he needs to interview them. It will be more difficult for the client in the commercial bribery case to provide access to seven sellers with whom he has made deals than it will be for the public official to provide access to seven employees.

As should be apparent (and as will be discussed in Part III), the presence of evidentiary sources in the client's organization has important implications for the possible defense objective of preventing disclosure of inculpatory information. Here one becomes aware of a distinctive element of white-collar crime: the dispersion of evidence among multiple sources. This characteristic can make defense work difficult because of the need for simultaneous access to different places. But if this is a problem for the defense attorney, it is equally a problem for the government, who must also obtain access to many sources in order to make its case against a target.

Observing defense attorneys at work brings into sharp relief characteristics of crime that correlate with defense opportunities: as the number and dispersion of necessary information sources increases, the opportunities for keeping the government ignorant of inculpatory facts also increases. During the defense investigation the defense attorney makes a picture for himself of the necessary information sources. As they increase in number and in physical and chronological disconnectedness, the likelihood that the government will obtain access to sufficient evidence diminishes. The attorney asks, can any one of the potential evidence sources provide completely incriminating evidence against the client, or would the government have to connect information from one source to information from another, or from many sources, to build the evidentiary case it needs? And what is the likelihood that the government will obtain the necessary access? The answers to these questions are preconditions to the defense attorney's fundamental strategic decision: to cooperate or to deny guilt. If information is dispersed, the likelihood of one source providing sufficient evidence to the government is low, relatively speaking. Then the possibility of winning, using the guilt-denying strategy, is high, relatively speaking. If information is not dispersed, the likelihood of one source providing sufficient evidence to the government is higher. Then there will be pressure on the defense attorney to make a deal.

It is important for the attorney to think of persons and documents as separate sources of information because he wants to know how numerous and how dispersed are the sources. But the problem of access is not only a function of number and location. It is also a function of influence over sources—the question is, who can get to them and get information from them? When this latter question is asked, the distinction between documents and persons is blurred, because access to documents entails cooperation of the person who holds the documents. The attorney must therefore also be thinking of the relationship between documents and persons because this bears directly on a second facet of accessibility, namely, the importance of possession and influence over sources.

5 Adverse Parties

Two sources of information have already been discussed: the client and the sources subject to the client's control. The third, sources to which the client has at best only limited access, can be divided into two broad groups: parties or entities with interests adverse to the client and parties or entities whose beliefs or institutional policies require that information not be freely communicated to outsiders. The former group is primarily constituted of government investigators, potential codefendants whose interest is furthered by taking an adverse stance to the client, and potential witnesses who are loyal to government interests. The latter group is primarily constituted of entities whose operating rules require varying limitations on public access for reasons of institutional integrity (government agencies of all types and business entities) and individuals who maintain a personal policy of inaccessibility for reasons independent of interests adverse to the client.

The information-gathering tasks of attorneys are determined not only by the number and dispersion of sources but also by the relationship that the client has to the particular sources: the key question is, how much influence does the client have over the source? This depends on the constellation of circumstances peculiar to the events that constitute the crime. In one instance, codefendants may view their interests as coextensive with the client's, or potential witnesses may cooperate with the defense rather than with the government because of organizational or personal allegiances. In another instance, involving the same offense, codefendants may view their interests as adverse, witnesses may be at odds with the client rather than allied to him, and there may be no organizational setting that facilitates client influence.

The range of persons and entities that constitute information sources its unlimited when the range of potential crimes is taken in the aggregate; for any one client, a defense attorney needs to define a determinate scope of sources that have become primary depositories of inculpatory information. Most cases require a combination of information-gathering skills and techniques. In some cases, the attorney may find himself primarily using skills described in the preceding chapters, related to situations in which the client has direct access to relevant sources of information. In other cases, the defense attorney will have to rely more on skills described in this chapter, because the information he is seeking is held by one or a combination of those sources to which the client's access is attenuated.

The Government Investigator as a Source of Information

One adverse source that will always concern the defense attorney is the government investigator. It may seem strange to think of the government investigator as a potential source of information for the defense. The government, after all, starts without any information and then presumably gets access to sources that the client certainly must have known about. Nonetheless, the government is an important source of information for two reasons. First, the client does not always want to give the attorney information or fails to recollect or recollects incorrectly essential pieces of information. If the government has already obtained information from third parties, then the defense may be able to learn important details not previously communicated by the client or other sources. Second, knowing what the government has found is an essential objective per se, even if the defense already has the same information. This enables the attorney to evaluate his chances of arguing lack of guilt. The attorney will always try to determine from the client and from third-party sources what the government has been told. But a skillful attorney will use his meetings with the investigator to get this information straight from the horse's mouth.

When a defense attorney is not able to get an adequate picture of the events being investigated from the client or from the client's sources, the government investigator may be willing to help or may inadvertently help the defense attorney. For example, he may say, "We are investigating kickbacks allegedly received by your client" or "skimming of profits" or "illegal agreements between this subsidiary and that company." And if the defense attorney learns that the government has already discovered certain damaging information, he is more likely to counsel cooperation. For example, the investigator may be willing to say something like this: "We have authoritative and reliable information that your client wrote this document." Such a statement may have a determinative effect on how the defense attorney handles the case. On the other hand, the government investigator may reveal through the questions he asks or statements he makes that he does not have an important piece of information. If the attorney is considering a noncooperation, information-withholding strategy, the discovery that there is a hole in the government's picture of events may confirm his decision to use that strategy. As one attorney put it, "After I met the assistant [U.S. Attorney] and realized what he didn't know, I decided to stonewall and move into a tight defensive position of righteous indignation."

Identifying the Agent

Although the defense attorney is looking for cooperation from the investigator, even without it the experienced attorney may gather helpful data by learning who the investigator is and what government unit and subunit he is part of and by listening to the way a refusal for information is delivered. One attorney reported that at a first meeting a client informed him that he was visited at home by a "federal agent and asked about certain business transactions." The first question the attorney asked was, "Which agency was he from?"

> It is an obvious question, but the answer may be more fruitful and more important than one would expect. The client knew the agent's name, but not the agency, because he had not dared ask further questions. Unable to proceed without better information, I had an associate spend half a day calling agencies in New York City, asking for a Mr. X.

The fact that one agency rather than another—the FBI, for instance, rather than the IRS—conducts an investigation may narrow the range of potential subjects being examined. And if the attorney is familiar with the agency's inner organization, knowledge of the department handling the case may further narrow the focus. Occasionally, it is known that Group X or Group Y in an agency is assigned, for instance, to "questionable foreign payment" cases, or that Agent Z is a member of the IRS department established to investigate taxpayer bribery of IRS audit agents. In IRS investigations it may also be important to know whether the agent is in the field audit department of the revenue division or a criminal investigator in the compliance and enforcement division.[1] One attorney, who generally waits until the last stages of an investigation to allow his own presence in the case to be known, often makes an anonymous call to an insufficiently identified agent to ask, "Is this the field audit department, or do I have the wrong telephone number?" Where an investigation is being conducted by an assistant U.S. Attorney, a few calls to other attorneys who handle criminal cases may quickly yield a detailed description of the subject matter that a particular grand jury or particular prosecutor is investigating.

Using Rapport

The attorneys I studied were clearly convinced that their ability to learn facts about a case depends significantly on whether they are known by the investigating agent and on their reputation for honesty. An attorney described his first meeting with an IRS criminal investigator in this way:

> I'm not saying that I get any special consideration from agents on the question of the merits of the case—the case for criminal prosecution. What I'm saying is that when I've worked opposite an agent already once or twice, and he knows me also from other agents, he trusts me. He knows I'm not going to lie to him or misuse what he tells me. In other words he just feels more comfortable with me as a human being.
>
> Let's say in one case he decides to give me some of the facts. First, he does this because he understands that I'm not going out to suborn perjury from witnesses. Secondly, if he has given me information in one case, it just

doesn't come off right if he takes a hardline, silent position in the next case. I think this is a real advantage of having practiced for some time, of knowing the ropes, so to speak.

When a new client comes to a defense attorney with a problem, the attorney often will tell the client that part of what he is paying for is the attorney's "familiarity" with agents and prosecutors. Such a statement increases the confidence of the client in the attorney's ability to handle the case. Some attorneys reported, however, that they also emphasize to clients that this does not mean the client is going to be given special consideration—"The assistant is not going to wink at anything because of this." On the other hand, one attorney said that he does not tell clients a fact that would decrease their confidence: that the agent who knows him or his "good" reputation may try harder to win the case.

Some defense attorneys believe strongly in the importance of rapport because of their own experience as prosecutors. A former assistant U.S. Attorney in the Southern District of New York described the potential benefits for an attorney who has achieved a trustworthy reputation.

> Let us say that the attorney is a defense practitioner, but there are a lot of defense practitioners, and he hasn't been at it long enough or visibly enough to have a reputation in the U.S. Attorney's office. He may have really tough sledding in getting his conversation to take place. This happens particularly if you're an unknown quantity. I know when I was an assistant there were lawyers whom I couldn't get a reading on whether I could rely on them. Then, I would never talk to them on the phone about anything important. About any matter, I would insist that they come to my office and I wouldn't meet with them alone. I didn't want to get misquoted. I didn't want somebody to say that I said X when I really said Y, or that I promised this or that. This is standard operating procedure for a prosecutor. You don't meet with defendants or defense lawyers alone. After a while there are some people you know and can trust and won't misrepresent what you say; then it is all right.

Another attorney commented about the effect of having worked as a prosecutor prior to becoming a defense attorney.

> MANN: How important is it to you in dealing with the U.S. Attorney's office that you worked there?
>
> ATTY: It gets you a hearing. Probably more readily than somebody they don't know. But you find out very quickly when you start a defense that once you get that hearing you have got to have something to say. So if I don't have anything to say which is particularly persuasive in the case, I do no better than any other lawyer that goes to that office.
>
> MANN: The U.S. Attorney is deciding whether you get a hearing or not?
>
> ATTY: I mean when I say a hearing, the assistants will listen to what I have

to say, if I am saying something. I am on a first-name basis with most of them and I can pick them up and say I just got retained by So-and-so and what is the case all about? They will more readily give me that information and listen to what I have to say in response to it than they will to the lawyer that they don't know. This is human nature.

Conducting the Meeting with the Government Agent

First meetings between defense attorneys and government investigators have one primary goal for both parties: information retrieval.[2] For a government investigator a meeting with the defense attorney is an opportunity to gather facts—what happened when, what the target will say about events, where documents are—and to learn the strategic defense position that the attorney will adopt in representing the client. As a result, the defense attorney often approaches that meeting with an opposite goal: to prevent disclosure of potentially damaging facts to the government and to conceal the defense strategy (unless the attorney has decided that an ultimate position has to be taken in the first meeting). Similarly, the government also has a second goal: to conceal what it knows and the legal positions it is considering. The course of these conferences between defense attorneys and government agents is dependent on the strategic decisions that each side makes about the amount of information it will disclose; success depends on the skill that each adversary has in persuading or tricking the opposite party into revealing more than he desires.

There were three distinct styles of dealing with government investigators that became apparent from interviews and observations. The first was based on passive listening, the second on proactive adversarial argument, and the third on a claimed intention to assist the investigator.

Passive listening. This approach centered on the assumption that the agent would be cooperative; he would supply information that would outline for the attorney the main subject of the investigation and would explain, at least in a general way, the role that the attorney's client seemed to have. A meeting with IRS agents in a criminal investigation was reported by an attorney this way:

> I went downtown to the Manhattan District Office on Church Street and met with the special agent and revenue agent. The revenue agent had done the initial audit and referred the case to the criminal side. After some bantering—I knew the agent—we got down to the very short conversation about the investigation.
>
> I said we didn't know what was going on, that I wanted to be able to speak to the client about the matter in a knowledgeable fashion and so I was there to hear what I could. The special agent said that they hadn't completed their investigation, but what they were looking at was whether the client's company had actually sold the tonnage of material that the company records showed. He said it just didn't seem realistic that our customers could have used so much

material, and wasn't more being billed than actually shipped? He didn't have to explain much more, but sonny-boy—that's the revenue agent—piped in and said that somebody in the company must be getting a bonus this way from the customers. So there we were. I said I'd have to discuss the matter with my client and that I'd get back to them.

If the attorney's client had not known or explained the subject of the investigation, the attorney was now equipped to question the client and the client's employees and customers; he would be able to develop more efficiently his own picture of the situation.

Later, the attorney was asked how this case progressed after the meeting with the investigator. His response shows that in retrospect he believed that the investigator, at the time of their meeting, had no proof of specific illegal transactions and did not yet know for certain that illegal payments had in fact been made. At that first meeting neither the defense attorney nor the investigator knew the facts about which adversarial argument would later take place. Nonetheless, the defense attorney felt that the investigator provided what could have been a useful lead by explaining to the attorney the subject area that was under investigation. The investigator helped the defense orient its investigation but was limited himself by his own lack of knowledge.

ATTY: The case was investigated by the investigative agency for about six months and investigated by the U.S. Attorney's office for about two years.

MANN: The U.S. Attorney's office had it for two additional years?

ATTY: In this case the investigative agency put it into the U.S. Attorney's office. The U.S. Attorney's office was not satisfied with the state of the investigation. They maintained control of the investigation but continued to utilize the services of the investigative agency, which they did on and off for two years, until they finally hit the jackpot by finding the supplier or the customer where the kickback was. Once they found out, it was easy.

MANN: So they were just working on suspicion that something fishy was going on in this company?

ATTY: That is right, which is a real pattern in the white-collar area. A lot of white-collar investigations are not all that specific. And a lot of them are really in the area of hunting for a needle in a haystack until they really hit on something. Sure, it happens that way a lot.

In contrast to reporting only an area of investigative interest, an investigator or prosecutor will sometimes supply the defense with a detailed account of the inculpatory information held by the government. This occurs when most of the information needed for charging has been gathered. The investigator then is an intermediary through which inculpatory information can be located prior to its actually being used against the client. Rather than withholding the information in order to draw the defense into deeper trouble, the investigator communicates it early, taking into account his own interest in efficiency, mutuality with known and respected lawyers, or, if a deal can be made, his need for information that the client may be able to provide about possible crimes committed by other persons. This is evident in the following situation, in which an attorney who specializes in commercial transactions was handling a criminal case with the assistance of cocounsel, a criminal defense attorney. These are the comments of the commercial specialist:

> MANN: You said you needed a criminal specialist in order to help arrange the plea. Why?
>
> ATTY: As I said before, I was more sure of myself with this hot shot helping me avoid pitfalls. I'll give you an example of a pitfall. There were five defendants. I was representing one, the only one who wasn't willing to cooperate. I went down to the U.S. Attorney's office with ——— [the defense specialist, a former assistant U.S. Attorney], and there at the meeting the assistant showed us films—tapes of my client taking a bribe. He said to me, "If you want to go to trial, it's up to you."
>
> So, we had another meeting with the client right here and I told him, "Look, Charlie, this is what they've got on you. You will either have to cooperate like the rest of the troop or almost certainly end up going to jail." I told him he was lucky they showed us the tapes. They had enough information from the other persons cooperating, they didn't need him.

Another attorney explained that he often receives essential information from the government about witnesses' probable testimony, which he needs to correctly advise the client whether to cooperate or resist.

> If I know the assistant and the assistant knows me, and we have a good relationship, I can often get help in the way of a signal about whether I should believe my client's story. I don't think this always happens to other attorneys, it doesn't always happen with me, but when it does you have really saved yourself a mess. Sometimes the assistant is trying to get you to go for a deal—you know, he's got so much stuff on your man that it's going to do you no good to hold out. So you deal. Other times it's just to save you and him the trial. But it's not going to happen where the witness is going to be shot the next day. You have to have a respectable practice.

Adversarial encounter. The second approach is adversarial in style. When the attorney has not gotten a satisfactory description of the problems from his client and only vague statements from the investigator, he may spark an argument to get the investigator to defend his position. Several attorneys stated that they used this way of drawing out the agent when he appears to be withholding important facts. The following "attack" took place at a meeting with an assistant U.S. Attorney who was investigating alleged payoffs by the client's company to government contracting agencies.

> DEF. ATTY A [speaking to the agent]: There is no way for us to adequately represent our client without knowing what's on your mind. We have examined books, daily accounts, the cash flow and find no indication whatsoever of expenditures that were not appropriate.
>
> DEF. ATTY B: This is a company that has an *excellent* record of cooperation with government agencies; it has voluntarily complied with all recent SEC optional reporting requirements; its executive-level staff has constantly taken internal measures to prevent any kind of improprieties in any of its divisions and subsidiaries.
>
> DEF. ATTY A: As far as we can tell, and without any further direction from you we cannot tell anything more, this company *has not* engaged *in any kind* of remuneration to any government official. We have made our case, we have met our burden of proof; if you attempt to get an indictment in this situation, then I say you are taking the role of judge, jury, and sentencer—and as a prosecutor you have no right to do that.
>
> DEF. ATTY B: A basic principle of our system is fair warning. You know that the issuing of an indictment in a case of this type causes very substantial damage. I ask you, how can you justify this to yourself without giving us a chance to examine the situation which you *suspect* constitutes a crime?

The assistant U.S. Attorney eventually explained that the government was examining the size and frequency of entertainment and meal expenses involving payments by the company for employees of the government contracting agency. When one of the defense attorneys was asked after the meeting whether he did not already know what was revealed about the subject of the investigation before his conference with the assistant U.S. Attorney, he answered:

> We knew that they were looking for some kind of gratuity payment. We also knew that certain high-level government employees had been given, by our client, favorable options to buy stock in another company on whose board one of our client's board members sits. What we didn't know is whether that stock option was what the assistant was looking at, or whether he was looking at something else, about which we might not have known. We obviously didn't want to go in there and say, ''Are you looking for fraudulent stock option gratuities?'' Now we *think* they are looking at expense accounts, not stock options.

The attorney was then asked whether he felt that he put himself in an unethical position by arguing that his firm had done its own investigation and found that the client had not made any improper payments. ''No,'' said the attorney, ''my client is the *company*, not the board member who arranged for another company to give an improper option.''

The adversarial approach can be used in varying ways. When the meeting between investigator and defense attorney has been called to enable the investigator to pose questions, refusing to cooperate can sometimes stimulate disclosure by the investigator. One attorney explained that he had accomplished this by refusing to allow his client to take what is called a ''blanket Fifth.'' A person who takes a blanket Fifth states that he will not answer any question, after which he is dismissed. There is no questioning by the investigator. When the client refuses to take a blanket Fifth but takes the Fifth Amendment on each individual question, the inexperienced investigator then reviews for the defense attorney much of his case by asking a long series of questions. He does this even though he knows he is not going to get substantive responses, apparently so that the target cannot later say that he did not refuse to answer certain questions.

The above procedure was observed at an SEC enforcement hearing, during the appearance of a corporate officer with two defense attorneys at his side. The SEC attorneys wanted the client to say that he would adopt the Fifth for all questions related to the subject matter the investigators wanted to talk about. When the attorney refused, the investigators went ahead and asked questions for more than an hour. At each question the corporate officer recited the same response: ''I refuse to answer, based on my Constitutional right not to incriminate myself.'' The attorney explained later:

> They really did a ridiculous thing there. Once they saw that we were not going to answer, they should have restricted their questions to those that they argued we couldn't take the Fifth to, those they said asked about corporate activities for which there is no Fifth Amendment privilege. All right, we took the Fifth to those too, to make them go to district court to get them enforced if they really want answers, but they could have forgone asking all those questions related to the *individual* activities. As they conducted it, each question they asked—in response to which they knew they were not going to get an answer from us—gave us valuable information.

He also later explained,

> Where I thought there might in fact be no Fifth Amendment privilege—and we took the Fifth anyway—I argued our position, the legal position, so that the record would show that we refused in good faith. We were coming close to the edge here and I wanted to make sure that we didn't expose ourselves or the client to contempt proceedings for improper refusals to respond.

Assisting the investigator. A third style of handling the information-gathering meeting can be used when the government has not been successful in obtaining what it perceives to be evidence essential for its case *and* when, given the nature of the case, it will be especially difficult and time-consuming to complete the task. In this approach, the defense attorney first makes an extensive and persuasive showing of how difficult, in the circumstances of the case, it is going to be for the government to collect all the information it needs. He emphasizes the large resource investment the government will have to make. He then states to the investigator that he is willing to aid the government investigation by having his law firm—and perhaps an accountant hired by him—gather documents, statements, and other information. The defense attorney thus voluntarily supplies to the government what the investigator believes he will need to determine whether to make a recommendation for prosecution and seek an indictment.

One attorney labeled this the ''junior prosecutor's role,'' an approach taken by him in an investigation of a pension fund and its trustees. The defense attorney addressed the investigating prosecutor:

> If you really think you are going to conduct a thorough investigation of this fund, you should know that it is going to take you all over the country. The fund has contributing companies and accounts in at least twenty different cities. We can get documents and testimony together in two months; it will take you two years to do this with subpoenas and interviews. We would like to suggest that you tell us what you want and give us sufficient time to put it together. If you are not satisfied, you can always do your own investigation.

Toward the close of this meeting the prosecutor agreed to allow the law firm four weeks to compile a set of documents. The documents were to include itemized reports, with supporting material, showing the work performed by accounting firms for the fund over the past five years and itemized bills of accounting work done by the trustees of the accounting firm for their personal finances. In short, when the defense attorney began the meeting with the prosecutor, he knew that improprieties in the management of the pension fund were being investigated. When he finished the meeting, he knew that the government was investigating improper charging of the trustee's personal accounting costs against the pension fund. ''Why would it take the government two years to collect the same information?'' the attorney was asked.

> ATTY: Because the government would have to issue subpoenas and then we or other firms would force them into delay and then perhaps litigate the scope of each subpoena—for documents as well as for testimony from the parties. It would be *more* than two years before they could complete a job that size.
>
> MANN: So why don't you stay out of the picture and leave them to do that?
>
> ATTY: That is still an option, depending on what we find. In the interim, we now know—more or less—what they are looking for. That's essential for us in order to evaluate what our long-range position is going to be. It's more impor-

tant for us to know this than to leave them to go about their business without our participation. All they need is one insider. They wouldn't necessarily have to go through all the accounts and all the trustee's financial papers.

By adopting this approach, the defense attorney shows the investigative agent that he can gather facts more efficiently than the government and that an unmanageable task would otherwise fall on the government. A fundamental assumption in this approach is that the investigator is burdened by a number of other cases. The extra resources of the defense can temporarily shift a major investigative load away from his limited capability. The investigator assumes that down the line he can always do himself what the defense attorney has offered to do, and that whatever he receives from the defense, orally or in writing, can only add to his knowledge.

The task-shifting arrangement, which has become increasingly common in white-collar crime investigations, has the potential to yield a substantial benefit for investigator or prosecutor and defense attorney simultaneously. The defense attorney may be able to provide documents and testimony that adequately explain the situation under investigation and thus save the investigator time and resources. It would also benefit the defense, for it would put a stop to a misguided investigation that could easily cause irreparable damage to a client even if a conviction were never obtained. In addition to these incentives, there are one-sided incentives and costs. The defense may slow an investigator's progress or may transmit knowledge about the subject of an investigation to clients who, by destroying or manipulating documents, make it impossible for an investigation to succeed. Or an unethical attorney may consciously mislead the investigator during a period when witnesses' memories inevitably fade and other priorities reduce the ability of the government to press the case with adequate resources. For the investigator, there is always the potential benefit that the defense will hand over unknowingly evidence that eventually constitutes a part of the proof of the client's guilt. It is well known that prosecutors' cases are often made by the mistakes and incompetency of defense attorneys who unintentionally or negligently disclose inculpatory information about their clients.[3]

There are cases, however, in which prosecutors would not rely on this task-shifting device. Again, the element of familiarity with the defense attorney personally and his reputation generally plays a significant part in determining the nature of the investigator-defense attorney relationship. If the investigator does not know the defense attorney, or if the client is perceived to be one whose general life style is suspect, the prosecution may not agree to allow the defense to assist.

Tracking the Investigator

An indirect but no less important method for getting information from the government entails tracking the movement of the criminal investigator to remain apprised of the places from which information is drawn. This aspect of the defense investigation was identified by attorneys in several interviews:

> But as we went along in the case, as the investigative agency began interviewing witnesses, every time they would interview a witness—since most of the people they were interviewing were in the company, they were accessible to us, they were friendly to us—so every time the investigative agency would come in and interview a witness, we would go in and interview the witness. And we would ask the witness what they were asked by the investigative agency. There, from doing that, we were able to figure what the areas of interest were.

And when another defense attorney was asked how he began to learn about the case, he responded,

> ATTY: What happened was that a subpoena was served for corporate records, and individual officers of the corporation were being subpoenaed to testify. Leading officers of the corporation retained my firm. Thus, we were aware who was being asked to go downtown and by debriefing our client and looking at the content of the subpoenas, we were able to form hypotheses as to what the investigation was about. It wasn't terribly hard; in addition, we were able to debrief grand jury witnesses who went down and did testify, who we didn't represent, but who were certainly willing to talk to us; and the prosecution can't prevent you from talking to them.
>
> MANN: Members of the company?
>
> ATTY: Employees, former employees, friends of employees, and so on. So we were able to learn the identity of people being called before the grand jury and we were able to go out and interview them or have investigators interview them and learn what they were being asked—"What were you asked? What did you say?"

Attorneys gain access to knowledge about the government's investigation by keeping abreast of the questions posed by government investigators.[4] The attorney may be able to determine exactly what the government is seeking, for instance, when a subpoena defines a specific document. Or the general nature of an investigation may be revealed when a range of documents are requested or a series of questions posed. On the other hand, it can also mislead the defense attorney if the investigator probes areas in which he is not really interested to put the defense off balance. How a government request can help an attorney develop a defense program emerges from this interview excerpt.

> It was already apparent that the government was going to try to make a fraud case by showing that the company failed to characterize properly the nature of

its expenses—as capital or business expense. However, it wasn't apparent how they were going to do it. Then we were told by purchasers [companies that bought from the client] that they had received summonses. We arranged for the purchasers to send us a copy of each record, that is, all of the papers that they turned over to the agent. So we were working parallel with them. Then they [the IRS] called and said, "We will give you an opportunity for a conference before it goes to district counsel with our recommendation for prosecution." So we were ready!

Debriefing persons who have been interviewed or given testimony before a grand jury is a method of getting a closer look at the government investigation. It is not as effective as being present at the interview, but it is a way of simultaneously obtaining information about the government and about what the interviewee knows. This method requires knowledge of the identity of persons interviewed and cooperation on their part. The more closely related the interviewee is to the client—within or on the fringes of daily life or business or occupational settings—the more likely is the client to receive knowledge about an interview and cooperation in debriefing. On the other hand, a defense strategy built on an expectation of successfully tracking information disclosures can result in a severely damaging backfire when a person with substantial inculpatory information secretly cooperates with the government.

How a debriefing is conducted—aimed at learning what the government wants to know—can be seen in the following interchange between a defense attorney and the client's regular accountant. It took place the day after the accountant was interviewed by an IRS special agent, who is a criminal investigator.

ATTY: I thought we had told you not to answer questions. What happened?

ACCT: Well, this man came to my house, about six o'clock in the evening. Showed me his identification and said he would like to talk to me; said he had just a few questions to ask. I said we were just sitting down to dinner and couldn't he come back later.

ATTY: So, you let him in anyway?

ACCT: He said he just had a *few* questions and if I wanted he would talk to me outside or would wait in the car outside while we ate dinner. I thought I'd better get it over with. I invited him in.

ATTY: So, what did he ask you? Chronologically, first things first.

ATTY: He wanted to know how long I'd been working for the company, what my general responsibilities were—you know, a general run down—and then he asked . . .

ATTY: And what did you answer to that first question?

ACCT: That I've been with the company eight years, first in the bookkeeping, then in the accounting department. I told him I've done all sorts of things, but now I'm responsible for payroll. That's about all I said.

ATTY: Then what did he ask, just after you finished telling about your general tasks?

ACCT: Well, he brought out these records—they were photocopies of old payroll books of ours—and asked if I could identify them. I said yes, I could, and then he asked me if those particular records looked like the ones I might have worked with.

ATTY: Describe the records, what were they exactly? [Records described] Go ahead, what did he ask?

ACCT: He asked whose responsibility it was to take the information off those records and make up the 941 forms, which is the employer's quarterly federal tax return.

When he asked at the end of the debriefing how long the agent spent conducting the interview, the accountant said, "Two hours . . ." The attorney, looking disgusted, said "Your dinner must have been cold." Although a more effective defense position would have been attained had the defense attorney been present at the interview, it was assumed that the accountant's description of questions and answers was not designed to cover up any information relevant to the investigation. The attorney was able to learn about the government's interest, to hear the accountant's responses to the investigator, and to carry out an independent interview. Nonetheless, it is always assumed that a great deal of potentially valuable information is lost in the retelling.

The government is of course the primary adversary. It is therefore something of a paradox that it can be used as an information source from which the defense attorney develops a defense strategy. From another point of view, however, this fact is consistent with the operation of the adversary system in other proceedings. Discovery techniques are devices well known in civil litigation for learning from one's adversary facts that will help one's own case. Indeed, information retrieval and control through manipulation of discovery devices is a large part of civil litigation. As with civil cases, discovery goes on at an early stage in certain kinds of criminal cases. When directed at the government investigating agency it is an informal discovery based on the skill of the defense attorney in manipulating a discussion with his adversary and drawing conclusions from his actions.

The defense attorney's role in relation to the government is similar to his role in relation to the client and to the sources of information in the client's setting. The attorney must develop strategies and tactics for obtaining information from sources who resist supplying it. The difference is that the ability to resist disclosure is much greater in the case of the government investigator, so much so that the attorney must always assume that there is a high probability that he will not be able to obtain any information of value. The difference can be illustrated by thinking of the attorney and the information source as occupying two autonomous territories separated by a boundary, where the thickness and opaqueness of the boundary determines the extent of access available to the attorney. When the government investigator is the target of the inquiry, the boundary tends to be thick and opaque. When a coparticipant is the target of inquiry, the boundary is thinner and more transparent.

Attorneys Representing Clients in the Same Matter

When the coparticipant or witness sees his interest as adverse to the client, the client is likely to lose access to him. Access may be reestablished, even though the relevant party remains adverse, if that party obtains his own attorney and that attorney decides to share information with the target client's attorney. Once a person has his own representation, his attorney becomes a repository of information. The attorney's confidentiality obligation requires that he not share information given to him by his client with anyone, but this rule, as the research findings indicate, is not always observed. In some instances the attorney who is doing the sharing gets prior consent from his own client. Such consent is not always intelligent, the consenter not being fully aware of the implications of his action. In other instances, attorneys share information with attorneys for other clients in the same matter without prior consent from their clients.[5] Pilot interviews indicated that information sharing among attorneys with different clients in the same matter is not an uncommon phenomenon. Thus questions about this issue became a systematic part of the research inquiry.

In the following excerpt, the attorney describes a case in which he represented the primary target and needed cocounsel to represent associates, who were officers in the same company.

> ATTY: I have had witnesses represented by lawyers who at least give me some information as to what is going on, consonant with their ethical obligations and their obligations to do as much as they can for their client.
>
> MANN: Can you tell me about a case in which that occurred, so that I can get a sense of how that information assists you as defense attorney in making your case?
>
> ATTY: Sure. Take a case in the Southern District which was a major mail fraud case. This was a company engaged in printing services, and the claim had been that they had violated a mail fraud statute by paying some bribes to a company to use their services. Some of the witnesses in the case came from the company—worked for the company—which I represented together with its president. And some of the employees were subpoenaed and I got them lawyers whom I knew well and trusted, good men. They got them immunity, but at the same time they felt enough—and their clients did, too—enough obligation to want to speak forth and tell us what they were testifying to. And that helped me because I didn't have to worry about what they were going to say. I didn't have to shoot craps. Very helpful. And by knowing what the prosecutor was asking them, I began to get an idea of how the case was shaping up, how

the case was being structured against my client so I could start taking steps to prepare for that.

Describing a broadly focused bankruptcy criminal investigation, another attorney (the lead defense attorney) made these comments.

MANN: Was there more than one defendant in the case?

ATTY: Oh yes, it was a multidefendant case. Our office was representing two out of seven people, defendants. There were three corporate defendants. Particularly significant was the fact that our office was coordinating the defense function, which is enormously time-consuming because even though there is separate representation, there is tremendous coordination and linkage that is very, very time-consuming in the preindictment period.

MANN: Is that something that occurs frequently, that a case of that scale requires coordination?

ATTY: Any multidefendant case, to the extent that there is not such an enormous cleavage of interest, ought to have some measure of contact between the attorneys because they could help one another while being absolutely true to the individual obligations of their clients. The number of cases where that arises to the degree in this case is very rare. This was an extraordinary case.

A third attorney described additional aspects of a relationship with an attorney representing another client in the same investigation. First, the attorney explained how the case got started.

MANN: How did the individual defendant get notice of the fact that he was involved?

ATTY: Oh, that was easy, a lot of ways. You get a subpoena from the grand jury, or let's assume you have an SEC complaint filed against you and at the SEC it doesn't go so well and you get a whiff they are going to refer it, or the FTC or the FDA or the IRS come in and they are doing an audit and it turns into a special audit, and then you get an idea that it may go criminal. There are several points along the way short of being arrested and slapped in the pokey where you know you may end up in a criminal case.

MANN: So this person got a subpoena. Is that what happened?

ATTY: His boss got a subpoena. His boss was in an SEC investigation and he got a grand jury subpoena, and then the lawyer for him was told, "Well, we want X," who turned out to be my client. And that lawyer called me into the case.

MANN: And then the client got in contact with you.

ATTY: Well, the lawyer did and said, "I am going to send you a client if you are willing—talk to him and then we will see." Of course you get into the problem here of who pays the guy's fee. The company or he individually and so forth. So the other lawyer had some involvement with that, too.

MANN: Now did this lawyer, when he sent this client to you, see the writing on the wall, that you were going to want information from him?

ATTY: I think he did in this case, yes.

MANN: That is a difficult situation to be in.

ATTY: Well, not really, because he too would rather have somebody there who was friendly, not just a hostile fellow who will not tell him what's going on. One of the great troubles or traumas in a white-collar case, any kind of a case really, but in white-collar cases particularly, is that you don't really know what the hell they are going to throw at you, what kind of statement may have been made in the last five years which will be turned against you in a complicated, very intangible case. What kind of document did your client fail to tell you about? And so sure, he wants to know, he wanted information also. So he wanted a friend in the case who would not turn this guy against his client. The understanding there really among lawyers who have some sophistication and decency is that you do whatever you have to do for your client but, at the same time, without injuring your client's interest, you can help your brother who represents somebody else, you do that. I do that anyway.

The above attorneys made general comments about the importance of sharing information with cocounsel. But what exactly is gained by the attorney who obtains information in this manner? One attorney who spontaneously began to discuss this issue was asked to be more specific.

MANN: For instance, what kinds of things occur between cocounsel?

ATTY: We would have a discussion of what the nature of the investigation was. I would ask him what questions did they ask your client and then I would tell him what questions they asked mine. And I would ask him what his responses were. And I would be curious to know whether or not the answers were similar or not similar. If they weren't similar I would want to know why. They could be dissimilar from an honest standpoint. It may be an honest mistake, an honest misapprehension on the part of a client. And it would be necessary to correct it. I would immediately get in touch with the assistant [U.S. Attorney] and write a letter. I would want to make a presentation to correct the testimony.

Another attorney started to specify the kind of information he shares but would not go into details.

ATTY: Well, I told the lawyer—my client wanted me to keep liaison with the lawyer who had the main guy—and so with my client's permission, I debriefed my client after he testified and I gave that information to the other lawyer.

MANN: I didn't quite follow that.

ATTY: My client gave me permission to relate what he said to me, and what he said to the grand jury, to the lawyer for the main target, and so I did that on that occasion.

MANN: For instance, what did you tell the other attorney that your client had said?

ATTY: "No comment."

Finally, one attorney—who was not experienced in handling criminal cases—provided a precise strategic reason for sharing information with another attorney.

ATTY: So what happened here is my client came in and I interviewed him. I immediately learned that he was a sitting duck. There was nothing to do but arrange some kind of deal, negotiate with the prosecutor. The officers working on the case for the IRS were very able, professionals, and they had done a thorough job. The goods were already in.

After a couple of meetings at the prosecutor's office, we arranged an agreement whereby we would talk and they would not prosecute our client for anything more than had already come out in the investigation—a kind of partial prospective immunity. All the time I was angled by ——— [another attorney].

MANN: What do you mean by the term *angled*?

ATTY: [Grimacing]: Well, I don't like that term at all. But you know, we often confer with other attorneys, friends, and those attorneys who have had experience in this area. I mean we just wanted to get a sense of how to best deal with the prosecutor and ——— was a natural person to do this for us. We work with ——— a great deal. All of our clients who have tax problems—criminal tax problems—we send to ———. He's the best in the city. There's no doubt about it when it comes to the tax area. We also agreed, early on, to let ——— know what our client was going to tell the assistant U.S. Attorney, because he was representing the main target.

MANN: Did your client meet with ———?

ATTY: No, no . . . not that! ——— would prepare questions and we would give him written answers. That way ————who was preparing to meet the assistant [U.S. Attorney]—was learning from us. He argued for his client on the basis of what we told him our guy was going to say.

In this case, the recipient of the information was able to make an informed argument because he knew what inculpatory facts had been given to the prosecutor by his client's associate. This knowledge allowed the attorney to decide whether or not he had a realistic chance of defeating the potential indictment; and he also was able to avoid making the critical mistake of arguing on the basis of a narrow set of facts when the prosecutor had already learned of a broader set.

There are many variations of multiple attorney cooperation in which essential strategic information is communicated from an attorney representing one client to the attorney representing another client in the same matter. For instance, an attorney who is informed that a client's business associate is pleading guilty might falsely assume that his client has been inculpated and unnecessarily counsel him to plead guilty. One way to increase the likelihood of obtaining early warning from an attorney representing another client in the same matter is to handpick that attorney. Frequently, at the start of an investigation one attorney will take on the main target, while choosing attorneys for other persons with the foreknowledge that all the clients are willing to join in an information-sharing defense program.

Government Records as a Source of Information

Aside from information the government collects in its investigation of a specific case, the government holds other information in the form of records and documents made by its agencies not investigating the case. In this highly bureaucratized society, government agencies collect a wide range of facts about the behavior and status of individuals and business entities. This information may be important to the defense attorney for evaluating the client's conduct and building a substantive defense. In addition, agencies keep records of procedures used to conduct investigations. Information of this type may be important for evaluating investigative techniques used by government and may form the basis for a procedural defense.

Individuals and business entities submit a large number of documents to government agencies. In the highly regulated industries companies have ongoing reporting relationships with numerous federal, state, and local agencies. Government agencies also research and carry out investigations of individuals and businesses that are not related to criminal investigations. For instance, research studies are done by the Food and Drug Administration on the need for and propriety of drugs; by the Federal Trade Commission (FTC) on the performance of industries; by the Civil Aeronautics Board on the safety of air travel; by the Bureau of Census on population characteristics; by the Social Security Administration on the needs of the aged; by the Environmental Protection Agency on the characteristics of industrial production methods, and so on. Such studies often solicit broad categories of information that eventually become part of the government recordkeeping bureaucracy. As will be illustrated below, information collected by these agencies, though it may seem neutral on its face, can be useful or even essential to a defense plan.

If government agencies collect vast quanitities of information that bear on questions of criminal liability, even if only indirectly, then the degree of openness of those agencies to public inquiry and the agencies' efficiency at information retrieval are critical to the question of whether crime is discovered and responsibility for it proved. On the one hand, inefficiency in government information management may be exploited by a perpetrator of crime and relied on by his defense attorney in making defense plans.[6] For instance, the IRS may not be capable of processing all the 1099 interest and dividend income reports it receives from institutions. Informed of this by his attorney, a person who has not reported income may decide to remain silent when he is audited. On the other hand, to the extent that the government is able to collect and recall information efficiently, the defense attorney, as well as the prosecutor, will want to take advantage of it. Certain information—such as systematic analysis of 1099s—will serve the law enforcement agency in its quest to locate and sanction law violation. But other information will serve the defense attorney in showing the absence of law violation.

Criminal defense attorneys interviewed in this study asserted that attorneys who are not competent in using the Federal Freedom of Information Act (FOIA) and the New York Freedom of Information Law to gain access to government records were often forgoing opportunities to establish defenses in criminal prosecutions. In one criminal defense firm, a manual for using the FOIA is circulated to all attorneys; in another, one among the several attorneys has developed special knowledge of FOIA procedures and is used as a resource by other attorneys in the office.

A defense attorney making a request to a government agency may want to retrieve several different types of information: information submitted to the government by the client himself for which there is no official documentation in the client's hands; information on the client collected by the government independent of the criminal investigation; information collected about other individuals or entities that bears on evaluating the behavior of the client; information collected by the investigators during the criminal investigation and passed on to other agencies; and information about the procedures used by the government in carrying out its investigations. Three cases described by respondents serve to exemplify different types of information retrieved from government agencies as part of the defense investigation. In each instance, successful handling of the case by the attorney was attributed to the response of a government recordkeeping agency.

Retrieving Information for a Substantive Defense

In one case, the attorney described a situation in which he used records obtained from the IRS. The records reported IRS opinions, based on data the agency had collected from the industry of which the client was a member, regarding how certain tax questions should be handled. The defense attorney, who prefaced his remarks by stating that he had prevented the Justice Department from referring the case to a local U.S. Attorney's office for prosecution, emphasized the importance of an opinion report that he had received directly from the agency.

> The report, based on an industry-wide study done by the IRS, said that many companies were using the like-kind provision of the IRC [Internal Revenue

> Code] to justify nonreporting of capital goods transactions, and that for the time being, the service [IRS] would accept that as a proper interpretation.
>
> Later my company did not report a large number of capital transactions, in spite of an IRS letter ruling received by them saying that they would have to report. When an audit showed the absence of reporting in this area, the case was referred to the criminal side [at the IRS].
>
> We had spent a long time negotiating with the special agent. By the time the case got to the chief counsel's office [an appellate review stage at the IRS] we had received a copy of that report through an FOIA request and argued that the service had previously approved nonreporting in this area, probably used data from our company in issuing that original report, and that in spite of the letter ruling we could not be held to a standard that the service had once said did not need to be met. The chief counsel turned it back [did not refer it further for criminal prosecution].

In the second case, an attorney described the importance of records he received from the FTC. The request had been made directly to the FTC, where it was denied. The request was then pursued in federal district court and two years later won at the circuit court of appeals in the District of Columbia. The case involved a price-fixing investigation carried out by the Antitrust Division of the Department of Justice. The report that was requested had been made by the FTC independent of the criminal investigation. The attorney, a chief litigator at a large midtown law firm, explained:

> At Justice they were trying to put together a price-fixing conspiracy among five major producers. Our defense required that we have production and price data from each producer. One of the producers was cooperating with the government, not with us. We knew that the FTC had done a study of these five producers for Congress, at a subcommittee's request. The final summary report was available, but what we wanted were the backup records compiled by the agency. Eventually, and with a tremendous amount of litigation time spent, we got the records we wanted and were able to figure the production and price data on the noncooperator from the report, not directly, but by using it in combination with the data of the other four producers. We've now briefed DOJ [the Department of Justice] using that data.

Retrieving Information for a Procedural Defense

The third case illustrates a different defense strategy in that it focuses on obtaining information about the procedures used by the government in carrying out its investigation rather than on the merits of the case against the client. Much as a case of street crime may be dismissed when evidence is excluded due to an improperly executed police search or interrogation, a case investigated by a regulatory agency or by a U.S. Attorney's office can be closed when the defense attorney is able to demonstrate improprieties in the agency's investigatory procedures.

One such procedural issue subject to substantial litigation effort in recent years is related to the division of powers between civil and criminal investigators in the IRS. Stated briefly, IRS civil division tax investigators, according to applicable legal standards, are not permitted to conduct criminal investigations. It is assumed that this would lead to misunderstanding among taxpayers about the consequences of any cooperation they offer. In order to show that an agency violated this separation of powers, the defense attorney must obtain information that specifies the circumstances of the government investigation. A defense attorney may be able to persuade a court to order an evidentiary hearing, or, as one attorney reported, the agency may unintentionally divulge that information when it is forced as a result of an FOIA request to disclose documents indicating that criminal investigators were involved during the civil audit.

The importance of using government-created documents to attack the investigative procedure was evident in a description of an attorney's handling of a securities fraud investigation. The attorney had mounted a comprehensive investigation of the business engaged in by his clients, a manufacturing company and the company's president. After meeting with SEC officers, the attorney's own investigation required that he spend several months collecting data from other manufacturers and from historical records of the market. Before the defense completed its investigation, the SEC recommended prosecution and referred the matter to the Department of Justice. From there it was referred to a local U.S. Attorney's office. Between the time of his original meeting with SEC officers and the referral to the U.S. Attorney's office the defense attorney had made an FOIA request. He asked for SEC internal data showing the amount of time that SEC compliance cases spend in the agency before recommendations for sanctions are made. After receiving this information, he was able to demonstrate that his client's matter had been pushed through the SEC without the normal amount of time allowed for presentation of the defense's factual case. The agency processing time in this instance varied so much from the norm that the defense attorney was successful in persuading the U.S. Attorney to send the case back to the SEC for further consideration.

Collateral Civil Suits

A source of information for both government investigators and defense attorneys are civil suits in which the parties disclose information relevant to the criminal liability of themselves or other parties. This is sometimes of paramount importance for a defense attorney seeking information from persons who would otherwise not cooperate with the defense. In any civil proceeding where discovery motions are made by opposing parties and court deposition orders are made, the defense attorney will be able to obtain a complete transcription of the deposition, unless a special sealing order has also been granted by the court. For example, a trustee in bankruptcy investigating the demise of a company in which fraud or culpable mismanagement is suspected may take depositions from all persons involved in the management and conduct of the company's business. Defense attorneys representing an executive of this company who is simultaneously the target of a criminal investigation may find that the trustee's depositions are the primary source of information about statements made by other people in the company. With this knowledge, the defense attorney is able to make informed strategy decisions and better prepare his client to give testimony. He will also be able to make his strategy decisions on the basis of prior knowledge of adverse and favorable testimony. One defense attorney stated that he prevented his client from attending a question-and-answer meeting proposed by an investigating assistant U.S. Attorney until after he had had an opportunity to examine depositions taken in parallel civil proceedings. As the attorney remarked, "After I saw what the others said, I had a strong sense that letting him talk could be helpful."

When parallel civil proceedings of any type are ongoing, there will be unique strategy decisions to make. Information disclosed through this means can be used as a sword or a shield, by the prosecution and by the defense. One defense attorney reported that he invested substantial resources to maneuver the delay of a civil suit against his client that threatened to force disclosure of damaging information. Conversely, another defense attorney explained that he has attempted to delay government decisions in a criminal investigation in order to wait for exculpatory information to be disclosed by discovery proceedings in an independent civil action filed by his client's company against a person who would be an adverse witness to his client. In still another situation, a defendant in a civil fraud suit brought by stockholders against him in his capacity as a company officer was forced to disclose his own role in certain business transactions, while being unaware that a criminal investigation was also underway. His testimony at trial corroborated—detrimentally to his own interest—the defense argument being made by another officer in the same company. A wary defense attorney might have stalled this action.

An unusual example of the importance of a civil legal action for information retrieval was provided by an attorney representing an officer of a corporation in an investigation that had potential criminal implications. What was distinctive was that this investigation was being carried out by the corporation itself. The subject was misuse of corporate funds by management personnel. When certain wrongdoing in the corporation's activities became evident, the board of directors decided to constitute an audit committee to investigate and make recommendations to the corporation. It was hoped that by taking this measure the corporation might avoid an investigation by the SEC, an occurrence that would be significantly more detrimental to its financial position. To conduct the operational side of the investigation, the audit committee hired an independent corporate law firm; it was to act as the independent investigative unit, under the supervision of the audit committee. Final authority to decide what finding would be made public to the stockholders and what actions would be taken was retained by the board of directors of the corporation.

During the law firm's investigation, many of the corporation officers were interviewed. Some asked to be given independent defense counsel, paid by the corporation, to advise them in responding to the audit committee investigation. After a debate on the issue and over strong opposition by a minority, the board of directors decided to provide officers who so requested with corporate-paid defense counsel. At this juncture several defense attorneys were called in. One related the following details about the corporation-sponsored investigation.

> There were so many suits going on here that the firm doing the investigation had a difficult time keeping control over things. The stockholders had a derivative suit going, and their attorneys wanted to interview the officers; an insurance company had an indemnity suit pending and they also wanted to interview officers. So did I.
>
> As the investigation moved forward, responsibility was beginning to be focused more and more on my client. I began to see that if this thing got out of the corporation into the U.S. Attorney's office there would most certainly be an indictment. So I had to keep the thing inside. No matter what they found on my client, I was determined to contain the issue within the corporation—strip his office, pension, fire him, give restitution—but keep the matter internal. We were prepared to offer anything in exchange for the corporation's not referring it to a law enforcement authority.
>
> Then the golden break came. The firm representing the insurance company began to uncover involvement in the problem on the part of two members of the board of directors. So, to make a long story short, I went to the chairman of the board and said, "Mr. So-and-so, we understand that there is a larger problem here. Let's keep it all in the family. Now, my client's willing to make restitution and he'll leave the company, but let's not have him and others splattered all over the business section . . . and so on."

Facts that the defense attorney was able to obtain as a result of the information retrieval efforts of other parties were used by the attorney to make it more costly to the company to continue with the investigation than to terminate it. While the particular interplay of parties in this situation may be infrequent, attorney use of the information from collateral proceedings is not. Whenever the role of an insider is litigated in a separate civil or criminal proceeding, the defense attorney and the government will have access to information that otherwise might not have been disclosed.

One difference among the sources of information discussed in this chapter bears significantly on the use that the defense attorney can make of the information. Retrieval of information from government recordkeeping sources and through a collateral private proceeding usually results in the government obtaining the information at the same time as the defense. In such instances, information disclosed must be integrated immediately into a defense position openly communicated to the government. Defense attorneys are thus careful not to motivate disclosure of information from these sources where there is a high likelihood that it will be inculpatory of their clients.

Information received from another client's attorney is significantly different. It can be transmitted to the defense attorney without being revealed to government investigators and therefore can be used to plan not to bring an issue before a government agent and to restrict the frame of adversarial interaction. The context of adversarial interaction is limited to a narrow subset of facts within a larger field of relevant facts not known to the government.

Conducting a defense investigation can be a long and complex process. It may take months or more than a year, requiring continuous information retrieval tasks, such as monitoring the progress of the government investigation, and concentrated periods of intense activity, when a great number of people must be interviewed or documents examined to keep pace with government investigators. As the process is described here it is one of information collection and analysis, in which the location of the information bears a direct relationship to the ability of the defense to evaluate exposure to criminal prosecution.

The defense office with large resources may approach many information sources simultaneously. A single practitioner, on the other hand, may adopt something like the following structured sequence. First he interviews the client. Next, he turns to the investigator to become better informed about the subject of the investigation and the identity of the targets. With this information he can better guide an intensive information evaluation program that focuses on the client's personal records, on testimony of persons in the client's organizational setting, and on records held by them. Finally, he will approach his most difficult sources—adverse parties and individuals and entities who restrict disclosure of information.

I have called this the precharge defense investigation and focused on the client, persons and documents subject to client control, and persons and documents not subject to client's control, in that order. This is, however, an abstraction of reality, because attorneys must be concerned with all their objectives at once. During a meeting with an investigator, in which the attorney attempts to get a sense of the government's strategy, he is also thinking about how he will arrange to examine the client's records and interview the numerous persons who are potential witnesses, tasks that he may or may not have already begun.

If the results of the defense investigation show that incriminating evidence is already held by the government, or is imminently about to be obtained, or is so exposed that it is unlikely that it will not be retrieved by a government investigator, the defense attorney may have to counsel cooperation. The client may be advised to plead guilty or to enter into a plea agreement with the government in exchange for a concession—immunity, a reduced charge, a favorable sentencing recommendation. On the other hand, where the defense investigation shows that inculpatory evidence can be kept out of reach of the government, the defense attorney will counsel resistance, that is, noncooperation with the government and denial of guilt. In the latter instance, the main defense task is to work to prevent the government from obtaining access to undisclosed sources. Implementation of control strategies generally requires that the defense attorney first determine the location of inculpatory evidence. As he progressively does this, his attention is trained more and more on information control tasks.

PART III
Controlling Access to Information

6 *Client Disclosures to Attorneys*

Two possible goals related to information control motivate the attorney in his meetings with clients. The first goal is to obtain adequate information about the situation being investigated. I have already shown that there are substantial obstacles to achieving this goal and that attorneys have developed special skills for overcoming them. The second goal, which can exist only in conjunction with the first, is to keep the client from communicating too much information to the attorney, information that would interfere with his building a strong defense.

There are some attorneys who say that they never facilitate a client's not giving them facts relevant to a criminal investigation. Others go further and say that they always actively probe the client for every piece of information that could relate to an investigation, even if some of it would negatively affect the attorney's defense plans. But many attorneys pursue the two goals simultaneously, encouraging disclosure of certain facts, discouraging disclosure of other facts. They want to extract all the information from the client that will facilitate good defense decisions: detail about the potential charge, what the government might use to prove it, and what the "worst case" picture for the client looks like. But they also want clients to conceal from them information that is not essential to these ends and that either limits the attorney's ability to argue certain defenses or puts him in a difficult ethical position.

Some attorneys, for instance, discourage the disclosure of facts that would negate a defense of lack of knowledge. They would not want to find out that a client actually had knowledge of a fact that would prove criminal intent—knowledge of a report or the action of another person—if the government was also not going to find this out. The attorney can then more forcefully argue that the client did not know of the report or action. In other cases, attorneys prefer not to know that the client is continuing to commit the very crime that the government is investigating. In still other cases, clients commit new crimes aimed at obstructing the advancement of an investigation. Knowledge of these acts could raise the problem of deciding how to respond to an ethical precept that allows the attorney either to report the client to authorities or to cease representation in midcourse, both of which would undermine the client's chances of avoiding prosecution.

Defense attorneys know that they walk a narrow line between helping and hurting their case when they facilitate or allow a client to hide facts from the attorney himself. Not having knowledge of an inculpatory fact that the government discovers can completely destroy a defense attorney's argument, which is why some attorneys reject this approach. But of the attorneys I studied, most either said that they sometimes preferred not to get certain facts from a client or showed by their actions that they felt this way.

Aside from the question of whether the attorney's ignorance of facts helps the defense or puts it at risk, there is the separate question of whether the attorney's conduct to discourage disclosure of information is ethical. If an attorney can learn of a fact from a client that will limit the extent of exculpatory statements that the attorney can make to an adversary or tribunal, is it ethical for the attorney to refrain from learning the fact? Before arguing to an investigator that the client never knew fact X, must the attorney probe and interrogate the client, or can he make this statement after a general discussion with the client about the investigation? Some attorneys probe. This chapter is about attorneys who do not.

The "nonprobers," if you will, do not believe that they are in violation of ethical standards. Most of them do not tell a client, "I don't really want to know if you saw the document, let's talk around that." They have more refined ways of accomplishing that goal. The refinement is essential to their own sense of the proper role of the defense attorney in the adversary system and of the ethical and moral standards that govern the legal profession in the context of a criminal investigation.

The deeper moral dilemma for white-collar crime defense attorneys is the question of what it means to devote oneself to defending persons who commit white-collar crimes—massive frauds on unsophisticated investors, breaches of trust given by voters to public officials, contrived misrepresentations in legitimate business transactions, and so on. Tension concerning this question, which either sweeps over an attorney from time to time, despite his normal ease with the job, or is ever present, can be significantly reduced by controlling information—by not knowing the true extent of misconduct, by not sharing in the continuing misdeeds of one's clients. To be sure, there are many clients whom a defense attorney handling white-collar cases can believe in and identify with—"there but for the grace of God go I"—but others provoke disgust. The job of defense attorney requires protection from becoming too involved with clients; information control serves this end as well.

Avoidance Techniques

If an attorney believes that it will be useful to a possible defense strategy not to be informed by the client of everything the client knows, he can simply not inquire.[1] A general apprehension about pushing clients to disclose all information about an alleged crime was expressed by one attorney in the following manner.

> I can remember years ago when I represented a fellow in a massive case of political corruption. I was very young, and I asked him, "Would you please tell

me everything that happened.'' And he said, ''What, are you out of your mind?'' Today my feeling is that I never ask anybody to tell me anything except what they want to tell me. I am not interested in fairy tales, and I am certainly interested in knowing at least what they [the clients] have told the investigators. But I think it is absolutely ridiculous for a lawyer to say I can't help you unless I know everything. If a fellow wants to conceal something, that is because if you probe unnecessarily, he is going to tell you what you don't want to hear and it is going to be devastating. Most clients, I think, have enough brains not to tell everything. It is understandable. And if they engaged in some kind of corruption, they are not going to tell you they are going to engage in another transaction tomorrow.

This attorney holds what is probably an extreme view on giving the client control over the extent of information disclosure. But even attorneys who proclaim that they actively interrogate clients for all facts demonstrate through their actions that they do not want to know everything that a client can reveal. The desire that some attorneys have *not* to know about ongoing criminal acts or all the details about completed crimes can be inferred readily from their reaction to the discovery of certain facts in the course of handling a client's case. For instance, two attorneys had been preparing to argue that their client had engaged in price-fixing activities only during a period when he was beholden to a certain superior in a corporation, who brought tremendous pressures to bear. The superior who applied the pressure had by then left the corporation. The defense attorneys were hoping to convince the prosecutor to exercise his discretion not to indict their client by arguing that his former superior had subjected him to irresistible duress. Just prior to the meeting with the prosecutor where this argument was to be made, the client disclosed to the attorneys that he had again begun to make similar price-fixing agreements. They reacted in this way:

ATTY A: The question is, can we now keep our meeting with the assistant [U.S. Attorney]?

ATTY B: We would certainly be better off if he [the client] had not told us about these new [price-fixing] meetings or waited until after our meeting with the assistant. I really don't understand him; he knew that we wanted to make this duress argument. I think we can go ahead with the duress pitch, but we will have to be much more careful how we phrase our statement. We'll say that he *was* under duress. But we should avoid all affirmative statements about the present. It's too bad, we are definitely in a weaker position now.

This conversation is a characteristic expression of inclinations found among attorneys not to be apprised of facts that limit the effectiveness of a planned defense strategy when it is believed that such facts would not be independently brought into the adversary arena. The ignorance of the attorney permits him to go forward with the strategy without any risk to himself and with a stronger advocacy position than could be taken with the additional information. The client's concealment of information allows the defense attorney and requires the prosecution (assuming the prosecution has not independently discovered the additional information) to argue their respective positions in a context more favorable to the defense. The defense argument that price-fixing was a *unique event* of the past related to pressure applied by a colleague is stronger than the argument that price-fixing occurred because of pressure applied by a superior. The absence of the term *unique event* in the latter argument is significant because a government investigator is likely to ask, "So, it is not occurring anymore, is it?" The attorney who has been informed by his client that it occurred again recently will not be able to give as good an answer to this question as the attorney whose client has kept quiet, unless the attorney is prepared to lie.

Even in the initial interaction between attorney and client, attorneys are aware that they may get more information than is good for the defense position. The usefulness of not being completely informed by the defendant was explained in the context of a "questionable corporate payment" case.

> Let me put the dilemma to you this way. We are representing a company being investigated for overseas—so-called illegal—payments to foreign government officials. We have decided to cooperate fully [with the government]. So let's say that I'm briefed thoroughly by the vice-president and others. I think there are some "questionable" activities, but they are not so serious that there will be a criminal recommendation [for prosecution by the investigator]. When I'm having a conversation, a conference with the agent, I now feel completely comfortable. But let's say I've also been told about one big payoff that looks ugly. Then I'm in trouble, I can't enter into a free-wheeling conversation with the agent as if being forthcoming. If your strategy is to imply that your client's actions were *de minimus*, you can't very well stop in the middle of the conference and say, I can't answer that question. You either have to be sure they are not going to ask that question, or you better hope that your client was savvy enough not to tell you about that payoff. Sometimes you are better off not knowing.

Attorneys must find ways to avoid inquiry that protect them from potential accusations of unethical misconduct by others and from a personal feeling of ethical impropriety that would make it difficult to perform their work. Attorneys do not want to be viewed by a client as unethical, nor do they want to go home thinking that their work is an obstruction of justice. To accomplish this end, they have acquired techniques for controlling what clients will talk about with them. Each of these techniques limits the frame of inquiry and can serve the attorney's interest of not receiving information.

Limiting the Time Frame

To define subjects about which they will not make inquiry and to communicate to a client what not to talk about, some defense attorneys limit their questioning to a particular time frame. While no attorney specifically identified this technique, it became evident from the way attorneys communicated with clients.

To prepare a case for indictment, a criminal investigator focuses investigative efforts on a discrete prior time period, the period he would eventually use in an indictment. This is particularly true in tax cases, where an investigator will say something like, "We are looking at tax years 1977–79," years for which the client's tax returns have already been filed. By the time the investigator has started the investigation and advanced it far enough so that a defense attorney is called in, it is 1981. The defense attorney then focuses his defense counseling on the earlier period. In his way of thinking, he has taken the client on for legal representation for the period 1977–79. No inquiry is made about other periods, including the present—so that even if the same illegal transaction continues to occur, the attorney will not receive knowledge of it on his own accord. The defense attorney creates a motion picture of his client's activities that stops abruptly where the investigatory period ends. It is a legal fiction the attorney uses to avoid attributing to himself responsibility for any action "not in the picture." One defense attorney explained the situation this way:

> If you have a client who has gotten involved in a lot of bad tax stuff, then you want to keep yourself trained on the period that the investigator claims to be examining. If you are going to argue to the investigator that what he is looking at either didn't happen or isn't a crime, you can do it better when you don't have all sorts of facts about other tax crimes the client is involved in. It is a delicate situation, sometimes it's important to know, other times it is better not to know. I can't make a generalization about it.

The idea of time frame control also comes through in the way in which attorneys describe the "completed crime" for which the client has sought counsel. A crime and acts of cover-up after the crime can be viewed as separate crimes or one continuing crime. A company that disregards negative results in product testing may be liable criminally for distribution of an unsafe product. A company that disregards negative test results and then destroys records of the results after a subpoena has been issued for them has also committed a crime prosecutable under an obstruction of justice statute. The criminal law provides more severe sanction for the latter company than for the former, in that the company can be prosecuted under two separate statutes and punished separately. There is, however, coexisting legal doctrine that would support a reasonable claim to define the destruction of documents as part of an original *ongoing* crime, not separately sanctionable.

If an attorney takes the view that evidence destruction is part of the original crime, not a separate crime, then he has no responsibility to the court or to the government to report it or follow up on hints of its occurrence. As one attorney stated, "Committing the crime originally entailed that it be concealed . . . continuing concealment during the period it is investigated does not seem to me to be any different than originally committing it." It follows that the attorney has no obligation to seek out evidence of cover-up after the investigation starts because he will be defending the client in regard to those acts as he is defending him in regard to prior acts. In this instance, the attorney extends the time frame of his representation to meet an informational control need, rather than shortens it.

Controlling the Client's Dialogue

In one situation an attorney simply said, "Stop, I don't want to hear about that." Even the thickest client is able to understand that message of information control. When a client begins to move into an undesirable area, other attorneys may say something like this: "I would prefer that we not talk about that subject area at this meeting." The subject is dropped, probably permanently. Still other attorneys accomplish the same end with a short lecture at the outset of a conversation. The following is a typical interchange, recounted from the time the client entered his attorney's office:

> CLIENT: I want to tell you what my parents and I decided to do after we understood that an investigation was going to take place.
>
> ATTY: Mr. Sweet, before we begin, I want to set out the ground rules, because we want to be very efficient about how we use our time—we can also keep your expenses down. I'm going to ask you questions, and when I think we are wasting time, I'll tell you to move on to another subject.

In another case, the following situation developed: The attorney began to discuss matters with a new client, who proceeded to tell about a scheme of payments to employees that was used for laundering unreported income. The client's company was under investigation for underreporting income to employees, thereby facilitating tax violations by the employees. In spite of the fact that the attorney had not wanted to discuss with the client the source of his unreported income, because that was not relevant to the subject of the investigation, the client blithely began to spew the story. The attorney plainly made an effort to direct the client away from that topic and on to how he arranged for payments to employees and who knew about it, but he was not entirely successful.

At the next meeting with the client, a new attorney was assigned to the case, but only after a discussion with the first attorney, who said, "This guy is for you—he needs a scolding from you because he is talking too much about his own personal matters. I think we are better off not knowing about his own problems now." As it turned out, the reason for not knowing about the client's "own problems'' was that the attorney could say to an investigator, if the case were to get that far, ''I assume that the source of the money for these payments was company profits.'' If he had known that they were personal profits of the client, then he could not say that, losing the strategic advantage of deflecting the investigator from the personal situation of the client.

Legal Advice and Lack of Inquiry

The attorney's desire not to know is perhaps most significant in the area of subpoena and summons compliance. The government is often dependent on documents to establish proof. Government investigative policy and in many cases Constitutional doctrine make search-and-seizure investigative techniques impermissible for obtaining documents. The investigator's use of subpoenas and summonses allows long periods of time for an answer, putting the attorney in a position where intentional avoidance of inquiry— by the attorney into the client's compliance with a government request for documents— yields a substantial defense strategy.

Here is an archetype scenario of the attorney in the inquiry avoidance role: a subpoena is issued by a court calling for the client to produce all documents related to a certain transaction. Upon receipt, the client takes the subpoena to an attorney and asks, ''How do I proceed?'' In the characteristic case of avoidance, the attorney begins by explaining to the client what is called for by the subpoena and what significance certain types of documents would have for the course of the investigation. He will not blandly ask the client what documents currently exist but will explain to the client what the subpoena indicates about the subject and scope of the investigation. Some attorneys go one step further and explain to the client what kinds of documents could be used against the client ''*if* they exist.'' For example, the attorney says, ''The government is trying to establish that officers in the corporation had knowledge of the improper evaluation of assets before the public distribution of the prospectus; if there are any documents which show such knowledge, these may be used by the prosecution as evidence for an indictment. Or if there is any document which indicates that an officer requested certain financial analyses that were not made, this may also be problematic.'' In this fashion, an attorney educates a client as to what constitutes a potentially adverse document. Subsequently, the client takes several weeks to conduct an independent search.

In many instances, such a discussion is the last detailed consideration of the type and possible existence of the requested documents. The client is later asked to report to the attorney whether any such documents were found. And then he is instructed how to make a formal reply on the date of appearance before the prosecutor to answer the subpoena. An attorney who is avoiding inquiry will not ask, ''Did such documents ever exist?'' or ''Was document X or document Y found?'' His interaction with the client is likely to be limited to a narrower question: ''Do you have anything to present in response to the subpoena?'' An attorney who was preparing to accompany his client to a U.S. Attorney's office to make a formal response to a subpoena explained his mission this way.

> The client's going to meet me here and then we are going down to Foley Square [location of U.S. Attorney's office in the Southern District of New York]. I'm not going to ask him whether he has all the books and records that have been requested. The assistant [U.S. Attorney] will do the asking. The only thing I'm going to do is to warn him about—explain to him—the dangers of a perjury charge. It's then up to him to handle the response.

In fact, the attorney explained to the client in detail how to answer the prosecutor's oral questions testing compliance with the subpoena, *after* the client said that he did not have anything to present. ''You do not,'' said the attorney, ''state anything more than 'The documents do not exist.' You do not say what kind of a search you made, or how you defined the nature of the documents you were looking for. All you have to say is that you read the subpoena and did not find anything that was described therein.''

Another attorney was asked directly about the attorney-client relationship in IRS summons compliance procedures. He stated:

> There are many cases in which one would surmise that documents summoned from the client existed at the time the summons was issued. My function in this procedure is a very limited one. I, of course, do not want the client convicted of an obstruction of justice charge, and I do warn him of the dire consequences of such a happening. But in the end it is the client's choice. I have no doubt that clients destroy documents. Have I ever ''known'' of such an occurrence? No. But you put two and two together. You couldn't convict anyone on such circumstantial evidence, but you can draw your own conclusion.

Still another attorney summed up the same views when he replied to an associate who seemed to think that a client was not being completely honest: ''What you are trying to tell me is that the client is not telling the truth. What I am saying is that the response is credible. We are not law enforcement agents.''

These interview comments represent the widespread view that it is not the attorney's task to enforce his client's compliance with the law. His obligation—even if it is an obligation not met all the time by all attorneys—is to refrain from actively facilitating or knowingly taking part in law violations. It is not a defense attorney's obligation to go into the corporate and personal records or send associates to conduct a search. Nor is it his obligation to find out what happened to missing documents. The attorney's limited role in this particular procedure is to serve his client by educating him. In addition to describing the evidentiary value of different types of documents, the attorney educates the client in the legal significance of the subpoena: ''The language in the subpoena encompasses documents of type A, B, and C, but not documents of type X, Y, and Z; you can legally refuse to hand over this document but not that.'' Or the attorney makes independent legal conclusions: ''The subpoena is overburdensome or excessive in scope and you can object to its enforcement.'' In essence, the attorney draws two diagrams for the client. One shows the client what is required by law and the language of the subpoena to be disclosed. The other shows the client which kind of documents are adverse to his interest and which are not. This is a passive role in which the attorney intentionally avoids proactive inquiry. The action—determination of whether the document exists and compliance or noncompliance—is left to the client.

Neutralization Techniques

When a client enters the office of an attorney and makes the following type of statement, the attorney is presented with a situation fundamentally different from cases in which the attorney's main objective is to overcome barriers to client disclosure. Says the client, ''I have a secret bank in Vaduz, in which for the past seven years I have deposited cash income. I am now in a position to make a major investment in this country. How can I bring these funds into the country without exposing myself to problems with the IRS?'' Very quickly, this client has distinguished himself from the large majority of clients. He has shown immediate willingness to disclose incriminating information and told the attorney he desires to be guided by his professional advice. There is no problem of withholding of information in order to prevent personal embarrassment or to influence legal strategy. The attorney does not have to manipulate the client in order to obtain information. Yet, because the client has revealed that he is currently committing a crime, the attorney has another problem. The new client has put the attorney in an ethical bind: can he provide legal advice without becoming a party to the crime?

Although it appears from my study that requests for legal counsel in order to cover up future criminal acts are not frequent, neither are they a rare phenomenon. Three attorneys reported dealing with it more than once in the year preceding the interviews. But a closely related situation is encountered more often. Not infrequently a client who is already the target of a criminal investigation or the subject of a criminal indictment will communicate to his attorney that he has not ceased the activity that is the subject of the potential or actual criminal allegation. That client, unlike the former client, typically does not directly request assistance in covering up the continuation of the crime. But the attorney is nonetheless faced with the same question. ''Do I act to prevent the client from continuing the illegal activity, or do I provide him defense counsel, ignoring the fact that he is still committing the crime?''

Some attorneys in these situations absolutely refuse to give advice or represent the client, relieving themselves of all concern about unethical behavior or complicity in the crime. One attorney who was asked by a client to participate in an illegal cover-up gave this explanation:

> ATTY: It is not an infrequent occurrence that clients suggest or intimate that we take steps that would be improper. By now I'm not surprised by this. What bothers me is that the people who do this seem not to care that they might be perverting, perhaps destroying, a law practice. I have no doubt that they wouldn't risk their business or profession for someone else, but they nonetheless make this request of me.
>
> MANN: Can you give me an example?
>
> ATTY: Okay. An uninteresting example, but one which is typical. A client says to me, "Well, I can get the company to issue a document saying that the funds in that account belong to the company, and that I've just been keeping them as a trustee." So you see, I have to be a policeman. I say, "No, we can't do that, that's perjury." It doesn't usually happen a second time with the same client. Somehow the message has been communicated.

It appears that some clients test their attorney's willingness to be drawn into an unethical strategy. When they see that the bait is not taken, their own approach changes quickly. They give up their plan or go to another attorney. In at least one instance, I observed great disappointment in a client who could not get his attorney's cooperation. From the attorneys interviewed and situations observed, however, it appeared that most clients did not expect that their attorneys would engage in blatantly unethical practices.

Does the attorney who refuses to handle a matter when the client is currently involved in illegal activities or proposes illegal means of crime concealment feel an additional duty to report the client's present or intended future criminal acts to law enforcement authorities? While this is a logical possibility, and it is permitted but not required by the American Bar Association (ABA) *Code of Professional Responsibility*,[2] it was not even within the range of alternatives considered by attorneys. It was simply felt to be impractical, unpragmatic, and unfair. One attorney who has handled a large number of securities and tax fraud criminal investigations, a partner in a large corporate law firm, explained what is probably a dominant norm of the legal profession.

> When a person comes to you and wants legal advice about a situation that may indicate that a crime is being committed, you, as an attorney, learn about the so-called crime in circumstances where the person perceives of what he says as being privileged—when in fact I am permitted to disclose it. But I don't see any major benefit in having lawyers snitch. It violates my sense of decency. People who come here believe that the privilege covers their conversations, and it would be unfair to act in a matter totally contrary to their understanding. I guess you have to say that I take a broad view of the attorney-client privilege.

While no attorney indicated that he would report a client to law enforcement authorities, many also said that they found ways of taking on clients who indiscreetly reveal ongoing or prospective criminal acts.

To take on clients who have already revealed a fact that should either prevent the attorney from offering his services or would make effective action impossible, the attorney has to do something to counteract the client's disclosure. There are several techniques attorneys use to accomplish this without having to be seen or seeing themselves as violating an ethical rule. "Neutralization techniques" seemed an appropriate descriptive term for these actions because it conveys the idea of counteraction—in this case, alleviating the effects of an inappropriate statement—and because it has been used in the past to describe a similar dynamic, albeit in a very different context. Gresham Sykes and David Matza in a leading article some years ago reported that juvenile delinquents learned and adopted in their own versions of principles of the substantive criminal law to maintain beliefs about the noncriminal nature of their behavior.[3] For instance, drawing on the idea of the affirmative defense of duress, delinquents were shown to be capable of justifying a law-breaking subculture because of self-ascribed duress. The similarity in the situation described here is that attorneys draw on customary and legal notions of responsibility to relieve themselves of the consequences of having been told facts by their clients that they did not want to know. They neutralize the knowledge—in the figurative and legal sense—and then proceed to provide defense services.

Admonishment

There were a number of attorneys who described in an interview or showed by their behavior that a properly emphasized admonition could eliminate the effect of the problematic information. When this technique is adopted, the attorney makes a clear, aggressive declarative statement telling the client to cease any and all criminal acts. One attorney noted that he gives a client a "stern warning," makes a memorandum of the conversation for the client's file, and then "forgets about that issue." "I am, of course, obliged not to aid the client in continuing. I tell him 'stop' and generally get at least a 'silent agreement.' " In essence, the attorney using this method of handling the ethical problem adopts a strategy of avoidance, after the admonition has been made. If present knowledge is not repeatedly forced on the attorney by the client, the attorney has protected himself by objecting and by noting the objection through the means of a memorandum to the file. The memorandum is meant to document that the attorney has properly responded to the information communicated to him by the client. The memorandum can always be drawn out of the file to protect the attorney from "false accusations" of unethical conduct.

This neutralization technique can work for an attorney when he is considering representing a client who is subject to a criminal investigation or indictment. In that situation, he can describe his connection to the client as relating entirely to past illegal acts, even where present or future illegal acts may also be disclosed. He no longer has responsibility for present or future illegal acts because he has admonished the client and is now focusing on past acts, which are of course fully protected by the attorney-client privilege. But when a client consults with an attorney for the declared purpose of maintaining a cover-up and there is no simultaneous investigation of criminal charges, this neutralization technique is ineffective. The attorney has no other reason to be advising the client except in regard to the possible prospective crime. If the attorney is to provide services to this potential client, he either intentionally collaborates with the client or finds a different technique for disassociating himself from the information originally communicated by the client.

The findings show that this situation definitely constitutes a problem for attorneys. They take seriously the implications of providing legal advice where they would manifestly be helping a person to conceal future illegal actions. Although interviews were successful in eliciting detached thoughts from attorneys on this subject, it could not be assumed that their actions comported with these descriptions. Through observation and discussion of actual cases I attempted to determine how attorneys actually respond when faced with the problem—when a potential client has presented a present or future crime problem and the attorney must make an immediate decision about how to act. Two additional neutralization techniques were identified—the use of ambiguity and hypothesizing.

Ambiguity in the Crime Situation

Certain situations do not readily demonstrate that a crime has occurred. One cannot make a reliable presumption that the elements of a crime are present, as one can when a bank manager finds a vault broken open. In situations of ambiguity, determining whether a crime occurred requires careful examination of fact and law. Many suspected cases of fraud—tax and securities fraud, for instance—leave open basic questions about whether criminal intent was formed by the so-called perpetrator. In the extreme, this phenomenon is exemplified by the potential client who thinks that he has committed a crime—say, he failed to report certain income—but the attorney can demonstrate that it was quite reasonable for the client to believe that an exemption or offset permitted the client's not reporting that income. There are at least two characteristics in potential criminal situations that create ambiguity. First, unclarity about the facts creates ambiguity. When the evidence to prove a crime is dispersed among many sources, the government's access to a limited number of sources may create suspicion but leave doubt. Second, and even where all the facts are known to the government, statutory definitions create ambiguity at their margins about what behavior is criminal and what is not. Certain kinds of statutes create more ambiguity than others. Attorneys interviewed said that white-collar crimes typically are defined in language creating a broad margin of ambiguity.

Faced with clients who apparently want advice about how to conceal prospective crime, defense attorneys exploit these factual and legal ambiguities by intentionally making interpretations favorable to the potential client. In other words, in order to provide advice on how to keep a particular scheme from being uncovered (where there is not already a criminal investigation underway or an outstanding indictment), the attorney defines away the criminal element. Neutralization of this type allows attorneys to believe that they are not "beyond a reasonable doubt" handling a present criminal situation, in spite of the fact that the client may have come into the attorney's office with a contrary assumption. One defense attorney hinted at the existence of this phenomenon when he made this comment.

> Particularly when you are talking about white-collar crime, you can't really say that there is a crime out there in the same way you can when someone comes in and says, "I've kidnapped X and I'm holding him in my house." You don't *see* the criminal act in the same way. You see a bit of behavior or bits of behavior which in the aggregate *may* show a violation. But you can't put yourself in the position of a judge on that question.

An attorney can thus define a set of facts as so ambiguous that he, like a judge in such a case, would have to acquit the client because of doubt. This was demonstrated most clearly when a client asked an attorney what to do about his company's leaving profits outside the country distributed among foreign subsidiaries and not taxed. The attorney said, "That's not a crime until the government gets a conviction in a court, and as long as that has not happened there is no crime there, as far as I have to conclude."

The point here is that attorneys exploit the ambiguity present in many cases, even when they themselves actually believe that the client has committed a crime. From a doctrinal perspective, one may have a reasonable belief that a crime has been committed without having to conclude that it is provable beyond a reasonable doubt. This distinction is used by attorneys to provide a basis for giving legal counsel.

Hypothesizing

The next technique of neutralization operates in a different part of the attorney-client relationship. When the former technique cannot be used because of the obviousness of the presence of a crime, this one can be effective, if the attorney believes in it. Rather than neutralizing the fact situation, the attorney neutralizes the connection between the advice and any prospective decision or action of the client. The technique, hypothesizing, can be explained most concisely by providing an example taken from observation notes. The following dialogue took place at the first meeting between attorney and client. The client started by explaining his problem:

> CLIENT: Several years ago, before the SEC started cracking down on overseas payments by corporations to foreign government officials, we created a fund, which is now held by a bank in Switzerland, in the name of a company which is owned by us, though the fact of ownership is not public record. The fund was created through large yearly business expense writeoffs for equipment that was never actually purchased by us or any of our subsidiaries. We are stuck in a strange position. Due to the SEC enforcement policy we feel it is imperative that we liquidate the fund, which now holds over four million dollars. It appears to us that any way we go about liquidating the fund other than continuing to pay out in the way we did in the past will eventually show up as a large expenditure by us for which we will have no legitimate record. Our question is this: how can we repatriate the fund without waving a red flag?
>
> ATTY: [after various questions about the fund and some extraneous conversation] It would appear to us that the way to handle this matter is for you to propose various programs which you have developed for repatriating or otherwise disposing of the funds. We would then be able to tell you what we would expect the consequences of such a program to be.
>
> CLIENT: What do you mean by consequences?
>
> ATTY: For instance, if you plan on reporting four million as profit from a particular foreign subsidiary we would be able to provide you with some sense of how likely—in the context of a particular subsidiary and its history—how likely it is that the report would become a red flag for a government auditor.

Another interview excerpt shows how a defense attorney responded to a request that appeared to require aid of concealment.

> ATTY: Mr. A was referred to me by his accountant. He came to me and said, in a nutshell, "I've got $25,000 in cash on which I have not paid taxes. How can I deposit it in a bank without creating a mess for myself?" He didn't tell me where he got the money and I didn't ask. I suppose this is the type of situation you are talking about . . . . First, I told him he had to report the income, what I said to him was, "Mr. A, it's my obligation to tell you, you have to report that income." He said to me, "Well, of course, but that's my decision, which I'll make, but first I want some answers to a few questions." And then he asked me, "What if I put it in the bank?" and I answered his question. And then he asked, "What if I buy stock with it?" and so forth . . . . I told him what happens when he does this or that; I don't see anything wrong with that, do you?
>
> MANN: What, for instance, did you tell him about what happens when he deposits it in the bank?

ATTY: I told him what anyone can read in the Bank Secrecy Act. Deposits of over $5,000 in cash are reported, with one's social security number, to the IRS.

MANN: There are those who would argue that that is an unethical practice of law. In what sense is it not for you?

ATTY: I don't see the issue. I've told the client that he's got to report the income. I've also told him what's going to happen when he does something with it and hasn't reported. Do you mean that I should report him? I don't think that's what you mean.

The dialogue and interview excerpt illustrate part of an attorney-client interaction that turns a direct request for aid in concealment into a request for analysis of hypotheticals. In its model form it occurs like this: first, the client makes a direct request for advice that puts the attorney in an untenable ethical position. Second, the attorney states that he must advise the client that the client has an obligation to report the concealed activity (and later makes a memorandum of this for the client's file). Third, the attorney invites or the client initiates hypothetical questioning. Where this kind of advice is given, the client may request assistance in concealing ongoing crime, prospective crime, or both, or, as in the above examples, the client may be seeking to take an apparently illegal situation and turn it into an apparently legal one. The attorney who answers the client's hypothetical questions does not believe that he is illegally assisting in laundering evidence or fruits of crime already committed.

Facilitation of Concealment

One critical question raised by the material in this chapter, perhaps an unanswerable one, is how far can attorneys go in actively facilitating concealment or destruction or other illegal manipulation of evidence? Is a passive disposition, when the attorney is explaining an information request to the client, in reality an active stance, given that the attorney knows that a particular client would be inclined to destroy evidence? Or is the use of the words *passive* or *active* of semantic importance only, because what really counts is the attorney's behavior, not his intention or belief about the actions that a client is likely to take? The normative question is discussed in more detail in chapter 11, but here I can state that two additional findings of the field research suggest that many attorneys remain passive when they believe that a client will take illegal action.

A large number of respondents indicated that some clients make open proposals to destroy or manipulate evidence. One attorney stated the following:

> When you have a client who's in a very bad bind and he's going to have to essentially convict himself by turning over bank records, or accountant records, or what have you, the client has a very strong impulse to do something about it, to save his own neck. From the client's point of view, there is not much to

> lose at that stage—he knows he's stuck if he doesn't do something. Occasionally, a client will say something like, "If I get rid of the records now, isn't it true that no one will know the difference?" He asks this because he believes he's been hexed and that anything he does will be found out, and he wants to know that it will work, that he can just get rid of something and everything will be all right. I don't think somebody like that is asking for my collaboration; he kind of forgets for a moment that I'm his attorney and wants a friendly, "Okay, go ahead and do it." I don't say, "Look, I can't allow you to do that." That puts me in a one-up moral position and is most embarrassing for the client. I usually say something like, "The penalties are very severe, and it is true that it may turn up later and cause you more trouble, so I advise you not to do it." That makes it seem more like I'm helping him protect himself rather than demonstrating some kind of moral superiority.

Another attorney described a similar type of encounter with clients.

> Sometimes a client will come in and say, "Here's my problem"—something like his bank account shows large deposits, and it looks like he's been covering up income, and he says to me that these are loans that his friend made to him and that because he has to pay them back this can't be income. He has a letter from a friend in the real estate business which says that loans were made so that the guy could buy property and wants to show the letter to the agent and so on. Now I can see that this is a total fabrication, and any agent is going to be able to see it, too, so I have to call the bluff, tell him it won't work, that I can't go out there like a clown and stand on my head; the whole thing will fall apart. Sometimes a guy like that goes and looks for another attorney, sometimes we get down to business.

Another finding related to evidence destruction is seen in comments by attorneys showing that many of them believe that the "smarter" and more intelligent clients conceal and destroy evidence. This is not to say that attorneys believe, or would respond if asked, that business executives are more inclined to destroy or conceal evidence than professional schemers and confidence men, or that there is any objective validity to such a proposition. What was observed was a theme in language and description of crime and clients that associated sophistication with various acts of obstruction of justice related to evidence. Two incidents, corroborated by later probing, originally pointed to the existence of this perspective on clients.

The first such indication appeared in a comment made by an attorney in an informal discussion of a case: "I hope he's smart enough to get rid of it, if he still has it"—referring to a client's daily diary of activities. While it was evident that this attorney would take no active role in aiding or assisting concealment, he thought that the client would be taking action in his own best interest, intelligent action, if he were to destroy his diary and that the client would be naive and lacking in savvy if he failed to do so. This attorney would handle the case to the best of his ability in either instance and would have no ethical problem if the client did not have the diary. As another attorney said, ''Take your victim as you find him,'' meaning that what the client does is his business—''Our business is defense.''

Sometime later, another incident revealed the same theme. The setting was a meeting with a new client who had come to the defense attorney with a letter and a summons from the IRS. The client explained, haltingly and with great pain, that he had not reported ''some part'' of his income and pleaded, ''Can't I just pay whatever tax I owe and won't they then be satisfied with fines, or what have you—there is no chance of prison, is there?'' After further questioning, it became apparent that the client had several hundred thousand dollars in brokerage accounts that had never been reported on tax returns and that yearly dividends were not reported. The client also divulged (provoking a tight grimace on the face of the defense attorney) that the agent had visited the client's accountant and had taken records related to the client. After more questioning directed at the client's background, probing to find out how the principal amount had been received, and after examining the balance sheet made up by the client (which estimated nonreported dividend income over the past three years at about $50,000 a year), the defense attorney made a general evaluation of the situation for the client.

> Mr. Black, what's going to make your case so difficult to handle, with the results that you and we want, of course, is that it's such an obvious and simple case. All the records, your accountant's work papers in particular, are now held by the agent. There's no complex accounting scheme here which would make it possible for us to work things through and come up with some helpful arguments. There's very little room for us to maneuver in. This is why I want to go into your medical background, to see if we can make some kind of psychological argument—at least to prepare ourselves for that if things go to the end of the line [that is, to sentencing by a judge].

Following the meeting with the client, the attorney made several statements about the client's pitiful situation, in each instance implying that the client had done a very stupid thing. Stupidity here meant that he had left his original records where they were easily obtained by IRS agents conducting an audit and, more generally, that the crime had not been carried out with a complicated scheme.

The finding that defense attorneys believe that the more intelligent and sophisticated clients obstruct justice through destruction and concealment of evidence is an important indicator of incidence, methods, and social location of crime as well as defense tasks. Defense attorneys have access to information about crime that is not available to any other observer or inquirer. They hear details and are exposed to incidents of crime that are not known to victims or to law enforcement agents or to social researchers. Thus, the belief expressed among attorneys that evidence destruction occurs among clients who tend to come from a high socioeconomic level and particularly among the better educated of the population needs to be treated as a special kind of research finding about crime. It adds weight to evidence already available that cover-up—using such means as alteration and manipulation of evidence—is not the special preserve of a marginally or generally deviant personality associated with violent or drug-related crime. It also alerts us to problems of prosecution and to the context in which defense tasks are carried out.

Justifications

There *are* attorneys who would probe their clients for inculpatory information, who would not use the techniques of avoidance and neutralization described here. It is less clear that they would make good defense attorneys in the present context of defense practice. The intrusive, whistle-blowing attorney is not appreciated by his client and it is doubtful that this attorney would compete successfully in the legal marketplace. If this is true, how do the attorneys who push the line of legitimate behavior, who use what appear to be at least questionable methods for pursuing the interests of their clients, justify their work to themselves? What allows them to do what they do? Are they just in it for the money? Have they no scruples about conduct in the interest of the client?

It would be completely inaccurate to say that the attorneys studied here believe that their work is ethically or morally improper, or that they believe that they are serving incorrect social ends by defending their clients in criminal cases. While they have different personal styles in dealing with clients, most of the attorneys believe that they operate in a system that requires attorneys to conduct themselves in the way described here. These attorneys believe that they should play by the rules, but that the rules have created a finely tuned system that must be used adroitly and with cunning in order that their opponents not triumph. Deeply imbedded in these attorneys is the idea of an adversary as a person who settles doubt in favor of his client, and therefore he looks for doubt and uses what may appear to be doubtful techniques and doubtful strategies, because it is part of his professional mandate. Unless there is an absolutely clear mandate to probe one's client to get information that even might be an obstacle to the client's best defense, the attorney can refrain from probing. Passiveness on the part of the attorney in the interest of not discovering undesirable information is just part of the nature of the adversary's role in the adversary system.

It was evident from the behavior and attitudes of many of the attorneys that they believed that even if the most passive attorney were joined with the most actively obstructionist client, there would be no ethical problem unless there were some kind of "direct" involvement of the attorney. What was meant by direct was not specified. What was found is that many attorneys would not see effective—as opposed to intentional—facilitation of evidence destruction as a malfunction in the system of adversarial representation, even if it were in fact partially the consequence of the way attorneys handled their clients. Rather, it would be seen as the inevitable by-product of an adversarial system whose higher value requires that the attorney be able to maximize his zeal for his client's cause while minimizing, if not eliminating altogether, any law *enforcement* role on his part. Attorneys believed this strongly and were prepared to defend it vigorously. As one stated,

> It's my mission and obligation to defend the client, not to sit in moral, ethical, or legal judgment of him. I cannot join him in transgressing the law, but whatever he does of his own impetus, whatever way he conducts himself in attempting to protect himself, is a decision he has to make independent of what I do. I must inform him of the consequences and significance of his action but not punish him or sanction him or in other ways initiate law enforcement actions against him. My role in the adversary system is to protect him.

This attorney was not concerned about potential backfire if his client were to be prosecuted for obstruction of justice. He explained that in the aggregate there is a high degree of certainty that some clients will help themselves by destroying or altering evidence and others will hurt themselves. From this perspective, the person faced with the tragedy of a criminal prosecution should not be told by an attorney how to handle the evidence that can lead to a conviction. As long as the attorney does not involve himself directly, it is the client's choice. By controlling the conversation, the attorney can protect himself from legal responsibility.

The attorneys who took an active stance by warning their clients about obstructive behavior and by making a diligent effort to discover the presence of all inculpatory evidence appeared to do so out of a long-range concern for the penalty exposure that results when a client conceals evidence or destroys it. One attorney put it this way:

> My job is to keep the client out of jail. Some of my clients have ended up in jail not because of the crime for which they were being investigated, but because they lied, or burned documents, or altered them in the course of the investigation. So I tell them right off the bat that if they want to stay out of jail, let me know what's there, and keep hands off.

None of the defense attorneys interviewed said that he attempted to get all the information from the client because he thought that there was an ethical obligation inherent in the public mission of the profession. The attorneys most committed to actively preventing their clients from obstructive behavior appear to be so because they are highly motivated to build and protect a reputation. A client who embarrasses the attorney damages his reputation. He must therefore conscientiously avoid being surprised and avoid making representations that may later be proved wrong. Above all, building a good reputation among the elite of the bar means that he can be trusted, not only by his client, but by his opponent. The test of his reputation is that when he tells an opponent that his client did not see a document, he is believed and relied on. These attorneys may also believe that they have an ethical obligation to actively prevent their clients from obstructing an investigation, but there was always a perceptible resistance on their part to making flat statements of moral obligation—"It is right for attorneys to find out what their clients intend to do with documents." Their stated concern rather was focused on their careers—"I do not want to be associated with a client who is concealing facts from me; my career is more valuable than any single client's needs." Attorneys were either openly dissonant with the idea of probing clients for information or pragmatic in their attitudes and behavior. None made a definite statement of ethical or moral obligation.

The Ethical Dilemma of Knowing Participation

The techniques of control used by attorneys to suppress counterproductive disclosures of information are based on interpersonal interview skills. Even the attorney's voice inflection can have an impact on what the client communicates and what the client does when he goes home and thinks—incessantly—about how to achieve the best possible defense program. Common to all of these techniques is the attorney's exclusive focus on manifest behavior. When the attorney asks questions of the client and gives legal advice, he measures his actions and his client's actions on the basis of what he does and what he sees the client do, rather than on the basis of what he foresees as the potential impact on the client's thinking and private actions. The attorney accepts that there are certain things he cannot and should not do—such as tell a client to alter his story—but if he explains to a client the legal significance of a particular story, manifestly a legitimate form of counsel, it is permissible even if he could foresee that given the particular client this explanation may result in client improprieties. While the immediate objective is to prevent the client from disclosing information to the attorney, the broader objective is to keep the client from disclosing inculpatory information to the government. In this sense, avoidance and neutralization techniques are ultimately directed at controlling access by government to facts that would prove the occurrence of crime and the client's responsibility for it.

The main ethical issue in these strategies turns on the question of what knowledge one attributes to the attorneys using techniques of avoidance and neutralization. According to legal doctrine, is a lawyer said to "know" that the client is concealing information if he uses any one of these avoidance tactics to keep from receiving knowledge that a piece of inculpatory information is held by the client? Does a defense attorney legally "know" that his client has a particular document when circumstances suggest that the client has the document but the attorney avoids being directly told so? Similarly, if an attorney answers questions about ongoing crime put to him by a client in a hypothetical form, does one attribute knowledge of the ongoing crime to the attorney even though he is not literally so informed? The scope of knowledge attributed to an attorney by legal doctrine—legislated law and ethical rules—has a great deal to do with whether the actions described in this chapter are illegal in the formal sense, and this will be explored more in the concluding chapter. But independent of what the law says, one can also ask what the law should be. Do the strategies used by the attorneys as demonstrated in this chapter seem to be the type of legal counseling that should be institutionalized by the formal rules as well as by custom and practice?

In answering this question, the defense attorney points to fundamental characteristics of the adversary system. He thinks not only of the rule requiring zealous advocacy of a client's interest, but also of the attorney's obligations to the public. For just as strongly rooted in the culture of the legal profession is the idea that the attorney is an officer of the court, serving the interests of the public, not just those of the client.

The underlying notion of an adversary system helps the attorney to cope with uneasiness he may have about specific actions he takes. The adversary system as a whole is assumed to serve the greater social good, even if some of its details do not appear so. Thus, if a rule mandates or permits a specific behavior—such as an attorney's answering questions posed by the clients as hypotheticals—that behavior is legitimate because it is part of a system that works. It is a deductive logic: if the system works, then the specific rules are right.

Another reason why strategies of avoidance and neutralization look so much a part of the adversary system, although the specific actions they entail may not, is because attorneys have transplanted the language of the substantive law. The time frame of indictments and the concept of continuing crime have their place in criminal law; so too can they be used by an attorney in defining the boundaries of his ethical obligation to the court.

As shown in this chapter, the idea of limiting one's inquiry and remaining measuredly passive toward a client is a mode of attorney work that can serve the operational goal of strengthening a defense effort. It also serves the goal of protecting the defense attorney from the larger moral dilemma of representing criminals—persons who defraud, bribe, and corrupt. This protective style has even deeper roots in the legal profession, for limiting one's willingness to hear a client's problem has to be a basic skill for any attorney. Any attorney—not just a criminal defense attorney—who cannot will be buried in the client's problem and made ineffective as an advocate or adviser. To handle more than a few cases, an attorney must remain to a certain extent detached and unresponsive. In this sense, the way of working of the criminal defense attorney is of a piece with the way of working of all competent attorneys.

7 *Client Disclosures to Third Parties*

It is common knowledge among defense attorneys that many persons give information to the government, even after an investigation is underway, that is eventually used against them to obtain an indictment and criminal conviction. Such information is transmitted in statements made through ignorant slips of the tongue, after improper advice from inexperienced legal counsel, and as a result of misplaced confidence in friends consulted and misconceived notions about government readiness to excuse persons who voluntarily disclose offenses. While there is a lack of consensus among attorneys about whether and how to control client communications made within the ambit of the attorney-client privilege, which was discussed in the preceding chapter, there is great consensus about a second information control task: keeping the client from disclosing inculpatory information to the government.

There are essentially two ways that defense attorneys can influence client communications with government investigators. They can instruct and educate clients how to keep quiet. And they can keep the government from making contact with and requests of clients. Thus the defense attorney has two focal points when he thinks about the danger of client disclosures—the client himself and the government. He wants to control the actions of both to maximize his control over the flow of information from the client to the government.

The intuitive assumption that the client can be easily managed because he wants to help the defense attorney achieve the goal for which he has been hired is incorrect. Just as it is often difficult to manage a client when the objective is to get him to relate facts to or to withhold facts from the attorney, so too it is difficult to manage the client's communications with third parties. The defense attorney has to work hard at educating the client in all the ways that he may inadvertently communicate with the government.

Controlling the government contact with the client is harder because the government has substantial legal powers for forcing the client to talk and because the government is pursuing an adverse interest. After all, the clients in this study are thought to be guilty clients and the government's interest is in discovering that guilt. Thus the attorney's objective in these cases is to prevent the government from using its powers to get information from the client that would accurately reflect the client's true behavior. The government is strongly motivated to prevent the defense attorney from achieving this goal.

Controlling Client-Initiated Communication

The Problem of Voluntary Disclosure

One way in which a person incriminates himself is by going directly to a government agent before going to a defense attorney. For instance, some persons decide to make full disclosure to the government, assuming that they can obtain concessions—an investigator's decision to recommend civil penalties only, or a mitigated sentence should an indictment be issued. This sometimes happens because the person believes that he is about to be investigated and that the government is likely to be successful. The theory is that self-reporting before an investigation will be favorably received by the government and lead to a decision not to act to sanction the person. But defense attorneys will tell you that this theory is invalid and voluntary disclosure should almost always be discouraged. The following, an account of a conversation that took place at a first meeting between a defense attorney, a client, and the client's regular civil attorney, shows a defense attorney discouraging voluntary disclosure. It demonstrates how clients begin to build a view of a legal strategy, including a concept of how information should be used. It shows also how a defense attorney acts as a brake on such a client. The effect of the defense attorney's advice in this case was to prevent an incriminating disclosure.

CIVIL ATTY: The problem is this: Alex has a substantial amount of income from a foreign business. That income has not been reported by him for a six-year period starting in 1972. We recently became apprised of the fact that Alex's ownership interest is being reported in a French newspaper because of a lawsuit brought by another company. The French government has also become part of the suit due to certain national regulatory issues that are involved. Alex has decided that he wants to report all this back income now, and he's willing to pay the penalty and interest and all. He is in a hurry to do this because he's currently undergoing a routine audit.

CLIENT: It's quite clear that if my foreign-ownership interest is discovered I'm a sitting duck. I want to get this thing out in the open under my own impetus before I'm asked about it. I'll pay the fine, whatever they want—penalty, interest. It seems to me that if I wait I'm putting myself in a much worse position.

CIVIL ATTY: I told Alex that I couldn't let him do this until we had obtained some more input from someone who knows the area, what to expect from the IRS, how they handle these matters. Alex agreed with me that we would consult you.

CLIENT: I'm very determined to get this thing resolved immediately. I also feel strongly that if I cooperate, show good faith, and so forth, I'll be better off. I'd rather have swift and certain punishment—a fine, penalties—than get myself in jail somewhere down the line because of this.

DEF. ATTY: How much unreported income is involved?

CLIENT: [Pausing, looking at civil attorney] Between thirty-five and seventy-five thousand a year.

DEF. ATTY: Where is it?

CLIENT: Foreign banks. Numbered accounts.

DEF. ATTY: All right. Let me start by giving you a short lecture in the IRS's voluntary disclosure program. It doesn't work, not any more. Back in the early fifties the IRS commissioner issued a public announcement that persons who reported income that had previously been omitted from tax returns might benefit from special consideration in that civil penalties would be applied but criminal actions would not be instituted, providing the disclosure was complete. That was a formal policy declaration but it was not binding even then. There were several cases—in the Supreme Court, I believe—in which the court decided that that declaration did not grant the taxpayer a *right* to this special dispensation. It was quite clearly declared to be a completely discretionary decision for the service. You must understand that since then even that formal "discretionary" declaration has been abandoned. It is true that there may be today an informal voluntary disclosure—well, I wouldn't go so far as to call it a policy—a consideration. Yes, informally they will sometimes take it into consideration. But there is no way anyone can depend on it. As for your case, I would not advise that you report your back income now. You have too much money involved and over too much time. If there is any mitigating effect for the IRS from the fact of voluntary disclosure, it comes in borderline cases, where the income is small, where the time period is short. You have a large amount, a long period, lots of evidence of intentional cover-up, of fraud. Judges in this district send people to prison for less egregious cases than yours.

Some clients, like this one, come to their attorneys with the intention of making partial or full disclosure of their wrongdoing to government agents. Rather than withholding too much information from their attorneys, they want to disclose too much information to the government—that is, too much for their own good. This desire is often associated with intense feelings of remorse and sorrow, even crying, and an asking for forgiveness. While it is certainly true that clients think of last-minute voluntary disclosure as a means for avoiding independent government discovery, with its serious consequences, it is also true that the specter of imminent exposure prompts some people suddenly to see what they have been doing from a different perspective. Some attorneys reported a desire among certain clients to disclose their crimes even though a viable defense plan was being proposed. The self-incriminating, cleansing catharsis could become an overwhelming impulse.

Clients who are told by attorneys that voluntary disclosure would not help their case or that cooperation with the government would be self-defeating often feel insecure with their attorney's advice. They are not fighters and do not like the idea of *openly* resisting government authority. There is also a tendency to disbelieve that enforcement agents are as tough as attorneys characterize them, and some clients are suspicious that criminal defense attorneys are overeager for a good battle and a large fee. The latter concern is demonstrated by a client's reaction to a defense attorney who advised complete noncooperation with the investigating agent. After several meetings the client reported that he had consulted with another attorney. The second attorney said that he "could arrange a settlement" by admitting and detailing the crime, without first waiting to see if the agent would locate enough evidence to refer the matter to the Department of Justice for criminal prosecution. The first attorney asserted that the client felt more comfortable with the cooperation strategy and that was why he chose the second attorney. Openly proclaiming innocence is a stance that some guilty clients do not have the courage for—they prefer an attorney who will help them plead guilty in favorable circumstances. Though he tries, the defense attorney may fail in persuading the client that he would be better off by not cooperating.

The Problem of Inadvertent Disclosure

Preventing ineffective confessions is part of the defense attorney's control of information. But more often clients would rather not make a confession, or after they are informed that a confession will not serve their interests, they want to follow the attorney's advice to abstain from talking with government agents. But even where it is clear that the client will not make a confession, the attorney must still prevent unintentional disclosure of information that would lead to or constitute a piece of inculpatory evidence.

Attorneys begin to educate the client to control information at the first meeting. One attorney explained a problem in doing this:

> A guy with a crisis in his life undergoes tremendous strains. There's naturally a strong inclination to talk to friends, family, business associates, to get sympathy, understanding, support, perhaps even ideas about how to deal with the situation. Family and friends talk to other people. Business associates are likely to be approached by an investigator—or invited down to the U.S. Attorney's office. Lots of guys don't know how to be quiet even after they have been warned by me with a pointed finger and harsh words. They're temperamentally talkers, and they end up incriminating themselves—by giving information to others who become government informants. For this reason I have to constantly monitor my clients, asking whom they are talking to, warning them again and again not to answer questions asked by associates, and making sure

they refer all official inquiries to me. If a guy hasn't already talked too much before he gets here, there's an impulse to do it afterward.

Because attorneys recognize that their clients often are accustomed to talking to associates as well as family about their private affairs, first meetings are used not only to examine what the facts are and who knows them, but to inform the client as directly as possible about the dangers inherent in communicating information to others. The attorney begins to assert control over the information as he is learning about it. The following is a typical first-meeting interaction between a defense attorney and a client who received an IRS summons; the client has told the attorney many details about his problem.

ATTY: How much of what you just related to me have you told to others also?

CLIENT: Nothing! I don't think . . .

ATTY: Have you discussed this with your wife, any of it?

CLIENT: Well, yes, I guess I have . . .

ATTY: So she knows everything, also.

CLIENT: Ahh, I did discuss some of it with her, I mean I told her that there's this problem I have and that . . .

ATTY: Can she be trusted?

CLIENT: Yes. I'm sure she can.

ATTY: What I mean is, can she keep from talking about this with—does she have a sister or brother?—them, with her girlfriends, and . . .

CLIENT: Well, I certainly hope so . . . I don't know.

ATTY: Now I want to tell you some of what *you* are going to have to do if we are going to work together. You have to stop discussing the situation—that means with anyone and everyone, including your wife, business partners, your intimate friends. Simply do not tell anyone that you have even consulted an attorney.

CLIENT: Jerry, you should know that I have talked, but not much, with my accountant.

ATTY: Talked? How, about what in specific? Details, I mean.

CLIENT: I told him that certain items on the company return were under question.

ATTY: Did you tell him which lines?

CLIENT: I think so.

ATTY: You absolutely cannot do this kind of thing any more. First of all, get the company return back from him. Does he do your personal return also? So get that back also. Bring them in here—send them by messenger. Accountants are stool pigeons, don't you know that? They ask questions, snoop around, get themselves knowledgeable and then have diarrhea when the agent comes. Let's not help him along.

Keeping the client quiet may seem to be an easily achieved goal, but attorneys frequently related stories of clients talking to friends and business associates who later were interviewed by government agents. One message that is difficult for clients to understand, defense attorneys said repeatedly, is that current "loyal associates" may turn on them and become informers for the government. As one attorney protested, "Keeping my client from debriefing his business partners, as well as me, was one of my biggest challenges. They were all in it together and I just knew one of them was going to break away and make problems for us. I wanted whoever that was to know as little as possible about my client." Another example can be seen in a conversation that took place after a client, a target in an antitrust investigation, had called another target in the same investigation to see if he could get any useful information about the progress of the investigation. During the conversation the attorney responded sharply.

CLIENT: I called David to see if he had been contacted . . .

ATTY: I thought I told you not to do that. This is ridiculous. You are going to have to do what I've told you or see us blow the whole matter. You're acting like an unruly adolescent. You have to cut it out. Now just don't do anything more than I've told you. Which means you sit tight and don't talk to anyone!

Later the attorney was asked if he frequently had trouble getting clients to follow his instructions. His response was this:

> It depends on the client. And the way I get control of the situation depends on who the client is. My tendency is to be demanding. I set the course and they are supposed to follow. If they don't, I let them know that the fate of the case is in their hands. . . . They have responsibility for the fuck-ups, not me. There are many clients who think they know better and they pull these shenanigans—talking to people to, if you will, "help me out." Other clients need their hands held a lot. They call up all the time and want to know if everything is okay—you know, one asks me, "Can I tell my secretary I'm seeing you today?" They can't take a shit without calling one of us. They are easier clients to manage.

Another easy client to manage is the one who legally is sophisticated before he comes to the defense attorney. One attorney sees this as a major factor in his work. As he stated,

> It all depends on the [legal] sophistication of the client. Executives in large corporations are accustomed to maintain a discreet profile. This doesn't mean that they don't talk among themselves—they do—but the likelihood of their not grasping the full significance of our request to keep quiet is very low. They are always guarding what they say in one way or another. Furthermore, the

large corporation executive doesn't do much of anything without asking his attorney first—his house counselor or personal counselor. When you are representing that kind of an executive, the personal counselor is keeping something of a daily watch. You may never have direct contact with the client after an initial meeting. You will have told the client's attorney what to do and leave it at that. Then you have other clients who are not accustomed to or adept at being quiet, and who we have ourselves to keep after all the time.

Because clients can so easily and inadvertently incriminate themselves, having an attorney who is experienced in how government handles criminal investigations and what should be done to protect targets is of paramount importance. Defense attorneys believe that when the target does not have an experienced defense attorney giving advice, he is often not able to resist a meeting requested by investigators and not able to resist explaining his way out of accusations of illegal conduct. To demonstrate the distinctive skill of defense attorneys, as compared to other attorneys, one respondent told the following story about an attorney who did not adequately perform his task.

This case was referred to us by a midtown firm that we work with often — specializes in commercial litigation. What had happened was that our client's secretary was met by an FBI agent when she arrived at work one day—this was before we got into the case—flashed his ID card, frightened her, asked for copies of monthly phone bills and for some other papers and she cooperated fully. Our client then went to this other firm and the attorney that got ahold of the thing thought that he knew how to take care of matters and went running down to the U.S. Attorney's office to "explain." What's worse is that he took the client with him—he thought the client "would be more credible." This is what I call malpractice. It is one thing to go to an assistant and talk about a matter, but to let the client do the talking, that is sheer incompetence. Now we are stuck with this transcript that the assistant made of the conversation—with the client's attorney a witness [to the conversation].

A target of an investigation is most effectively protected from making damaging disclosures of information when he has an attorney whose specialty it is to control information. By placing himself between the client and government agents who would seek to get information from the client, the defense attorney becomes the intermediary through whom all communication flows, at least in the ideal attorney-client relationship. Where the attorney does not conceal his involvement in the case to keep from arousing government interest, he informs the relevant government agencies that he is representing the target so that the ethical obligation to contact the attorney, rather than the client, is formally establshed. From that point, direct contact should not occur between agent and client without the attorney first being apprised. But how effective the attorney is depends to a large extent on how sophisticated the client is in understanding all the ways he can inadvertently disclose information or otherwise frustrate the attorney's efforts to restrict communication between the client and government agents. There is a great variation in client type and in effectiveness of information control.

Controlling Government-Initiated Communication

As the most direct way of obtaining inculpatory evidence, government investigators may make their first inquiry with the client himself. The agent may appear at the client's home, for instance, or send a letter requesting the client's appearance at a government office for the purpose of "answering some questions." Once the attorney has situated himself as an intermediary and educated the client, the client will refer the agent to him or contact him before agreeing to discuss the matter. It is then the attorney's decision how to proceed.

When a client turns away an agent by referring him to his attorney, it is possible that the agent will not press his request for an interview with the client. If there are other parties thought to be able to supply information, the agent may turn his attention to them, expecting less trouble. On the other hand, he may pursue the possibility of getting information directly from the client by asking the attorney for permission to interview the client or by issuing formal process—a summons or a subpoena.

How to handle the government's request to interview a client is a major decision for the defense attorney. It is generally believed that an outright refusal is an invitation for an intensified investigation. Thus the decision requires evaluating what a client might be forced to divulge were he interviewed and what other sources would be accessible to the investigator if cooperation were not forthcoming from the client. Part of this equation is also the ultimate concern with penalty, should the investigation lead to conviction, for it is widely believed that noncooperation aggravates the harshness of a sentence meted out by most judges. As indicated earlier, when the government has received or is about to receive evidence determinative of guilt, there is great pressure to cooperate and plead guilty in order to earn the available sentence mitigation. But where a reasonable chance to avoid exposure to indictment or to reduce the seriousness of a charge is believed to exist, a strategy of control is likely to be adopted. The strategic question is whether there is a high enough probability of the client's silence resulting in the government's not finding the information that will be concealed by the client. This must be weighed against the potential negative impact of the client being revealed as a noncooperator or accused of obstruction of the investigation, should the government get the information independently.

Bluffing

One of the techniques used for information control is bluffing. When the defense attorney uses a bluff, his goal is to create the impression that there is no inculpatory evidence to be found or that what would be found is so insignificant that it is not worth continuing with the investigation.

The first strategy of this type entails using the Kovel accountant to reply to the government's information request. As described in chapter 4, the Kovel accountant is employed by the defense attorney to help prepare the case by examining the books and records of the client, and he is protected from government questioning by the attorney-client privilege. In addition to performing technical analytic functions, Kovel accountants are sometimes used as surrogate attorneys during the initial stages of an investigation, in order to conceal the fact that a defense attorney is working on the case. The attorney who uses an accountant in this manner assumes that informing a government agent at an early stage that a criminal defense attorney is representing a taxpayer has the effect of increasing the agent's suspicions. By using an accountant who represents himself as the taxpayer's accountant, the defense attorney creates a facade of business as usual. Some defense attorneys also believe that Kovel accountants are better at obtaining information from investigators than the defense attorney himself because an investigator is assumed to be less protective of his own position than when dealing with attorneys.

One attorney demonstrated the use of this strategy in an IRS civil audit. Civil audits are performed randomly and on the basis of neutral criteria. They are to be distinguished from criminal audits, which take place only after some evidence of wrongdoing has been discovered by a civil auditor or obtained from independent sources.[1] Here the attorney used the accountant to conceal his own involvement while ascertaining whether the IRS civil auditor had discovered all or only part of his client's problem.

> ATTY: After we met with the client, we realized that we didn't know whether the agent had the whole picture or whether he had only touched the tip of the iceberg. The fact that the [client's tax] file was still with the civil auditor was some indication that he [the investigator] was not fully informed. So our decision was to handle it with a very low profile at the beginning. We would delay surfacing until we saw that the revenue agent had come onto richer paydirt, and we hoped that he would not. At that stage he had apparently only a computer printout from a TCMP [Taxpayer Compliance Management Program] which showed some irregularity in the client's tax return. Smith [the Kovel accountant] was going to call the agent and get him to explain the problem and then suggest that the agent send us a thirty-day notice [civil penalty assessment].
>
> Our hope was that the agent would respond positively to an approach by the "taxpayer's accountant," who would be expressing his willingness to pay up. There was a lot more out there for the agent to run into, and we thought we just

might be able to deflect the agent's attention from doing a bigger job on the matter by getting across our client's readiness to pay. But it wouldn't have been the same for the client to do it himself—that would look strange. Revenue agents are more accustomed to dealing with accountants.

MANN: What do you mean by surfacing, exactly?

ATTY: Coming up with our guns manned—the accountant's more like a periscope.

Delaying the appearance of the attorney was designed to deflect the agent's attention from a more thorough search. In adopting this strategy, the defense attorneys assumed that the revenue agent had indications of only modest taxpayer irregularities; the agent could be encouraged to issue a deficiency notice, assess a penalty, and charge interest, rather than referring the case for criminal investigation. If the irregularity shown on the TCMP output was similar to irregularities on other tax returns, the attorney said to himself, the IRS should be inclined to interpret the situation in a nonalarming manner—as a "common" taxpayer negligence error, against which a civil penalty is assessed. The defense attorney wanted to exploit the opportunity to have his client's matter treated unexceptionally, so that the very large deficit and potential fraud prosecution that lay behind the apparent facts would not be discovered. The accountant later described his conversation with the agent this way.

ACCT: I wanted it to look like we understood that there had been some careless mistake on the client's and my part and that we would "kindly" rectify the matter. So I called the agent and said, "This is Smith, I'm ———'s accountant. Now, I understand that Mr. ——— received a letter requesting some kind of records. Ah ha . . . Mr. ——— has not been feeling well lately. Anyway, I want to get this thing taken care of immediately, so it doesn't disturb him too much. Let's see, I understand that there's been some mistake. What did you say the deficiency is here?" He said, "We have found some problems here and would like to get the bank books and checks, so we can make an examination." So I said, "I don't have Mr. ———'s tax return in front of me now—what is it that you're concerned about?" Then he said to me that they had a larger W-2 figure than we reported. I said, "Yes, there had been some mistake there" and "just send us a deficiency notice for the difference. I'm sure your figures are right." The agent kept saying that he would like a meeting with me or the client. So I then said that I didn't have my calendar with me right now and I would get back to him. He hasn't gotten back to us yet.

MANN: Why didn't you take the client's records with you? You purposely didn't want to have the tax returns with you?

ACCT: Because I'm talking to the agent as an accountant. As such, I have an ethical obligation to cooperate. By not having the tax returns with me, I could put off any questions he might have wanted to ask me then.

A deficiency notice is an order to pay up an assessed liability. When paid, it terminates the disputed matter as far as the IRS is concerned, unless at a later date some additional reason appears for reopening the matter. When a client is concerned about a criminal investigation because an audit has been taking place and he has much to hide, receipt of a deficiency notice—a trauma to other taxpayers—is a victory for the defense attorney. Maintaining a low profile and a business-as-usual appearance through the use of Kovel accountants is among the principal strategies adopted by defense attorneys at an early stage of a tax investigation. The more widespread an attorney's reputation as a specialist in handling criminal matters, the more essential is a person who can function as a front—who can carry out attorneys' tasks without appearing as an attorney. Indeed, some general practitioners will keep a client's case in their office for a similar reason, concerned that by turning their client over to a criminal specialist they are communicating to a government agent their extrasensitivity to the investigation. Criminal defense attorneys, however, say that while a potential defendant may benefit by staying with his civil attorney because he may avoid stimulating the agent's suspicion, he will be disadvantaged because he is likely to over-cooperate; attorneys without adequate defense experience may allow a client to supply records, witnesses, and admissions, without realizing the consequences.

Obviously, the bluffing strategy involves at least some misrepresentation by the attorney to the government. The attorney is essentially saying, "There is nothing here so you don't need to look" when he knows that the government probably can make a case against his client. The strategy is not, of course, dependent on the use of a Kovel accountant. In some instances, the attorney himself makes representations to the government that are not entirely accurate; his skill is in creating an impression that there is nothing for the government to be looking for, without actually saying that in so many words. The attorney has to protect his own ethical position.

A technique used to accomplish this is the nonresponsive answer. Assuming that an attorney is not ready to make an outright misrepresentation (and surely some attorneys are), he carefully dodges the question but creates the impression that he has given an appropriate answer. For instance, when an investigator asks, in regard to certain tax years, whether the client had any foreign bank accounts, the attorney replies, "The client has no foreign bank accounts." While this is obviously a nonresponsive answer, defense attorneys rely on investigators being overworked and sometimes incompetent, which can cause them to miss important details of the investigation.

Nonresponses and Controlled Responses

Invoking the self-incrimination privilege. Asserting the Constitutional right against self-incrimination is a primary way to prevent the government from getting information from a client directly. Deciding whether and how to assert this privilege appeared to be one of the most frequent judgment tasks performed by defense attorneys. The extent to which attorneys permit a client to make a so-called blanket use of the self-incrimination privilege, refusing to answer any question, depends on the kinds of client and the nature of the potential evidence. It is axiomatic that the worse the client's situation—the answers he would be forced to give would be unambiguously incriminating—the more likely the attorney is to advise asserting the privilege. Weighted against this is always the negative effect that the use of the privilege has on investigators or prosecutors, who read it as a message that the client has something to hide. An attorney representing a ''guilty'' client would much rather have him appear to be cooperating, letting him talk to investigators and respond to a grand jury subpoena. But there are great risks involved in allowing such an appearance. Some defense attorneys are more conservative than others, tending to take fewer risks; they are less likely to allow a client to make responses.

The most straightforward situation is when an individual is issued a grand jury subpoena to give testimony about matters related to private affairs, for instance, how he handles his own funds. In such instances, there is no question that the privilege applies to the subject of the investigation, there being no records asked for and no business entities involved, two major areas where there are broad exceptions to the privilege.[2] When attorneys know that honest answers to likely questions would incriminate their clients, the usual decision is noncooperation.

In spite of the fact that an attorney comes to an unequivocal decision that it is best not to respond to questions, some clients are reluctant to agree to such a strategy. This was stated by an attorney who handles a large number of clients who are subjects of subpoenas, some of them targets, others ostensible witnesses who know that they have something to conceal. He tended to take a conservative approach to the issue.

> One of my problems in this area is getting businessmen to take the Fifth. They think it's unbecoming, embarrassing, humiliating, and, as one client asked, ''What do I tell my boss?'' ''I can go in and explain the matter,'' he said. Well, he was in the grand jury for three hours and by the time he got finished he had supplied the prosecutor with testimony to make a dozen perjury charges. So my policy, except in very rare situations, is to not permit clients to go into the grand jury. It's very bad practice to do that, and I almost always recommend against it. That's one of my biggest raps when I speak before these Practicing Law Institute groups on ''white-collar-crime''—don't let your man in there, he won't come out alive.

The attorney knows that the interviewer will make every effort to get the client to make damaging admissions. The client will be examined intensively by the interviewer and there will not be a judge or, in federal jurisdiction, a defense attorney present to restrict the content of questions or control the interviewer's style. When an attorney feels that there is a high likelihood that his client will be cornered into making damaging statements, he cannot allow him to appear, or, if he must appear, he will make sure that the client does nothing but assert his self-incrimination privilege.

Preparing a client for interview. Sometimes the attorney will decide that it is better to have the client appear and respond, as long as appropriate preparations are made. One such situation is when the attorney concludes that his fight against the issuance of indictment will be lost unless he allows the prosecutor to question the client. This usually occurs after a prosecutor has completed his investigation and has decided that without some explanation from the target there is no choice but to indict. If the case is borderline, and the client has a reasonable explanation, the client's appearance might tip the scales in his favor. The attorney's aim is to have the client present exculpatory information. One attorney described such a situation:

> At the preindictment stage one of the hard and fast rules is that you never let your client go to talk to anyone, any investigator, and you don't let them go into the grand jury. Any attorney who does this is not doing his job well. There's one exception, an infrequent one, but one that I've been part of on at least two occasions. In a case in which I think the evidence is borderline, but I don't, for one reason or another, want to expose my client to a trial, I have made a deal with the prosecutor whereby I agree that my client will testify in the grand jury in exchange for the prosecutor's promise not to indict him for perjury. My client then gets the chance to convince the grand jury not to issue the indictment through his testimony, and the prosecutor gets the testimony, which he knows he will be able to use at trial. The benefit for the prosecutor is that he gets a preview, one might say, a chance to test his case against the testimony that the defendant will make. My benefit is that I get a chance to convince a jury of my client's version before issuance of an indictment, without exposing him to perjury. Now in this kind of case, it's clear that I'm not going to take my client to trial if the indictment comes out, but I don't say this directly to the prosecutor. I did this once with ———, when he was still in the Southern District. I had this net worth case and my client was a professional man. He was saying that he had lost track of the money—taking the professional scatterbrained defense position. The only problem was that the excess income was about $80,000 and that seemed like a great deal of money to lose track of and to convince the jury. So I wasn't confident of how they would take to the case, but I thought I should let him go in [to the grand jury] and tell his

story. Now in spite of the fact that I didn't tell the prosecutor that we were going to plead guilty if we got indicted, when this kind of a deal is made a smart prosecutor will know that we are going to plead. I'm sure ——— knew this.

Control is not always fully exercised. Defense attorneys sometimes allow partial exposure in controlled settings. In the above example, the attorney allowed his client to go into the grand jury on the condition that he obtain the agreement of the assistant U.S. Attorney not to prosecute his client for perjury. If we take this description at face value, the prosecutor had agreed to allow the defense, in any manner it chose, including the possible fabrication of facts, to argue for an immediate termination of the case. Controlling information meant not only containing it, but disclosing it in a measured manner. Some attorneys allow clients to go into a grand jury to "make explanations" without such prior agreement, because they have nothing to hide, or because they have everything to hide and are not above facilitating perjury. But it is probable that the more usual situation finds the defense attorney preventing disclosure altogether or carefully planning its context.

Planning the context of disclosure means that the attorney must plan with the client exactly what will be said in the interview. And the attorney must be present at the interview, if possible, to insert himself as a check against improper questioning by the interviewer or ineffective answering by the client. In a federal grand jury appearance, where defense counsel is not allowed, the attorney must educate his client to be ready to assert his right to leave the room and consult with his attorney outside. When this situation is anticipated, some attorneys drill their clients and have them participate in a mock grand jury interrogation in the attorney's office.

An invariable principle of competent defense work is that the attorney prepare his client for questions that will be posed by the interviewer. Here attorneys walk an extremely narrow line between insufficient preparation and improper influence. It is certainly true that highly ethical and competent defense attorneys have clients whom they honestly believe should not be indicted, but who also believe that the clients could fail to demonstrate this through confused and unintelligent explanations. The attorney has to bring such a client to understand how to organize his thoughts and what to emphasize. But it is also true that other attorneys—perhaps committed less to the truth and more to their client's winning the case—improperly influence a client by letting him know, even if only by hinting, what to leave out and what to include and how to shape facts so that an appearance of propriety is created where in fact wrongdoing occurred. An attorney in a large midtown law firm handling a complex criminal investigation gave his view this way:

Sure I prepare my witnesses before they go into a grand jury. Take for instance now, where we are representing a company and its officers. All the officers

> —at least ten—have been called before the grand jury. I've prepared them in this sense: with each one I go over the facts of the matter extensively. I let each one know what the other one has said or is going to say. This is not with the intent of suborning perjury or getting them to fabricate anything. If my theory of the case is true, and I believe it is, then I want to have it presented in the strongest way. It's a fascinating process. I love doing this.
>
> There is no better feeling when you are a litigator than coming back from a deposition session in which every question asked by the prosecutor you had asked your client in preparing, and every answer came out as you expected. It gives you a real feeling of triumph.

Careful preparation of a client can obviate the need to use the self-incrimination privilege. So can the attorney's presence and active intervention in the questioning. His skill in helping the client provide noninculpatory answers to each question is important to achieving this end. Another attorney expressed this view about responding to requests for interviews.

> Certainly it's axiomatic that you don't let your client appear alone to answer questions. This is why the rule against appearing in a grand jury hearing is observed by most of us. But if you're talking about an administrative summons or subpoena, an appearance before a hearing officer of some kind, you are often better off to go and attempt to answer questions even where your ultimate position may be weak. You can get around the questions by giving indirect answers, sometimes nonanswers. A lot of these officers don't know how to ask a decent question, and that goes for assistants [U.S. Attorneys], too. You can put your guy through a two-hour session, jockeying with the assistant all the time, without putting your client in a bad spot. Once you are there, they expect you [the defense attorney] to try and interrupt them, at least when they are dealing with me, so it's no indication at all that we have something we are not telling.

Still another attorney expressed a similar view regarding a case in which his client was in danger of a perjury charge. In the context of an investigation of illegal corporate political contributions, the client had earlier been requested to respond in writing to the "eleven questions" presented by the IRS as part of their investigation.[3] In answer to a question whether the client "knew of any documents that show the size of contributions to campaign funds," the client, after consultation with his regular attorney, had written "No." Later in the investigation the IRS discovered that such a document existed and that this person probably had known of the document. An additional issue in the case then became whether the client would be prosecuted for perjury or false statements. Shortly after a subsequent meeting with district counsel at IRS in which a new attorney (a defense attorney) had argued that the client could not be prosecuted for an "exculpatory no" response, that attorney stated,

> This [case] teaches one a lesson about how not to advise clients to respond to an agent's questions. Rather than a short "no," the answer should have been complicated, open to a dozen or more interpretations. I found out how hard it is when I was a prosecutor to make a perjury case out of a long response. I got sucked into a terrible round of interchanges with a defense attorney before a judge and jury and I came out looking very bad. Whoever allowed ——— to respond in this way certainly didn't know what he was doing.

An even sharper picture of how a defense attorney controls information flow when the client is allowed to appear and respond can be seen in the transcript of another investigative interview. The client, an accountant for a medium-sized New York-based service company, was being questioned in connection with a fraud investigation. He had not at that time been identified as a target of the investigation, though the attorney's evaluation of the case after several meetings with the client was that he could easily become a target. The attorney had considered making a proffer for an immunity deal but rejected it on learning that the client had ownership shares in the company being investigated and a high level of executive responsibility.* In preparing for the meeting with the investigator, an assistant U.S. Attorney, the defense attorney and the client had several meetings to discuss how the client would respond to likely questions. In particular, they had discussed whether the client would have to admit knowledge of the contents of certain company documents. The interview excerpt presented below is from the actual interrogation carried out by the assistant U.S. Attorney (AUSA). At this point in the interrogation, the assistant was trying to get testimony about a document that would have implicated the accountant in the case.

> AUSA: But have you ever seen this document, or is this a copy of a document which you have seen?
>
> CLIENT: It is a copy of a document that may have been part of the records of the company, and if it was, it would have come across my desk in the normal course of our daily affairs, yes?
>
> AUSA: Could you describe for me what this document is?
>
> ATTY: Objection to a question asking for a description of a document which explains itself. I object on the grounds of the best evidence rule. I think the question is not a good question, the document speaks for itself, furthermore, it is not a document in evidence.
>
> AUSA: Not in evidence . . .
>
> ATTY: So you cannot ask what a document that is not in evidence says. You can ask is it a contract, is it toilet paper, is it a window shade, but you cannot tell him to read it.

*As it is used in this context, a proffer is a statement by a defense attorney that he and his client are ready to provide information to the prosecution in return for a concession, which includes some indication of the nature and reliability of the information. The art in making proffers is to convince the government of the value of the information without actually divulging the information.

AUSA: This is an evidentiary deposition!

ATTY: May we go off the record for a few minutes?

AUSA: All right. You're off the record. [Confidential conference takes place between attorney and client, achieved by whispering.]

ATTY: We are ready.

AUSA: So what is your response now?

CLIENT: It looks to me to be an agreement of some type between a supplier and the company. I haven't studied it in the last five years or so, I suppose so, I don't know what it is.

AUSA: What was your understanding of the agreement when you were familiar with it?

ATTY: Objection, it has not been shown that the witness was in fact familiar with a particular agreement when he was familiar with "it"!

AUSA: You did testify that you did receive a copy of this agreement, this agreement or a copy of this agreement.

CLIENT: I said it was received at the company.

AUSA: What did the document provide for?

ATTY: Do you mean what did it say?

CLIENT: It says whatever it says. I turned it over to Mr. D and asked him what it said and then he was—I don't know what happened to it from that point on, I read it and it looked to me like it was an agreement. I am not a lawyer, I don't know what it says, you people should be able to tell what it says.

AUSA: To the best of your understanding what did the agreement call for?

ATTY: Objection, the document speaks for itself. [Second off-the-record confidential conference between attorney and client.]

CLIENT: I don't remember what it called for.

AUSA: Do you remember seeing such a document?

CLIENT: I remember seeing such a document.

ATTY: Objection on the ground that it is not clear whether or not the questions and the answers relate to the document the witness saw some years ago, or whether he is talking about the document that he holds in his hand. [To the client] Clarify it by saying it was a copy of a document you saw years ago.

CLIENT: This is a copy of the document I saw years ago; it appears to be a copy of the document I saw years ago.

AUSA: When the document was sent to you years ago did you know who sent it to you?

ATTY: Objection, unless the foundation has been laid for any such knowledge.

AUSA: We can't go on like this. Your objections are groundless. [Third confidential conference between attorney and client.]

CLIENT: I don't recall exactly who sent this and it is not clear in my mind whether this was sent by—[interrupted]

ATTY: Say you don't recall.
CLIENT: I don't recall.

As described by the attorney after the interview, the questions posed by the prosecutor brought the attorney close to having the client refuse to answer on the basis of his self-incrimination privilege, but because the client was not pushed at the critical time this strategy was avoided.

> Our client, for instance, never admitted understanding the content of that document. He did volunteer, eventually, and certainly didn't need to do that, that he read the document, but whether he ever knew what was in it certainly can't be proved by that deposition. Yes, we could have taken the Fifth, but we would have undercut our earlier presentation in which we explained the regularity of the procedures. In the end, we've got to give the assistant a reason to drop our guy. He can't justify that to his superiors if we throw him the Fifth.

Marginal Use of Privileges

In addition to using the Fifth Amendment to control disclosure of information, defense attorneys use other privileges that function for the client in the same way. Each privilege of confidential communication—attorney-client, husband-wife, doctor-patient, for instance—can constitute a screen behind which information is protected from disclosure to government agents. What was found from interviews and field observations is that these privileges often were invoked by attorneys even when they were aware that current legal doctrine tended not to support their use or raised serious questions about their applicability. They made it clear that, in spite of legal doctrine, where they felt that a particular interpretation of a principle "should apply," they would adopt that interpretation until required by a decision of a court to act otherwise.[4]

In discussing these marginal positions defense attorneys offered several explanations. The main explanation was that the case in question was "different from any previous case on the same issue," an argument drawn from traditional legal reasoning as it is applied in adjudicative decisionmaking. Attorneys used this reasoning for taking adversarial positions, though the facts of their cases quite perceptibly lay outside the boundary in which the principle they advocated had been declared to be applicable. For example, where controlling appellate decisions clearly stated that a taxpayer's records are not protected by a privilege of confidentiality when in the hands of his accountant, an attorney repeatedly would take the position that as long as the particular document being sought in his case was not the exact same document required to be turned over in a prior case, he could withhold a client's document and claim the privilege. Thus in spite of the fact that the court had made a broad declaration of principle, the attorney would argue that his case was distinguishable on the facts. But even where the facts of the prior cases palpably included the facts of the case currently being handled, the attorney would take the contrary position. When pressed for an explanation of this adversarial strategy, one respondent commented,

> If I believe that the current state of the law is wrong, then I can and should fight it by litigating the issue any time my client can afford it and it serves his interest. And this goes, notwithstanding a line of previously ''bad'' decisions. How do you think the law gets changed, anyway—because attorneys with guts fight it . . . peck at it, push on it, until something budges. Now it's a luxury to be able to do this because lots of clients can't afford it. It's very expensive to brief and argue issues if you're serious about doing it. And let me tell you a fundamental principle that underlies all our work, one we've formulated out of experience—you lose cases you thought you should have won, and you win cases you thought you should have lost. This means that you have to take every possible step, every affordable step, in every case. Otherwise you're giving up cases. If the agent or assistant doesn't like the way I handle the case, it's up to him to fight it. I don't need to start by taking the position he wants.

The views of defense attorneys studied include two assumptions about the adversary system that not only allow them but require them, if they are to be accomplished advocates, to take marginal positions: first, the rules of the system are open to change and do change; and second, when the system operates correctly, it is able to check and stop any improper use of the law by one of the parties. If the defense attorney takes an improper position, his adversary should be able to counter it and prevent it. So defense attorneys are checked just like the government. As stated by another attorney, ''Until my adversary goes to court to get an order, I can adopt any position for which I can demonstrate good faith. When the court decides my case, then I have to respond accordingly.''

An additional fact that makes this strategy particularly effective was noted by a few attorneys. One stated that prosecutors and agents ''often do not understand that my position is open to attack,'' and when they do, ''they often don't have the time or resources to argue the matter.'' In other contexts, too, defense attorneys stated that lack of competence and resources has a significant impact on the ability of the government to prepare and argue its cases adequately. Thus, while defense attorneys are keenly aware that the ability of their clients to pay often determines whether they will take and defend a marginal position, they are also aware that when they do take marginal positions, the government is often unable to respond properly. ''Some of my cases are dropped,'' said one attorney, ''because the assistant just didn't see the hole in the argument I was making.''

A political corruption case. Illustrative of the marginal use of the privilege against self-incrimination is the following case, a grand jury hearing where an assistant U.S. Attorney posed questions to a company chief executive. The company involved in the investigation was a medium-sized public corporation engaged in a business that enjoys certain congressional environmental concessions.

A grand jury investigation had been ordered by a U.S. Attorney's office after information was received from a government informant that corrupt relations had developed between members of Congress and the industry of which this particular corporation was a part. What had in fact been occurring, though the grand jury did not have evidence (no indictments were issued during the tenure of that jury), was that certain corporation officers had been granting themselves yearly bonuses and from the bonuses transferred a percentage to intermediaries working for members of Congress. This was done in exchange for favorable action on relevant environmental legislation.

When the grand jury subpoena went out, it was addressed to the corporation in care of the chief executive. The subpoena called for "any and all corporate records" that would show the "disposition of any and all corporate funds" for the purpose of "obtaining or influencing . . . any congressional legislation or the conduct in office of any member of Congress." The chief executive met with corporate counsel, and then corporate counsel brought in a criminal defense attorney. The immediate defense matter was how to respond to the subpoena.

In the original subpoena, thirty days were provided for response. By the time the subpoena arrived on the desk of the criminal defense attorney, who had not himself at that time met with the chief executive, ten days had elapsed. The defense attorney handling the case discussed with a partner how to proceed. One unstated assumption held by the attorneys, necessary for understanding the significance of the discussion, was that corporate documents are generally not protected by the privilege against self-incrimination even where they incriminate individuals.[5]

> ATTY A: There's no question about what records are available. There are records of the bonuses being given, and the individuals who received them have their own records. But other than that, nothing. As far as we know, there's no direct connection to ——— [client and chief executive] or the company. None of the congressmen have been subpoenaed, and they are not likely to be unless something definite is turned up from the industry side.
>
> ATTY B: Now I understand that the bonuses were paid to our client and to several vice-presidents as far back as ten years ago . . .
>
> ATTY A: But they were raised when the payoff started, raised more than the payoff . . . at the same time.
>
> ATTY B: So the funds went into their company executives' private accounts, and from the private accounts cash was taken and deposited in a numbered account.
>
> ATTY A: That's right.
>
> ATTY B: Do we know which congressmen?
>
> ATTY A: No, and corporate counsel says the client would rather not provide that information now, unless it's absolutely necessary.
>
> ATTY B: Well, we ought to be aware of anything any of them [the con-

gressmen involved] do. . . . I mean that might indicate to us that they are going to name names.

ATTY A: We have been assured that corporate counsel is taking care of that matter. They'd like us to stick to the subpoena issue at this juncture. Also, they very much want to avoid having ——— go into the grand jury if it can be prevented in any way. Suggested that we might talk to the assistant and make some kind of deal where ——— could provide answers without appearing.

ATTY B: Well, I've been thinking about that . . . We might start out with a letter.

ATTY A: You're jumping the gun. Okay, a letter, but what kind of response are we going to make?

ATTY B: Our response will be this: there are no corporate records and we'll take the Fifth to any other question. The bonuses were legitimate payments to officers. I assume they paid tax?

ATTY A: Yes, on the individual returns.

ATTY B: So our position is that there are no corporate records. The only records of the funds' transfer are the individuals', that is, our client's and the vice-president's. Those are individual records and we can take the Fifth. Do you agree?

ATTY A: That's the obvious way of handling it. But what about exposing ——— and the company to a contempt proceeding for perjury—if it is determined later that the records of bonuses are corporate records and therefore encompassed in the subpoena?

ATTY B: I think we can back off a bit, make it an advice of counsel letter. I know the assistant [U.S. Attorney] won't like that, and it's a bit wishy-washy, but I think it's the only way to handle the matter.

ATTY A: Give me an idea of what you mean, for instance . . . how?

ATTY B: "After making a diligent search and consulting with counsel, we have found no corporate records and so forth. . . ."

With twenty days left, the matter was then dropped. About three days before the day for appearance in response to the subpoena, the lead defense attorney arranged for a postponement of appearance ("We need more time to fully comply with the subpoena") and then a week later the following letter was sent.

To: ———, Assistant U.S. Attorney,

I am responding to the subpoena of . . . in regard to . . . After conducting a search and upon advice of counsel, it is my position that there are no corporate records as so described in . . .

Signed

———, President of Corporation

Some time subsequent to the discussion between the attorneys, the word "diligent" was omitted and the phrase "it is my position" was added.

Approximately one week after this letter was sent, and a few days prior to the second date on which the client was supposed to make a personal appearance to respond to the subpoena, the assistant U.S. Attorney called to inform the defense attorney that "since this is a subpoena for records your client will have to appear in person to respond; we expect to see you on the date set in our previous conversation." For the attorney this meant that the client would be exposed to more questions than those contained in the subpoena, because "that's the way it always works when a client gets into a grand jury," and he would have to prepare the chief executive for a personal appearance that was then unavoidable. A few days later, the defense attorneys met the client for the first time. The following is part of the conversation that took place.

ATTY A: They are going to ask you questions about the whereabouts of the records, and probably other questions which we can't predict at this time.

CLIENT: What am I supposed to tell them?

ATTY A: There are a few questions that you will have to respond to, but in almost every instance you will tell them nothing, you will do nothing but read out loud what I have on this slip of paper [paper reads: "I respectfully refuse to answer based upon my Fifth Amendment right not to be a witness against myself"]. You read that just as I have written it and say absolutely nothing else. At the beginning of the session you will be asked to identify yourself, and you will do that. Give your name and identify yourself as chief executive of the company.

CLIENT: Just my name, or something else?

ATTY B: Nothing else.

CLIENT: But what if they say, "State your name, address, and telephone number"?

ATTY B: Give them your name and stop. Take the Fifth to anything else. Now, next they will probably ask you what records you have brought to present them pursuant to the subpoena. To that question you are going to respond exactly as we did in our prior letter to the assistant. I have written that on this piece of paper, which you will have [second piece of paper reads: "After conducting a search, and upon advice of counsel, it is my position that there are no corporate records as so described"].

Finally, there is one other question that they are going to ask, and I'm not yet sure how we are going to answer that. They are going to ask you something like, "Have you made a 'diligent search'?" We will decide later how to handle that question. If you are asked that or any other questions, you come out and talk to me. You can always come and talk to me; you can be excused for a conference with your attorney at any time. I'll be waiting outside the grand jury room.

The response of the corporate officer had to be carefully planned in order to comply with the wording of the subpoena. The attorneys would not make a palpable misinterpretation of the subpoena's language or openly and clearly fail to turn over documents that obviously came within the scope of the subpoena. On the other hand, their analysis of the transaction used to make the corrupt payments led them to believe that it would not be an unreasonable interpretation of tax and corporation law to define the inculpatory records as outside the scope of the language of the subpoena. To the extent that the attorneys experienced any trouble in making their decision in this case, it centered on the question of whether the interpretation eventually adopted was, as one attorney put it, "reasonable enough." Once they decided that it was, they experienced little problem in deciding to use it. As phrased by one of the attorneys directly involved in making the decision,

> Certainly I knew that the government wanted that document, and certainly I knew that the truth would be better reflected if that document were made available to the government, but I also knew that I had an obligation to the client, and that obligation required that I do the best job for him I possibly could. Doing a good job required that I take the view I did on the nature of the transaction. I think it is a perfectly defensible position, don't you agree?

A securities fraud case. The following investigative agency interview further illustrates the way in which marginal positions are taken. The case involved an SEC investigation into an alleged 10(b)(5) investor fraud in which a referral for criminal prosecution was eventually made. The agency was claiming that "manipulative and misrepresentative" statements related to the activities of subsidiaries of the American parent corporation were made to persons who purchased shares of the parent corporation in reliance on those statements. At the hearing were the vice-president of the parent corporation, an attorney from a defense firm representing him, a house attorney representing the corporation, and two SEC agency officers, one of whom had issued the administrative subpoena.

In the part of the interview presented here, the agency officers were questioning the vice-president about his knowledge of the activities of the foreign subsidiary. To the extent that the vice-president had such knowledge, it had originated in the chief executive of the subsidiary, an attorney by profession. When the SEC officers began probing, the vice-president declined to respond based on a claim of attorney-client privilege, asserted by the corporation attorney to apply to communications between the chief executive of the subsidiary and the vice-president of the corporation. The interview is presented at length with an excerpt from the interaction that took place prior to the raising of the attorney-client privilege issue, because it supplies an instructive view on the contentiousness of the adversary relationship during questioning and the active role a defense attorney takes in protecting his client from the government's probing. In the first part of the excerpt, the prosecutor is attempting to determine how much involvement the vice-president had with the subsidiary. The prosecutor's approach was to get the vice-president to define exactly how "independent" the subsidiaries' executives were from the parent corporation.

SEC: To use your language, in regard to subsidiaries of the corporation, would you always accept the position that this was *their* company [the subsidiaries' executives', not the corporation's company]?

CLIENT: Let me answer that question in this way. As a senior officer of the corporation, when visiting any subsidiary corporations of the company, I never took it upon myself to give instructions to those people as to how they were to run their business. It was not only understood that these people were responsible for their business, they were being measured on their own performance. The staff people and I were very careful not to offer advice to any of the people running these subsidiaries, other than in the limited field of their relationship to what I was doing in the corporation.

SEC: That was in regard to all subsidiaries?

CLIENT: All subsidiaries.

SEC: What were you doing at the corporation where you would have an interest in regard to a subsidiary?

CLIENT: Well, as I have already testified here previously, I was treasurer.

SEC: Could you for my sake tell me again what your concerns were?

CLIENT: I would be more than pleased to. I was concerned about those normal functions that a company has and running the very complicated financial affairs of the company where we were borrowing money in a dozen different states, we were having exposure to various risks, transferred funds back and forth amongst the companies and between the parent company and the subsidiaries. To be sure that the assets were properly secured, to be sure that the relationships with the banks around the country were coordinated, that was the responsibility of the treasurer, to be sure that we did have this coordinated banking arrangement. By "coordination" I mean to know at all times with which banks we were doing business and what our exposure was with each bank. This was my interest as it related to the corporation or as they might relate to banks here or in other states, for instance. That was my relationship with these subsidiaries.

SEC: Are you saying here then that to your knowledge, Mr. S [chief officer of the subsidiary] did not report to any department on a regular basis at the corporation?

CLIENT ATTY: Objection to the form of the question in that the term *report* is one of mixed meaning, therefore it is vague and ambiguous.

SEC: Read the question back for the witness, please. [Question read back.]

CLIENT: I cannot . . .

CLIENT ATTY: Same objection to the extent that the previous answer has not already answered this question; I object to its form, because the term used in the question, the term *report* has a different meaning to the examiner than it does to the witness.

SEC: Read the question back.

CLIENT ATTY: I object to that question because that is not what he said; he said quite the opposite.

SEC: I asked him if that's what he said; he could have answered the question.

CLIENT ATTY: The answer to the question is "no," that is not what he said.

SEC: I would appreciate it if you would stop—

CLIENT ATTY: You are misleading the witness by telling him he said something he did not say. He did not say the facts you set forth in your examination.

SEC: I wish you would stop deliberately trying to interrupt my direct examination of the witness. You have taken long sidebar conferences to have drawn-out discussions with the witness. You have suggested answers to him!

CLIENT ATTY: If that's what you feel after two hours of total irrelevancy, I'm going to now instruct the witness not to answer any irrelevant questions further because we have sat here, and the first half hour was taken up with what high school he went to, something which is not relevant to any issue in the complaint, but I let you go on, I let you go on!

SEC: I have to ask those questions.

CLIENT ATTY: I let you go through his college education, postgraduate courses, and his career, all because I thought it would be gentlemanly. This witness did not say he [Mr. S] never reported to nobody; I object to the form of the question and I instruct him not to answer. Please frame a new question.

SEC: I would like the record to reflect and for you to realize that I am conducting this examination, and the questions that I have to put to the witness are preliminary questions that are generally put to the witness, that this deposition may be used at a trial, and that I fully want the background of the respondent on this record. I would ask that you stop instructing him in regard to what answers he should give. If you would exercise your role as a lawyer and not as a witness in this case, it would be appreciated! At this point, let the record reflect that Attorney R suggested an answer to the witness off the record that he should refer to Mr. S as an attorney for the subsidiary.

CLIENT ATTY: I object to this man eavesdropping on me. One, that is not what I said, but I will not tell you what I said, and two, I intend to continue to advise my client about his answers to your questions.

SEC: I would like to make it clear that the conversation was audible.

CLIENT ATTY: Please don't eavesdrop on my conversations with my client.

SEC: I would like to make it clear that the conversation was audible.

CLIENT ATTY: Avert your eyes and turn your head when you see me talking to my client.

SEC: I feel no obligation to do so.

CLIENT ATTY: Don't eavesdrop!

During this interview, the defense attorney repeatedly broke the flow of the questioning to have conferences with his client, to prevent him from giving an immediate response to correct improper interpretation by the investigator, and to plan the content of the client's response. As the interview continued, the attorney then invoked the attorney-client privilege to prevent his client from giving any responses. The impression created was that the client was ready to talk, but the attorney put the brakes on.

SEC: Let's go on! Now you had conversations with Mr. S about the operation of the company. What did he say to you when . . .

CLIENT ATTY: This is the place where the answer to the question will disclose a confidential communication between an attorney and a client.

CORP. ATTY: Insofar as the corporation is the client to whom you are making a reference, we certainly invoke the privilege against disclosure of any communication between counsel and client.[6]

SEC: Just for the record, I would like to clarify that. Are you saying that the respondent gained such knowledge from an attorney, a person acting in an attorney capacity in regard to the corporation?

CORP. ATTY: Yes.

CLIENT ATTY: Wait a minute, are you asking him what the content of the conversation with counsel was?

SEC: I did not ask him the content of it; you invoked the privilege here.

CLIENT ATTY: We have not, they have, we are servants. I move to strike the answer "yes" and refer you to the answer to the previous question, which was made by me as the result of the invocation of the attorney-client privilege by the corporation.

SEC: I would like to ask some preliminary questions of the respondent in regard to this matter without getting to the substance of it.

CLIENT ATTY: Certainly.

SEC: I would like to clarify the nature of the privilege that is asserted so that a determination can be made as to whether or not such a privilege is properly invoked. That is why I asked the previous question and I will put a similar question to the respondent. Did you gain information subsequent to April — that Mr. S may have been aware of the possibility that the subsidiary was [receiving funds directly from the corporation] — from a person employed to your knowledge as an attorney of the corporation?

CORP. ATTY: I object on the ground that the corporation has invoked a privilege against disclosure of any communication whether directly or indirectly between itself and any of its counsel.

CLIENT ATTY: And that question would disclose it!

CORP. ATTY: It calls for disclosure itself, in fact, it states the disclosure.

SEC: We would like two minutes. I would like to state on the record that we have not asked the respondent to reveal what conversations he had, if any, with counsel for the corporation or anybody else at this point. The corporation cannot merely, and no one can merely, invoke a privilege without laying some foundation for invoking that privilege. If this were before the court, the court would probably conduct a voir dire to see to what extent the privilege, if any, might be available to the corporation. They have the burden of demonstrating at least in some fashion to some extent that such a privilege exists, and they must do this beyond merely stating on the record that they have the privilege. The asserter of the privilege must demonstrate that the person who communicated the information subject to the privilege was an attorney retained by the person asserting the privilege or the company asserting the privilege and that such communication was made in his capacity as an attorney employed by the person or company that is asserting the privilege. Furthermore, one that would assert an attorney-client privilege must establish that the person to whom the information was communicated was a high-ranking officer or employee of the company.

CLIENT ATTY: Not in this circuit; we have the duties of employment test here.

SEC: I wish [lawyer] would not interrupt!

CLIENT ATTY: I am going to interrupt because I don't understand what is going on here. I have never before in my not so inconsiderable years of practicing heard a speech be put on the record in the course of an interview. This is a place for questions and answers. If you want to make application to the court, make it, and make that speech to the court and not to me!

SEC: I would like to finish this, I would like to finish what I am saying if you would give me the courtesy.

CLIENT ATTY: I mean this is extraordinary.

SEC: If I might proceed and you would give me the courtesy, I would appreciate it.

CLIENT ATTY: I'm not paying for this record, so you go ahead.

SEC: I understand that, and if you would not interrupt me, maybe we could proceed faster.

CLIENT ATTY: I am interrupting you because your procedure is anomalous.

SEC: I'll put the question this way: what did you ask Mr. S in regard to the subsidiary?

CORP. ATTY: Oh, no, no, no! If you are asking about communications between Mr. S and my client, I object again on the ground of privilege of such disclosure. I request that the witness not answer the question.

SEC: The witness has already testified about Mr. S. I think that to the extent that he has already testified, any valid objection that you might have is waived and that he should be allowed to continue to answer.

CLIENT ATTY: We are not going to get involved in it, say "Same response."

CLIENT: Same response.

SEC: I would like to clarify the record again: Mr. S is one of the three directors of the corporation, and he also, at least nominally, owned shares in the subsidiary, and the matters which are the subject of this litigation relate in a substantial way to the performance of his duties as an executive officer, not as an attorney. He has, I am informed [by corporate attorney], performed some lawyer function for the corporation, but certainly all of the matters which are of issue here, that we are trying to gain knowledge about, were not matters which he performed as counsel for the corporation. He was in fact a fiduciary and an officer of the subsidiary, and to that extent, I think the testimony should be allowed. Read back the question, please.

CLIENT ATTY: The witness will not respond for the same reasons stated earlier, he is the stakeholder, and he has been directed by counsel for the corporation not to respond to that question. Subject to some order of the court or some agreement between him and counsel for the corporation, we will remain silent.

SEC: I would ask attorney if he will be willing to clarify that for me.

CORP. ATTY: We are invoking a privilege on behalf of our client as to the disclosure of any communication in Mr. S's capacity as counsel for the corporation. Since I certainly don't know the content of the answer of this witness if it were to be given, I cannot myself go beyond merely asserting that privilege and objecting not only to a question that would call for that kind of answer but to any clarification if in fact such a communication would be revealed in the course of the answer.

The multiple set of relationships that S had with the two corporate entities was used by defense counsel to construct two defenses. First, the attorney claimed that the subsidiary is independent from the parent corporation and therefore the parent corporation and its officers are not responsible for having knowledge of financial details about the subsidiary. S, as chief executive of the subsidiary, is not intermingled with the parent corporation. Second, what S does communicate to the parent corporation is privileged because S is also an attorney and has an attorney-client relationship with the corporation, in addition to being chief executive of a subsidiary. The two defenses are based on independent statuses. One entails independence, the other a fiduciary confidentiality. Each has the effect of making information inaccessible to the government.

In the preceding examples, defense attorneys were concerned in each instance with how much information a client would be forced to supply to the government. They interposed themselves between the prosecutor and client as monitors and controllers and they used the privileges to prevent the client from answering questions that would disclose inculpatory evidence. Where there was a serious question about the applicability of a privilege to documents or testimony requested by the government, the attorneys, without substantial discussion of the issue, decided to assert the privilege. In so doing they protected documents and testimony from immediate disclosure, though they also signaled the government that there was probably inculpatory information to obtain and in a sense challenged it to question the defense's use of the privilege. While a prosecutor would have no way of knowing prior to a court inquiry whether a privilege was being used properly, marginally, or improperly, he had the opportunity to move in district court for an enforcement proceeding.[7]

One reason that marginal positions—and positions actually contrary to legal doctrine—can be effective for defense attorneys is the widely recognized fact that few disputes are brought before a court for official determination. Although there is always a threat that the prosecutor or investigator may test the defense attorney's position, it may be months or years before the issue is finally determined in an appellate court. In the attorney-client privilege dispute illustrated here, a court could examine the relationship of the subsidiary and the parent corporation and decide whether the vice-president was entitled to invoke the privilege to prevent disclosure. There are clearly cases where this kind of enforcement procedure takes place, and, if the government's position prevails, uncooperative respondents are required to testify or to face a contempt charge if they do not. But if systemic factors work against and actually prevent judicial clarification of the issues in all but a small number of instances, then the dispute is resolved as a standoff or through negotiated compromise between the adversary parties.

Where resolution of differences on critical information control issues takes place informally, one might say that there is an informal law determined in a large part by the comparative ability of defense attorneys and government agents to bring nonjudicial authority to bear on each other. Prosecutors and other government agents often make accusations of illegal or unethical behavior against their adversaries, attempting either to call on the attorneys' ethical sensibilities or to make a veiled threat of enforcement proceedings. But attorneys know from experience that such proceedings occur infrequently; if their position is not vindicated by the court, they are not likely to lose anything that would not have been lost by immediate compliance. In any event, they have gained time and all its potential benefits, so there is little incentive not to take marginal or even doctrinally wrong legal positons.

Undisclosed Legal Decisions

Where the defense openly opposes a prosecutor's version of a particular legal doctrine, the issue can be disputed between them and clarified in a judicial setting if the appropriate commitment and resources are present. The sine qua non of a standoff, a negotiated compromise, or a judicial determination is the recognition by a party that his adversary is in fact taking a contrary position. Where the defense attorney asserts a privilege or moves to quash a subpoena or otherwise declares why he refuses to communicate requested information, the government is put on notice and can act to correct the situation. However, where the defense attorney takes a position on an issue without openly communicating that position, no opportunity arises for adversary dispute on the matter. Formal requests for information disclosure in which substantial time is allowed for response allow the respondent to determine the substance of the response without notifying the investigator of the legal position adopted in regard to that request. This makes dispute and judicial clarification not only unlikely but often impossible.

Probably the most common situation in which the respondent can adopt a legal position without communicating that fact to his adversary is when the government issues a subpoena or summons for records. Here marginal positions often go undisclosed because the client and the defense attorney are able to make a decision without communicating essential features of the decision to the adversary. One attorney provided the following example. The FTC had referred for criminal prosecution a company distributing a product that injured a statistically high portion of users. The FTC's own investigation of the company indicated that requisite testing had not been performed and that there may have been concealment of significant negative test results. The local U.S. Attorney's office decided that additional factual investigation had to be carried out. It issued a subpoena requiring the company to turn over "all and any records" of "tests or opinions" about the product's "effects, safety, side effects" and "any other information" related to "product testing" "done by" or "acted on" by the company.

Shortly after the subpoena for records was received, a criminal defense firm was asked to join a large corporate law firm in handling the investigation for the company. The reason for bringing in the criminal defense firm was that the attorneys at the corporate firm felt it would be beneficial to have an attorney on the case who was formerly a prosecutor in the district where the case was being considered for prosecution. A meeting was convened at the offices of the company, attended by several managerial level officers, an attorney from the company legal department, attorneys from the corporate law firm, and the defense attorney.

These persons focused their discussion on the question of whether and how to comply with the subpoena, reviewing details of product testing methods, the procedures followed by the company in this instance, and the arguments that had been made by the corporate law firm at earlier meetings with FTC officers (the firm had a department that specialized in handling administrative law problems and appearing before federal regulatory agencies). The participants in the meeting reached a consensus that the subpoena had been broadly drafted and required that a great quantity of routine memoranda be turned over as well as reports and letters relating to the product. Eventually they narrowed their discussion to a number of documents that had been collected by the product safety division of the company, reporting clearly negative findings on certain qualities of the material used in the product, directly related to the injuries that led the FTC to order the product recalled and to institute the investigation.

All the attorneys present felt that this set of documents—reports by independent laboratories done several years prior to the development of the company product—would be very damaging to the company's case. A memorandum attached to the documents showed that the documents had arrived at the desk of the corporation's safety divison director. Knowledge of the danger, it would be argued, had been transmitted to the company prior to marketing, yet the marketing plans went ahead unaffected. The central question for the attorneys in making the decision about how to comply was this: with close attention to the precise language of the subpoena, were these documents encompassed in the subpoena? It was decided quickly that because the negative reports were not "done by" the company, they would not have to be produced under the first clause of the subpoena.

A more difficult question was whether they were included in the "acted on" clause of the subpoena: were the negative reports acted on by the company in distributing its product? Discussion on this issue opened with a split in opinion. One group of attorneys began by observing that, in spite of the technical ambiguity in the term *acted on*, the subpoena would no doubt be interpreted by a court to include all records that in any way related to the safety of the product. They concluded that *not* to turn over these reports would expose the company and the law firms to heavy liabilities if the documents somehow were disclosed at a later date. The second group of attorneys held a different view. They said that whether or not the spirit of the subpoena was that the company turn over related documents, there was little question that the term *acted on* was unartful and that if it could be open to more than one interpretation—and it was, they said—they could adopt the narrower one. They advised not including the outside reports because they were not "acted on"—they were disregarded. In response, the first attorneys said that they understood that position but were not comfortable with it and would want to disassociate themselves from it if it were taken. The second group of attorneys then made an alternative proposal: they suggested maximizing the amount of documents—routine reports, memoranda, letters, circulars, and so on—in a large, unclassified submission so that these particular questionable documents might stay buried. One attorney said, "I envision two complete file cabinets of documents turned over, and I think there's some chance these reports will not be recognized for what they are, if indeed they ever get around to looking at everything we turn over."

What actually happened in this situation was that the original position held by the second group of attorneys was adopted as the legal stance of the client in responding to the subpoena, and the negative reports remained somewhere in the files of the company. The defense attorney handling the matter arranged for submission of all other documents, declaring that "a diligent search for records had been made," and that "all records in the possession of the company called for by the subpoena had been produced." The investigating prosecutor was therefore not apprised of an essential legal interpretation made by the company's representative and did not have the opportunity to litigate the question of whether the subpoena covered the documents in question.

The Defense Attorney's View

The objectives of information control and the strategies used to achieve them embody the essential nature of the defense function: preventing the government from meting out sanctions against a client irrespective of what all the facts would prove. The defense attorney's goal is not to do justice, in the sense that he strives to protect the client from undeserved sanctions. The defense goal is disconnected from any measure of just deserts. The attorney is committed, rather, to the objective of winning, where winning means minimizing sanctions.

For the defense attorney, winning almost always entails helping the client to conceal facts. To the seasoned practitioner and the student of law, it is elementary that a defense attorney would not disclose information about a client to persons seeking to determine whether an offense has been committed. Two of the most basic tenets of the Anglo-American legal system are the confidentiality between client and attorney and the principle prohibiting government-forced self-incrimination. Though some lay readers may think that the self-incrimination privilege and the attorney-client privilege are strange—after all, why shouldn't the perpetrator of crime have to explain to the police what he did?—practicing attorneys rarely if ever question their propriety. They assume that concealment and cover-up are fundamental parts of the attorney's role in the adversary system. They are integral to the mandates to act zealously and to resolve doubt in favor of one's client.

The attorneys studied here would agree that difficult ethical questions can be raised by the type of actions taken in these cases, when proper limits are not observed. An attorney can improperly influence a client when he prepares him for an interview or for testimony, improperly ground his claim of right to the self-incrimination privilege, improperly apply law in making marginal and undisclosed legal decision, and improperly bluff. But all these strategies have their place in the adversary system, if done correctly. The question is, where does the boundary lie?

These attorneys see themselves as correctly carrying out their tasks, that is, without ethical violations. Whether they are right in making this assumption is a question that cannot be answered without actually litigating the issues raised in the specific cases. As I will suggest in the final chapter, the ethical precepts of the profession provide no straightforward answers. The behavior of these attorneys is so close to the boundary between correct and excessive advocacy, and authoritative interpretation of ethical rules are so few and so ambiguous, that no clear determination could be made.

Whatever one concludes about what the ethical rules demand, it is important to understand that these attorneys view their behavior as ethical. Their views are not based on an expert knowledge of the ethical rules and the decisions under those rules, because most of the attorneys did not possess such expertise. Rather, they are based on the assertion that the skills applied in these cases are customary, time-tested skills that most competent litigating attorneys use and accept. And underlying this assertion is the more important assumption that the adversary system is self-checking. These customary ways of conducting litigation must be integral to the adversary system, for if they were not, the adversary process would have kept them from becoming entrenched and widely accepted.

8 Third-Party Disclosures to the Government

Controlling information held by third parties is vastly more difficult than controlling information held by one's own client. The goal is the same: keeping inculpatory information from reaching the government. But the means must be different because the source of information, whether a person or a document, is not directly controlled or possessed by the client. Third parties holding inculpatory information may be friends or associates of the client, who are willing to cooperate if they are located in time and proper requests are made. Or they may be persons with directly adverse interests, who perhaps are loyal to government interests or who have other reasons for wanting to provide information to the government that inculpates another person.

The extent of the difficulty of obtaining control or some influence over information held by third parties depends on how many parties there are and how adverse their relationship is to the client. These circumstances will also determine the strategies the attorney will use to attempt to assert control. In some cases, control over a third party is simply accomplished by explaining to him or her what to do. In other instances, the client and the attorney may have to shrewdly maneuver themselves and the third party to obtain even a modicum of control —for example, delay in making a statement to the government, which would keep certain facts concealed while the defense attorney attempts to get the case closed. In still other cases, control is impossible. This may force an attorney to counsel immediate plea negotiations.

There are several strategies used by attorneys to attempt to control the statements made and documents held by third parties. The defense attorney may use the client's power and authority to control third-party interactions with government agents, or he may try to influence third parties through representation of multiple clients. Here, the attorney's turning a third party into a client creates influence over the information held by that person. Another strategy involves multiple attorneys, so that one attorney may obtain some control over information inculpatory of his client by coordinating defense work with the attorney of another client.

It is important to maintain a proper perspective on how the strategies described in this chapter fit into the larger picture of defense tasks. Recall that information access tasks are discussed in one part of this book and information control tasks in another, principally to emphasize two significantly distinct goals pursued by defense attorneys. One goal is gathering information in order to determine what overall and what specific defense strategies should be used. The other is influencing the disposition of information, because the basic defense strategy has already been set: deny all or some of the guilt attributable to one's client. In handling the real case, there is some chronological ordering in these tasks. Information gathering often takes place before a full-fledged information control campaign. But there is also a great interweaving of the tasks, which is particularly important in the defense attorney's handling of third parties. Often an attorney will be able to obtain only one meeting, if any, with a potential witness. Thus, while he is learning what the third party knows he is simultaneously exercising whatever influence he has to persuade the witness to act favorably to his client. In this sense, information access and information control are meshed in time and execution.

Using Client Control over Third Parties

The first resource for the defense attorney in his effort to control third parties is the client himself. The client often has ongoing relationships with third parties. Depending on the ability of the client to influence the party, control may be established informally. Business colleagues and employees of a client are two sources of information often drawn on by government agents in a criminal investigation. They are also routinely regarded by a defense attorney as potential sources of information for the government's case. One defense control tactic is to suggest that the client cultivate feelings of loyalty among these persons. For instance, in an investigation of a possible bribery scheme, government meat inspectors were being questioned about the exercise of improper influence by a company accused of giving personal gratuities to the inspectors. The president of the company, the main target, informed his defense attorney that certain employees probably were familiar with meetings that the president had had with inspectors in circumstances that "would *not* be helpful to the defense." The following discussion took place between the attorney and the client,

CLIENT: There are division chiefs and quality supervisors who were certainly aware that I had developed a close and friendly relationship with the inspectors. I suppose that they may have overheard my planning to meet one of them for dinner, or talking about a show we had seen together at a resort. I don't know what was overheard and what they would have made of it.

ATTY: If we don't know what they overheard or how nosy and curious they are, let's assume the worst for the moment: one or two of them have followed your machinations to the extent that they could and have put together their own picture. If an agent were to come to your supervisors and divisions chiefs, what's the likelihood of their giving you a bad reading?

CLIENT: For most of them, I would say that I would get a good reading. There are, however, one or two whom I'm less sure of.

ATTY: What do you mean?

CLIENT: Well, I've had some trouble with them, and we've had some mild disagreement on salary.

ATTY: Look, let me put it to you as bluntly as I can. You need all these men on your side. Now is not the time to be concerned about cost efficiency and work productivity. If I were you, I would see to it that the salary issue is resolved and that you are on very good terms with all these people.

The message was well understood by the client, and he became solicitous and supportive of his division chiefs and quality supervisors. In addition to being instructed himself to keep quiet, the client was made to understand that he could keep others quiet. In general, how a client achieves this is left up to him—whether he offers bonuses, threatens to fire an employee, or simply refrains from alienating someone who could do damage.[1] This is a task that many clients would and no doubt do carry out without any coaching from their attorney; but some attorneys assume, and rightfully so, that clients fail to do the obvious when they are under the pressure of a criminal investigation.

Keeping an employee or business associate from supplying inculpatory evidence also may entail retrieving records that he might voluntarily hand over to the government or be forced to hand over as a subject of a subpoena or summons. One such recordholder who is often requested to return material in his possession is the accountant; he is not protected by a confidentiality privilege, so whatever remains with him after his accounting tasks have been completed is easily accessible to the government. Defense attorneys are less concerned about the final product (for example, a tax return) because that has already been filed with the government. Their concern focuses on the underlying work papers in the possession of the accountant. One defense attorney illustrated his reasoning.

> Let's say I'm handling an income understatement case, and the accountant has the work papers. And let's say, in addition, that the defense argument we want to use is first, that we turned over all income records and that the accountant neglected to use some of them, and second, the client was not aware that foreign income already taxed in a foreign country has also to be reported as income here. Now assume further that the accountant's work papers have a detailed list of the materials transmitted to the accountant on the day they were received—a kind of receipt. What if the stuff we say was given to the accountant is not on the list. Even worse, what if the accountant has noted on his own daily work sheet the work he's done on the client's account each day, and on one day he's written, "foreign income accounts requested," and he has no record of their being turned over.

Even though an accountant was loyal to his client and not likely to provide damaging information in an oral interview with an investigative agent, if he were forced to turn over records of the kind indicated by the attorney his loyalty and goodwill toward the client would be for naught. So the client, on the advice of the defense attorney, has to move quickly to beat the government to the accountant. In that race the client has the advantage.

There are many other third-party recordkeepers who are largely out of reach for the client, including banks. A client can close his account, but he cannot retrieve past records that a bank is required by law to keep.[2] Even records held by persons in the accounting division in a large company may be out of reach to an executive in the company, despite great powers of influence he may wield over persons lower in the hierarchy who head an accounting division. Where standard operating procedures require that records be kept in certain ways, the mere absence of records may be used by the government to build a prima facie incriminating case on circumstantial evidence. Company personnel therefore are not likely to be willing to cooperate with the target in these circumstances. Such violations are too easily identifiable and would lead to immediate implication of the person controlling the records. On the other hand, were an employee or associate requested to alter or dispose of records outside the pool of standard or required forms, fewer telltale signs might be created. Cooperation is more likely to be forthcoming.[3]

One alternative to taking complete control of records held by third parties is to change existing records or create new ones. An attorney described a case he worked on:

> I received a case from an out-of-town law firm after that law firm had already advised the client, a manufacturing company, to go back and change certain records. They had felt that the [original] records created an impression that was not an accurate portrayal of the company's true financial situation. Rather than trying to explain the inconsistencies, they changed the records. Now that I've looked at the records I can see that it is not at all apparent that the new entries were made recently. My very difficult question is whether to give the records to the agent without informing him that they were changed. He may never realize the difference between the early and late entries. Or should I say, "We changed the records and here's why"? If he's to find out about the change, it's of course better that he finds out from us rather than on his own. But if he's not going to be inclined to accept our explanation, then the risk in not telling him is worth it.

Research findings showing outright acts of concealment were infrequent; I did not observe any instance of an attorney altering existing records, but merely heard attorneys recount instances of record manipulation by other attorneys known to them. However, there were other instances, directly confirmed, in which attorneys made new records based on old records, without destroying or altering the old records, and submitted the new records instead. Such actions were not considered by attorneys to be technically improper where they were responding to a general request for records, even where the content of the records requested was specified in detail. Unless the request definitively stated "original records," a new set of records could be constructed with no indication that they constituted new summaries. New summaries can redefine information in a way beneficial to the client, and it is not necessarily true that redefinitions are illegal. The first definition is made with one goal in mind, the second with another. Where financial accounts are the subject of the new record, execution of this defense strategy requires an acute understanding of the ambiguities in the substantive accounting laws. For this reason, professional accountants are often made part of the defense team.

Defensive Interviewing of Third Parties

One minimal way that a client can act as a resource for the defense attorney in asserting control over third-party information sources is to facilitate attorney access to those sources and, most important, access prior to the government. The client's role is to prepare the third party to meet the defense attorney, cooperate with him, and resist cooperating with the government until later. In addition to drawing on personal or corporate loyalty, the client often is told to explain to the third party that the defense attorney who will interview him—who is going to ask many questions about the person's work and relationship to the client—is not going to threaten his interests. The client therefore is an essential intermediary in the defense attorney's direct intervention. In describing an initial meeting with a client, an attorney emphasized the importance of his access to third parties, which was made possible when the client first "imposed security."

> It is extremely important that the client impress on his employees that if an agent comes to interview them they can refuse to be interviewed at that time and ask that a later, "more convenient" date be set. This gives us more time to complete our own interviews first and allows us to arrange to be present when the agent does his interviews. Now that may sound like a straightforward thing to do. But it's difficult. I'll ask a client, "Can you impose security on your employees?" He'll say yes, and the next thing you know three people have been interviewed. That's always bad for the defense.

Once the attorney has obtained access to a third party—an employee, a colleague or business associate, a customer, or any other person—he will conduct an interview. There are two basic types of defense interviews. One has already been discussed; it can be called the debrief interview and is a central part of the defense investigation, used primarily when the government has arrived first and conducted a prosecution interview. The aim of the debrief interview is to determine what the third party has told the government in its interview. It is largely a tool for measuring current exposure of the client to a successful government case. The second type of defense interview is an adversarial interview. Its aim is to flush out interpretations of facts that are favorable to the defense position; in this sense, it is one of the defense's information control strategies.[4]

The fundamentally important question is whether the defense attorney's interview takes place before or after the government's. If the investigator is skilled at his job, there may be little value in a defense adversarial interview following a government interview, because of the basic working principle that he who arrives first gets a better interpretation of the facts. It is assumed that after the first interview the respondent's perceptions have been influenced by the interrogator's construction of questions and that interpretations adopted during the first interview are difficult to overcome in a second, particularly when statements have been frozen in an affidavit.

Research has identified two distinct types of third-party interviewees. One is cooperative, the other uncooperative.

The cooperative third party. This interviewee either wants to help the client, or is uncommitted to a particular version and by personal disposition is open to being swayed. If he is not sure what he wants to say, or what he has seen, or what he knows, the preparatory remarks made by the attorney prior to questioning can have a critical impact on his answers. Or an interviewee may be gushing with enthusiasm to give the ''right'' answers, but he may not know what they are. The attorney can have a substantial impact here, too. In other instances, so attorneys believe, persons come to interviews positively bent on giving a favorable version and are ready to fabricate whatever is necessary. This readiness can be taken advantage of without the attorney manifestly taking part in the creation of a false statement. Many times the attorney will not know if the interviewee is telling the truth or creating a favorable version.

A question which is phrased, ''Now, isn't it true that you would give files to John before John left for the evening?'' is more likely to stimulate a positive answer than the question, ''Did you always give the file to John before John left in the evening?'' If the former question is a defense inquiry looking for a positive response, then the latter is a prosecutorial inquiry looking for a negative response. Similarly, when the defense attorney wants to establish that a certain record (for example, a record received from a South American subsidiary in July) was dealt with *routinely* at the company, the attorney will not start by asking, ''What did you do with a file received from the South American subsidiary in July?'' Instead he will put the question in a form something like this: ''Now let's talk about how files are handled. Let's say you receive a file from a foreign subsidiary—what do you do with it?'' With this question the attorney wants to establish a standard operating procedure from which, if the interviewee is open to it, he can slowly tease out a general statement that all files were handled ''the way they are supposed to be handled.'' The explanation of what happened to the South American subsidiary file in July is then more likely to fit into the routine pattern. The interviewee is interested in characterizing himself as a properly performing employee and also wants to give a favorable version for the client.[5]

The situations most favorable to a defense interview are when the interviewee has actual exculpatory knowledge and is willing to use it, when he is so devoted to the client that he spontaneously bends facts to his favor, or when he fears for his own potential target status and is therefore motivated to present a picture exculpatory of the client in order to protect himself. In each of these instances, the main goal of the defense is to draw out as much as possible the full range of exculpatory facts, encouraging the interviewee to embellish them and carry out beneficial implications as far as possible. The attorney may attempt to correct apparent "inaccuracies" in the interviewee's statement. Throughout this interview, the defense attorney is preparing notes that will supply the content of a sworn statement in the form of an affidavit that the interviewee will sign. The purpose of the affidavit is to protect against inculpatory versions that the prosecutor will try to extract from the same person during a later interview. The witness will have frozen himself into a position that he will want to protect because he has a self-interest in being consistent.

The uncooperative third party. The more difficult situation for the defense is when the informant is hostile. The uncooperative third party is one who is either openly hostile to the client or committed to telling "the whole truth and nothing but the truth," even when that truth is contrary to the client's interest. He can refuse to meet with the defense attorney, provide partial and misleading statements if the interview does take place, or make outright and sometimes false accusations. It is as important for the defense attorney to interview hostile informants (and first, if possible) as friendly informants. With a properly aggressive approach the hostile informant often can be drawn into an interview and caught in a contradiction, or he can change his story, provide exculpatory information unknowingly, or otherwise supply material that the attorney can use to impeach his credibility. Here is an attorney's explanation of how he conducted an interview with a hostile client:

> ATTY: I knew that this associate of my client's firm was in a position to destroy me and that he was likely to give to the government the information it wanted.
>
> MANN: So I understand you went to interview him. Why did he even agree to meet you?
>
> ATTY: Because he wanted it to look like he was cooperating; he didn't want my client to know that he was going to squeal.
>
> MANN: How did the interview go?
>
> ATTY: Quite well, though I didn't realize just how well when I was talking to him.
>
> MANN: What do you mean by that? Can you explain?

ATTY: I told him that I would need to take a written statement and at the outset he agreed to do that. Then I decided to play his game. I let him believe that I thought he was on our side and then I fished for the best possible story for us. He gave me a good story and I helped him build the story by supplying facts here and there that were consistent with what he said to me but which I knew not to be true. I had the statement written up immediately and he signed.

MANN: So what good did this do you?

ATTY: When I later met with the U.S. Attorney I showed him this statement. He was caught off guard. He saw his best source crumbling on the witness stand.

Even if the attorney would not use the affidavit to establish the exculpatory rather than inculpatory version, an action that would raise serious ethical questions, he could at least use the affidavit to impeach the credibility of the interviewee as a supplier of reliable information.

Another example of how an attorney attempts to persuade a potential hostile witness to hold back if and when an investigator approaches him can be seen in the following short lecture given by an attorney to an employee of the attorney's client, whom he had just interviewed. The attorney thought that this employee might try to make an immunity deal with the government, particularly if he were to get his own attorney. He also believed that the employee was participating in the client's illegal activities, but the employee had given answers to a series of questions that were exculpatory of himself and of the client. The attorney seemed pleased at this but was visibly frustrated by the interviewee's later hesitation about signing an affidavit. After much discussion, they agreed to hold another meeting a week later, at which time the affidavit would be presented to the interviewee for his signature. Then, as the first meeting came to a close, the attorney straightened his back and, looking like a commanding officer, bluntly "hinted" to this person that he should invoke the privilege against self-incrimination if anyone from the government attempted to interview him.

> Don't worry about this at all. You know we are not prosecutors. We are trying to help your employer, Mr. ———. Now let me give you a little friendly advice. Don't start searching around in files trying to find answers to questions I just put to you. If you ever have to answer these questions for anyone else, it's okay to say, "I don't know!" And if you get a call from the IRS, you call us . . . put off the meeting. We may join you at the meeting or else find you an attorney. Now I'm not telling you to take the Fifth or anything like that, but just remember that the rights that the Supreme Court in the sixties made for blacks are for you also, those rights that the Supreme Court is erasing one by one now. The worst thing in the world that happens to middle-class people is that, where they had no problems, later they find themselves with more than they can handle because they talk too much.

His implied but not ambiguous message—"You too have a problem and you'd be better off keeping quiet."

Establishing Presence at a Government Interview

The careful and aggressive defense attorney will always attempt to be present at any interview the government carries out. In cases with a large pool of potential informants—such as salesmen in a land sale fraud—there may be no way that the attorney can interview all the potential informants prior to the government. But if there are channels through which the defense can arrange to receive early notice of interviews, the defense attorney may simply "happen to be present" when the investigator shows up to conduct his interview. If the witnesses are hostile, such early notice will be difficult to obtain. If they are cooperating with the client, then the client may be able to arrange an early-warning system whereby each employee or each customer agrees to give the client notice of an investigator's attempt to set a meeting and may agree to attempt to put off the investigator until a later date so that the defense attorney can be present.

A defense attorney's presence at the interview of a third party or his advice to that party creates a delicate conflict-of-interest problem. Legal doctrine is not unambiguous in this area, and the intervention that an attorney can make with a third party is limited. Federal courts have held that an attorney for one client cannot advise a third party who is not his client to take the Fifth, to remain completely silent by invoking the privilege against self-incrimination.[6] If a third party is requested by a client's attorney to assert the privilege, it may be said that that party was kept from providing evidence to the government for the purpose of protecting the client rather than for the legitimate purpose of serving the third party's interest. Several attorneys stated that they had exposed themselves to reprimand in the past by advising third parties to invoke the privilege even when it had appeared to be in the best interest of the third party. They were accused of both compromising the interest of the third party and obstructing access needed by the government. Nevertheless, defense attorneys do attempt to intervene in a government agent's contact with third parties in limited ways, directed to restricting the amount of information the third party will share.

When an attorney plans to be present while the investigator interviews a third party, he has to prepare himself for trouble. Most government investigators do not like the idea of having a defense attorney present, for they believe, rightly, that the interviewee will be influenced by having a representative of the client (who is probably a friend or business associate) listening to all the answers. Defense attorneys believe that their presence is important, even for the most favorable and loyal defense witness. As stated by an attorney,

> There's no reason why I can't tell the witness, even in midinterview, that he

can get himself a lawyer if he wants one, and he has a right to stop the interview while he arranges for his own attorney. Also, people forget themselves when they're in a small room with an interrogator. So, there's no question about it, I'd always rather be there.

If it is useful to be present when a favorable witness is interviewed by the government, it is essential to be present when a wavering or potentially hostile witness is interviewed. This often can be achieved even if the interviewee would not have chosen it of his own volition. Such a witness may feel obliged to allow the client's attorney to take part in the meeting if asked by the client, rather than alienate a longtime associate. Thus, it is always better if the third party has not found his own attorney. Once another attorney is involved, there rarely will be room for direct involvement of the target's attorney at an interview.

Representation of Multiple Defendants

At the stage when information control is most important, representation by one attorney of more than one person involved in an investigation may provide him with important influence over how information is dealt with by putative third parties. A typical situation is as follows: an officer and employee of a company is involved in making illegal market control agreements and is being investigated by the antitrust division of the Department of Justice. An associate is also involved in the negotiations, and a secretary has knowledge of meetings and conversations that took place between officers of participating companies. These conversations are inculpatory of the first individual. The secretary also knows where inculpatory records can be found. Where one defense attorney represents all three individuals in an investigation, he can do many things that will affect the readiness of each of these persons to cooperate with the investigator. When the defense attorney uses his position to facilitate noncooperation on the part of more than one person in an investigation, it is said that a "stonewall" strategy has been adopted. Using the colloquialism of the profession in discussing particular cases, it was not uncommon for an attorney to say, "I am stonewalling," meaning that he was conducting a defense in which he was attempting to keep all persons holding inculpatory information from talking to government investigators and thereby defeat the criminal investigation.

There are many benefits to a defense based on multiple representation, including close coordination of statements given to the investigators, early warning of investigatorial contact with third parties, and the making of uniform legal arguments. The major benefit of multiple representation has been described this way:

The sharing of all information regarding both the subject matter and progress of a grand jury investigation may well be the most vital element of a stonewall defense. Certainly it is the element most effectively facilitated by the use of a common attorney. Prior to the witnesses' appearances before the grand jury the attorney is in a position to gather all the relevant facts and to eliminate or at least minimize any inconsistencies produced by faulty memories. Perhaps more important, he is in a good position to assess the progress of the investigation at all stages by virtue of his access not only to the testimony of witnesses but also to information revealed by the prosecutor in his questioning.[7]

Representation of multiple defendants raises difficult legal problems, even though the ABA *Code of Professional Responsibility* permits it. The relevant rule states that

> a lawyer may represent multiple clients if it is obvious that he can adequately represent the interest of each and if each consents to the representation after full disclosure of the possible effect of such representation on the exercise of his independent judgment.[8]

While multiple representation is in principle permitted, not all advice given by an attorney representing more than one person in the same investigation would be ethical. It would be unethical, for instance, for an attorney to advise one client not to make a plea agreement with the prosecution palpably beneficial to the client because of the damage it would cause to another client.[9] On the other hand, when informed consent to multiple representation has been given by all clients and as long as there remains a prima facie benefit to all clients, many courts have chosen not to intervene in multiple representation.[10] There are, however, decisions holding that waiver by a client may be irrelevant. Court rulings in this area have been so far from uniform that there is no clearly recognized standard that attorneys can follow in deciding whether the multiple representation that they want to engage in is ethical or not.[11]

The Court of Appeals for the Second Circuit, for example, has created a presumptive rule allowing multiple representation. In a leading case, *In re Taylor*, the court faced a challenge to multiple representation brought by an investigating prosecutor against an attorney representing four defendants in an investigation of day care centers in New York City.[12] The prosecutor argued that the defense attorney was going to obstruct the investigation by influencing all four targets to remain silent. As the court stated, "In effect, the government is attempting to bring about the compulsory disqualification of [the attorney] as a tactical maneuver to compel [one of the defendants] to testify and to prevent what it anticipates will be efforts to 'stonewall' the work of the grand jury."[13]

The court addressed the government's interest in pursuing the investigation unhindered by an attorney who simultaneously advises several persons to remain silent, and it set down a broad rule permitting multiple representation:

> When a potential or actual conflict of interest situation arises, it is the court's

duty to ensure that the attorney's client, so involved, is fully aware of the nature of the conflict and understands the potential threat to the protection of his interests. Once the court is satisfied, however, that such a client knowingly and intelligently wishes to proceed with joint representation, the court's responsibility is met, and it is without power unilaterally to obstruct this choice of counsel.[14]

In spite of this broad endorsement, there is a difference of opinion on the question of multiple representation, which can be seen by comparing a recent opinion from the Central District of California (Los Angeles).[15] There, multiple representation was examined in the context of an antitrust investigation carried out by the attorney general's offices of several states against major oil companies. Employees of the corporate defendants received subpoenas to appear for interviews, as potential witnesses, and were then represented at deposition hearings by a single corporate law firm that was also representing the targets of the investigation, the corporations. The corporations, relying on *Taylor*, argued that there was no impropriety in the multiple representation and that as long as consent was obtained from the clients, the court lacked the power to disqualify the law firm from representing targets and witnesses. In granting the motion for disqualification, the court explained why multiple representation could not be allowed and raised a serious question of whether it should ever be allowed.

Under the circumstances here discussed, plaintiff's counsel [the attorney general's offices] who contemplate deposing a presumably independent prospective witness suddenly find that neither they nor their representatives may properly seek to interview him without the presence, or at least approval, of opposing counsel, who suddenly have become the attorneys for the witness.[16]

The court said that the witnesses probably did not know that they needed an attorney until they were told so by the corporation and that the interest of the corporation in providing the representation was to restrict communication between the witnesses and the attorney general's representatives. It cited coaching of witnesses as an obstacle to proper fact-finding procedures and pointed to the phenomenon of frequent interruptions by attorneys at depositions, both of which would be aggravated by permitting multiple representation.

In the course of a deposition, once it occurs, counsel for a witness can find many ways of protecting his client through objections, requests for clarification, instructing the witness not to answer, etc. Such interjections always are disruptive of the train of thought of the interrogator. Sometimes they are appropriate for the protection of the witness and his testimony; occasionally they are unnecessary for this purpose but nonetheless serve the interests of the interrogator's adversary. If the latter is also counsel for the witness and instructs

> him not to answer, a question necessarily arises as to which client's interests he is serving.[17]

For this the court required that counsel for the corporate defendant not represent witnesses in the investigation. Similar results have been reached in other cases.[18]

Conflicting legal doctrine explains to a large extent why defense attorneys will often continue with multiple representation even when there is doubt about its propriety. Very few attorneys act as one attorney in the research group did when faced with an opportunity to represent more than one person in the same investigation. He sent one of the potential clients to another attorney for an outside opinion before taking him on as a client. He asked the attorney, "Would it be proper in the particular circumstances for me to take this person on as a client when I am representing this person's employer in the same investigation?" After getting an affirmative opinion from the outside attorney, which he put in the client's file, he felt he could represent both clients until "additional factual questions were clarified." It appeared to be more typical that defense attorneys would take on multiple clients and represent them until forced to withdraw by a judge or by the threat of a motion on the issue from the investigator. As one defense attorney said, "We are, after all, mandated to resolve doubt in favor of our clients."

A second important reason why multiple representation continues is that defense attorneys know that the government has great difficulty in raising effective opposition. Multiple representation may take place for some time prior to the government's becoming informed of the fact. It becomes known when the attorney has contact with the government as representative of more than one person in the investigation. This may not occur until the government requests an interview with or subpoenas or summons two or more persons represented by that attorney. In a complex investigation it may take the government months to discover the fact of multiple representation.

Yet even where the government becomes aware of multiple representation, extraordinary action may be required to do anything more than raise the issue informally with the attorney. A motion for disqualification must be made; this requires a commitment of resources and the assumption by the government that the issue will not be mooted before a court decision. There also appears to be an informal norm in the legal profession, applying to prosecutor and defense attorney alike, that requires an attorney to resist making accusations of unethical behavior against another attorney except in the most egregious situation. And, again, the unclarity of the current legal doctrine leaves the outcome of such a motion in question even when the facts are undisputed. Multiple representation is not itself impermissible. Thus the government has to be prepared to make a special showing of conflict.

Attorney practices. Where inculpatory information is held by more than one person, it is always to the advantage of the defense attorney for the main target to represent as many of the persons as possible. The usual condition of multiple representation is the belief by more than one of the evidence-carriers that professional legal representation is needed. The coperpetrator situation is the most obvious, but many potential witnesses who are holders of relevant information often feel they need legal representation even though they are not themselves involved in the wrongdoing. A friend or associate of a target may find it easier to stick by his story when he is counseled and accompanied by his friend's or associate's attorney.

Once a multiple representation situation is established, the attorney is faced with the problem of deciding how to represent each client without compromising the interest of the others. In one possible situation, each client holds inculpatory evidence against the other, and the government has just enough evidence to consider asking for an indictment against each, but not enough to dismiss the option of granting immunity to one client in order to get determinative evidence against the other. In this evidentiary context, it is difficult for an attorney to act without compromising one of the clients' interests. If he advises neither to make a deal because he believes that he may be able to win the case for both, he is sacrificing a certain success for one of them. And he clearly cannot advise one to make a deal against the other's interest. Some attorneys are able to obtain informed consent in this situation, after explaining the implications of the multiple representation. They then continue to represent all clients in a strategy based on total noncooperation. It is often the case that no client is willing to voluntarily become an informer against other clients. The stonewall defense continues until the government decides to force immunity on one of the clients, at which time the attorney will then have to divide representation.

In the second situation, each client holds inculpatory information against the other, but the prosecution appears to be far from making its case and completely off track. Here both clients may be able to hold out and save each other the humiliation and embarrassment of becoming either an informant or the subject of a criminal prosecution. In this situation, the position of conflict is less severe for the attorney. The prospect of success for both clients is high. Yet the difference between this situation and the former may disappear quickly. As the government's investigation progresses, one client may be presented with an opportunity to make a good deal with the government, to the detriment of the other client or clients. When an attorney is enthusiastically trying to manage a stonewall defense he may fail to give proper attention to this opportunity and compromise the interest of the client who is the potential beneficiary. An attorney representing multiple clients must constantly reevaluate the relative position of his clients, making certain that each client is well informed of his individual opportunities.

In interviewing, my sense was that many attorneys put a gloss on the situations that raise doubt, while taking as much advantage of control opportunities as possible. Where doubt does exist, the attorney may behave as if it does not. Projection of an attitude of certainty about the propriety of multiple representation is believed by attorneys to be a key factor in preventing the prosecution from asking for disqualification. One attorney explained how he handles multiple representation opportunities:

MANN: How early were you able to get into this case?

ATTY: Very early, before anyone went into the grand jury. Sometimes I get a case only after other lawyers have made mistakes; then I have trouble. They may have put people in the grand jury. I am very, very leery of putting anybody in the grand jury. In this case I got in before anybody had gone in the grand jury, immediately postagency. Usually I get in during the agency investigation.

MANN: Well, when you got into this case immediately postagency, I imagine that you then went directly to the assistant [U.S. Attorney]?

ATTY: Oh yes, I made my presence known, and the issue was who I would represent. There were many, many people involved here, and the U.S. Attorney wanted lots of lawyers so he could sort of divide and conquer. And I represented everybody at first, and then I broke them off one by one. There was a great deal of argument and discussion over multiple representation here. My own belief is that the more information you control as defense lawyer, the more effective you are, meaning that the only weapon you have as a defense lawyer in my view is control of information. You do not have much else. The prosecution has all the cards—they have the grand jury, they have in effect the presumption, they have all the investigative agencies, they have awesome powers. The only thing you have is sometimes you can stonewall an investigation. Now some people claim that that is obstructing justice. I don't, if you do it ethically and you do it out front, it's not. There are certain things you cannot do, and I suggest that you read the Fayer case—Albert Fayer. You can't tell people you don't represent to assert the privilege [against self-incrimination], for example. But I operate on the grounds that I can represent as many people whom I can ethically represent, meaning telling them whom else I am representing and discussing with them the conflict-of-interest problems. I say to them, here's what I am doing and I am doing this because I believe that you people have many interests aside from just the case [such as not informing against an associate or friend]. And sometimes they do have just the case, and you have to make that clear to them, too. And when you deal with a prosecutor, I think you have to set a high price, meaning that if he wants information, you want immunity. I've seen cases where, for example, the guy goes in and has his client spill his guts and plead to two felonies, without getting a good deal, where if the client would have gone to trial it would have ended up no worse. The client ends up alienating everybody he ever worked for and his friends. That is stupid. But if you make the prosecutor say, ''Well, look, I'll give you immunity,'' then you may want to cut the client loose. I think the group banding together for defense sometimes has a great advantage, sometimes it is dangerous.

MANN: Well, who were you arguing with in this case about multiple representation?

ATTY: The prosecutor. The prosecutor said I shouldn't do that, it is wrong—

MANN: The assistant U.S. Attorney?

ATTY: The assistant in the office, sure. Their argument is you are obstructing us because you represent everybody; it is unethical; you are not doing them a service, and ''We won't talk to you and it's not fair.'' Usually I say in effect, fuck you. You think it is not fair, I say it is fair. You want to make a motion, you make a motion. I say you have got to establish that what I am doing is wrong. I think the law is by and large going in my way, but there are some disturbing trends.

Whether this attorney disregards conflicts of interest among clients could not be determined. The prosecutor felt that early in the investigation the multiple representation kept him from obtaining access to persons from whom he desired information. He also thought, or felt it effective to argue, that the attorney was acting unethically. The defense attorney, in speaking of ''interests aside from the case,'' meant that the informant's role into which the prosecutor wanted to draw one of the clients might result in severe sanctions for the client even if immunity from prosecution were granted. The defense attorney was concerned about his client's professional future, his ability to return to the marketplace and his career position. Although the prosecutor could prevent the client from being exposed to criminal sanction through the immunity grant, he could not neutralize the sanctions of the marketplace that often follow a person's providing incriminating information against business associates.[19]

Another attorney made a similarly strong statement about the conflict he has with prosecutors over multiple representation.

MANN: What about the problem of conflict of interest during an investigation—how do you react to prosecutors who argue that you've got to split the defendants up early so the stonewall phenomenon doesn't occur?

ATTY: They call it turning a guy out—I call it turning a guy over, that is, my own client. You can understand why I don't like that situation. I tell the prosecutors to keep their hands off of my business; it's for my clients to decide, not for them to decide, when it's time to bring another attorney into the matter. This is my prerogative and the client's. As long as I can freely inform my defendant, there is no place for the prosecutor to get involved. In one matter I've got now, I'm representing two defendants whose interests may conflict down the line, but in the meantime, I've shown each why it would be better for both of them to stay with me. My evaluation of the situation is that it may be worse for both if one of them talks. In order to protect each from the other's potential sellout, I'm meeting with them separately and not divulging to one what the other has said. I constitute a Chinese Wall between them and their communications with me. If X eventually makes a deal, he won't know what Y has told me, and vice versa. But these guys are up to their necks in trouble, and I don't expect that the dual representation will end. I want you to understand I'm ready to end the dual representation should it appear that one of their interests is being compromised.

A third attorney described a case in which he was able to hold two targets together as his clients long enough to make a deal beneficial for both of them.

ATTY: I had a matter recently, a very difficult fraud case. I was representing two of the primary targets, but I knew that the government wanted to get certain other people. So I decided that I wouldn't let them talk to either of my clients. And I said, "Okay, you may have a case, but we can help you," and I wanted to get them both out of it because I knew that if they went, they would go down hard. And yet there was one sort of fly in the ointment, and that was that a colleague of theirs was somebody who would be hurt badly by their statement. So I got this colleague a lawyer, and I effectively worked out a package deal for everybody, meaning my clients and their friend.

MANN: What does that mean?

ATTY: Well, I got both of my clients immunity, and I got the prosecutor to agree, in effect, with the lawyer I got for their friend, to agree to take one count and no jail, in effect. No promises of no jail in this instance, but pretty much a promise, if you know what I mean.

MANN: So that they wouldn't have to testify———.

ATTY: Against a friend, that is right.

MANN: There were other defendants in the case?

ATTY: Yes, there were many others. There *are* many others. But my guys are out. They are witnesses, but not against their friend.

Still another situation in which multiple representation takes place is the case of a targeted employer or company who hires an attorney to represent a number of employees who will be questioned in connection with an investigation of the employer or company. The target of the investigation may have a different attorney, but what is significant here is that the target pays for the employees' attorney, discusses the case with the attorney, and then dispatches him to the employees. It is not uncommon that the employees are confronted with an attorney who is, on the one hand, supposed to represent them but who, on the other hand, acts in the role of a company superior. Early in an investigation an employee may not be able to distinguish his best interests from the company's or employer's interest. If the defense attorney does not have these interests separated clearly in his own mind, the source of his fee will determine his actions, rather than the interest of his client. A prosecutor told me of a witness who came to him without his "assigned attorney" (company-supplied) in order to give his version of the matter in question in an "atmosphere free of the intimidation" exercised by his attorney.

Representation by Associated Attorneys

Where inculpatory evidence is held by a client's associates, the next best attorney-client format, after that in which one attorney represents all persons holding inculpatory evidence, is when closely associated and cooperating attorneys represent all or a large portion of the persons who can provide inculpatory evidence against each other. While one attorney will probably not be able to bring direct influence to bear on clients of other attorneys, there is a widespread feeling among the attorneys studied that they benefit substantially from friendly, associated attorneys representing other targets and potential informants in a single investigation. The major benefits of this kind of representation can be identical to those gained from multiple representation by a single attorney. The difference is that control is weakened, because the interested attorney now deals with the third-party potential informant through an intermediary, another attorney. One goal of the interested attorney is thus to influence the choice of attorneys made by other clients, aiming at an associated attorney who can be relied upon to effectively control his client and to provide proper forewarnings and coordinate strategy.

In looking at this mode of representation, the preliminary question is whether there are different legal boundaries respecting the coordination of defense efforts by two or more attorneys representing multiple defendants or witnesses in the same investigation. In other words, if by choice or because a single attorney is disqualified, two or more attorneys attempt to reach the same goal that would—coordinated control of information—does the law raise different restrictions?

The rule of the ABA *Code of Professional Responsibility* allows an attorney to disclose information to third parties received in the context of representing a client when permission is obtained from the client. It states, "a lawyer may reveal confidences or secrets with the consent of the client or clients affected, but only after a full disclosure to them."[20] If a coordinated defense effort is being made through a stonewall strategy, one attorney receiving information from another can act on that information to control his client's disclosures as long as such actions are minimally consistent with the client's interest. In this respect, the attorney representing a third party over whom control is desired is in no different a position than the single attorney representing multiple clients. The scope of permissible actions should be identical. Thus two attorneys can have the same impact as a single attorney carrying out multiple representation if effective cooperation can be developed.

There is one exception to this principle. Some jurisdictions prohibit disclosure of information learned in connection with grand jury proceedings.[21] This prohibits an attorney from disclosing the details of testimony given by his client before a grand jury. In the federal courts, however, there is no such prohibition. Sharing of information disclosed in a grand jury proceeding has been held to be protected when it is given to another attorney who is preparing a common defense. Such disclosure is held to occur within the zone of confidentiality. This means, first, that investigators cannot inquire into the communications between attorneys with different clients that are made for the purpose of developing common strategy. And second, it may mean that client permission is unnecessary, inasmuch as confidentiality is not breached.[22]

A leading case on this point, *Continental Oil Company v. U.S.*, involved a grand jury investigation of the Continental and Standard Oil Companies.[23] Executives of the two oil companies were called before the grand jury to testify. Before and after their appearance they were interviewed by their respective attorneys. These attorneys, members of two major law firms, prepared memoranda concerning the testimony of their clients before the grand jury and exchanged memoranda in order to apprise each other of the nature and scope of the inquiry. In response to the investigator's attempt to subpoena the memoranda, the defense counsel asserted a common confidentiality privilege. The Ninth Circuit Court of Appeals upheld the defendant's claim, stating that the privilege asserted "is a valuable and important right for the protection of any client at any stage in his dealings with counsel."[24] Similarly, the Court of Appeals of the Seventh Circuit recently upheld a similar claim to confidentiality, making this general statement:[25]

> Uninhibited communication among joint parties and their counsel about matters of common concern is often important to the protection of their interests [citations omitted]. In a criminal case it can be necessary to fair opportunity to defend. Therefore, waiver [of the confidentiality privilege] is not to be inferred from the disclosure in confidence to a coparty's attorney for a common purpose.[26]

With court approval of multiple-attorney defense strategy, there is no apparent reason to conclude that such efforts are not pursued regularly. The only caveat to such a conclusion has come from two authors writing in the *Columbia Journal of Law and Social Policy*, who concluded that attorneys do not know just how liberal the federal court rules are on this issue. Their research was based on a questionnaire sent to a sample of attorneys. They found that there was a "general lack of awareness among attorneys as to when the attorney-client privilege will apply to interattorney exchanges of information" and went on to conclude that "this confusion and uncertainty, combined with normal legal caution, is probably the principal explanation for the restricted use of joint conferences."[27]

The findings I present here suggest that their conclusion is naive and inaccurate. By its nature, coordinated representation, including sharing of information, is difficult to detect. Unlike the case of the single attorney representing multiple clients, the fact of coordinated representation among multiple attorneys is not revealed when two or more of the clients appear at a hearing or other investigative meetings with their attorneys. In this sense, there is a defense advantage in coordination among two or more attorneys. Government's concern is less likely to be stimulated. Interviews and observations of the attorneys in the research group indicate that there is substantial coordinated representation, at least in certain kinds of criminal cases. Underestimation of its frequency is also a result of defense attorneys' resistance to report on a research questionnaire that they participate in that form of representation.

When one attorney wants to bring in another attorney over whom he will have some influence or someone whom he can trust, that attorney will call on personal friends, former professional associates, and persons with the same prior professional experience. One attorney who often represents multiple defendants during the early part of an investigation makes it a practice to bring in friends or other acquaintances only when irresolvable conflicts become actual. Another attorney attempts to decide from the outset of the case whether it is likely that he will be able to represent all the persons involved in an investigation through to the end and makes it his practice to refer immediately to friends and associates anyone who may have a conflict.

One strong network through which persons involved in the same investigation are referred for counsel, and the one most often encountered in this research, is made up of former assistant U.S. Attorneys. At the core of such a network for each former assistant are the other assistants whose tenures in the U.S. Attorney's office overlapped his or who served under the same U.S. Attorney. These attorneys worked together on the same cases as prosecutors, and still meet each other in the corridors of the courtroom as defense attorneys and civil litigators, commune once a year at the U.S. Attorney's reunion gathering, and have regular contact through other bar committees and professional groups. Somewhat less closely related but still part of the same network are former assistants whose tenure did not overlap. But the sense of having common expectations about how a case is handled and about cooperation remains strong among all former assistant U.S. Attorneys. One former assistant, now a partner in a major corporate firm, described it this way:

> Occasionally, we have to get defense counsel outside of the firm. We either have a conflicts problem—we've got the corporation and need someone else for the chief executive—or we have decided not to handle the case. In either instance, I'll refer the matter to one of the large number of former assistants

now doing criminal defense work. Their competence and work quality are high, and I know how they are going to handle the case. And if *we* are also in the matter, I know I can expect maximum sharing of information and co-planning of strategy. One firm, whom I often refer matters to, I considered joining myself at one time.

In chapter 5 I showed how defense attorneys can use a friendly relationship with another attorney whose client is involved in the same case as a conduit for obtaining access to information. In that context, the attorney's goal was to learn the facts of the case to make the strategic choice between bargaining and withholding cooperation. In this chapter, the sharing of information serves a control objective. Several attorneys told of situations in which they received a client on referral and gave tacit agreement that the referring attorney, who continued to represent one of the targets, would be given early warning of a decision by the receiving attorney to have his client cooperate and give inculpatory evidence. The receiving attorney would thus be better able to protect his own position. Receipt of early warning may lead the first attorney to offer cooperation simultaneously or let him avoid making cetain statements because they would contradict what the prosecution would learn from other cooperating persons. Early warning of cooperation by third parties might, for instance, lead a defense attorney to prevent his client from giving "exculpatory" statements that eventually could be used as proof of fraudulent intent. A strategy of complete silence would be adopted. One attorney described a joint effort this way:

> I can remember a case when there were eight defendants. All of them had white-collar specialists [as attorneys]. We collaborated at the beginning, and in the joint meeting we talked out this problem straightforwardly. We agreed that if anyone was going to make a deal, he would give us early warning, so we wouldn't get caught by surprise. We also agreed that each of us would attempt to hold out as long as possible, not cave in to the temptation of immunity too easily. Implied in this conversation was the assumption that one of us might have to take immunity, that it could be the right answer for at least one of us in building the proper defense. Whoever did that would be squealing on the rest of us, but we understood that if this had to be done, it would be done later rather than earlier, and that we would know about it before it happened.

Most of the attorneys studied believe that using friends and acquaintances as associated counsel helps them control third parties. They assume that friendly attorneys will have their clients resist cooperating with the government, whereas other attorneys might facilitate cooperation. In the following excerpt, an attorney relates how he experienced the expectation from other attorneys that he would cooperate with them by keeping his client from cooperating with the government.

I've run into this problem with major law firms frequently. What happens is that they are representing a corporation, and as the investigation moves forward, they realize that they've got to get outside counsel for individuals because they want to represent the corporation, or they want someone to take on the vice-president while they continue with the president. Now here I am with a relatively small practice compared to theirs. I need their referrals; there are a number of defense attorneys who have kind of become adjuncts to big firms—they always get their criminal referrals, and it makes a big difference to the economic stability of their offices. Anyway, I was called by one of these firms in a very major bankruptcy fraud. I very badly wanted to be in that case. Well, I didn't get it. Why? I got the rumor back that they thought I "wouldn't play ball with the team." They were no doubt afraid that I would have my guy spill beans on the corporation. I consider it a compliment, a real compliment to my integrity as a lawyer that they think I'm too independent. I don't take it as an insult at all that I didn't get the case.

Whatever pressures there are to cooperate, there are clearly counterpressures to take an independent position. Independence, indeed, seems to be a hallmark of a defense attorney's identity. This is apparent in an attorney's description of a multistate corporate embezzlement scheme.

MANN: Can you tell me what you did when you first got into the case?

ATTY: Yes, what I did is I learned as much as I could about it, and I began moving to get the subpoenas quashed. By the way, this is typical of a white-collar case. There were lots of lawyers in the case, and immediately one of the lawyers tried to get a conference going with all the lawyers, where we would cut up the work and divide responsibilities and share. This has certain benefits and also certain disadvantages. The benefits are that you get insights from other lawyers and you get certain work products out of other lawyers, and you know what is going on. The disadvantages are that you end up perhaps subjecting your own individual client's interests to a group interest, and you form relationships which at some point may be antithetical to an individual creativity. And I really don't like to work in groups. I have done it, and done it successfully at times, but then again I think in all fairness I like to have something to say about what the group does. I don't like to lean on somebody else. It's not the nature of my practice or my time.

MANN: In this case you didn't respond favorably to the invitation of one of the other attorneys?

ATTY: Well, I did, I cooperated to some extent. But I did not respond to the point where I allowed anybody to tell me what I should do.

MANN: What did this attorney want with a group?

ATTY: Well, one attorney had decided what subpoena motions ought to be made, and he was going to assign them out to various attorneys, and most people bought that. I did not, I did my own. I was willing to share my work product in return for other people sharing theirs, but I didn't want anybody to tell me what motions I could make and not make, or to be the spokesman for me with the U.S. Attorney, so I was my own spokesman.

MANN: Did he argue that this would make your case, total case, weaker because you wouldn't cooperate?

ATTY: Well, he tried to extol the benefits of cooperation, but under his flag. I was cordial enough about it, but in point of fact I didn't go along with him. I attended some meetings and I told people what I was doing, but I went ahead and did what I wanted to do myself, and eventually my guy got out of it.

MANN: Did you do something different than they did?

ATTY: I made different kinds of motions, yes. And I had different discussion with the assistant.

MANN: How did the situation of your defendant differ from that of the others?

ATTY: Because he was mine, and because I wanted to do things my own way. Because I don't like to do things other people's way necessarily.

MANN: Can you be more specific about that so that I can understand what you did that others didn't do?

ATTY: I did not rely on other people's paperwork. I did not rely on other people's analysis. I used it. I listened to it. But I made my own bottom-line decisions and did my own bottom-line writing, and did my own arguing and my own negotiations.

The attorneys studied made evident repeatedly that they cooperate by sharing information given to them by their clients, by sharing legal research and briefing tasks, and by discussing strategy. In many instances, legal positions are formulated jointly for a number of clients; letters to investigative agencies are drafted jointly. One attorney stated that when he drafts a defense document in cooperation with another attorney representing another client in the same matter, he will make it appear as if the work product is actually emanating from two sources independently, so that neither of the attorneys opens himself to charges of conflicts of interest.*

There is less certainty about the degree to which attorneys bring pressure to bear on their clients to choose a strategy beneficial to clients of other attorneys. Attorneys did state that they often experience pressure to cooperate in ways that might appear to compromise their client's best interest. This suggests that those who apply pressure or express expectations have some reason to believe that they will get what they want. Certain attorneys operate on the assumption that their colleagues will participate in a coordinated effort at defending a group of clients

*One attorney stated that he will occasionally bring his own letterhead stationery to the office of another attorney when "I expect the other attorneys to do the writing and me the signing."

where an independently conducted defense program might lead the attorneys to take different positions. But despite the messages communicated between attorneys that they are prepared to influence their clients, the actual occurrence of this kind of cooperation was more difficult to capture than perhaps any other research topic. The findings did not reveal directly any instance of an attorney who appeared to resist providing information to the government where it would help his client, in order to serve the interest of another attorney's client, nor did any attorney state that he actually ever did this or saw others do it. The question left open, then, was whether these attorneys simply feign this kind of cooperation while always acting in their client's own best interest or whether the particular cases did not provide instances of this kind of cooperation in spite of the fact that it does occur.

One reason for feigning, as well as actually providing, extensive help to associated attorneys has to do with the dependence of certain attorneys on other attorneys for client referrals. Where one investigation involves a number of potential targets who have a hierarchical relationship among themselves grounded in their business, occupational, or other organizational setting, it appears that the persons at the top of the hierarchy—a president of a corporation, a crime boss—may wield substantial influence over the legal representation of those lower on the hierarchy. The subordinates look to those higher for recommendations and tacit approval of their own counsel. They may also wait for their superior's attorney's decision on the issue of *when* independent counsel should be sought. Parallel to this stratification of potential clients is an apparent stratification of law firms. Where ''establishment'' clients are involved, the larger and more prestigious law firms determine which of the smaller and less prestigious firms or attorneys receive referrals.

A large number of the attorneys interviewed recounted instances of small firms and single practitioners going out of their way to wait for the lead to be taken by a large firm or putting extraordinary resources into documents that they knew would be read by their more prestigious associated counsel. The associated firms and attorneys would also, it was said, orient their work in a manner that would appear to be consistent with the lead counsel's conception of the correct emphasis of a legal position. Thus, while major corporate law firms, who do not frequently or ever handle criminal matters, sometimes are dependent on the specialist's knowledge of criminal procedure and his access to the prosecutor's office, specialists are often dependent on the big firms for referrals. Some of the attorneys interviewed have a deeply ambivalent attitude toward the larger, more prestigious firms. They would like to build their practices independently, without obligation to a large firm's influence. To the extent that they do so, their clientele will include fewer corporate executives and large business entities, and more smaller cases will have to be handled, matters that generate smaller fees and force the attorneys to handle lower-status clients.

PART IV
Substantive Legal Argument

9 *The Precharge Substantive Defense*

During the period of investigation of a potential criminal case, before a decision to charge is made, there may be opportunities for a defense attorney to present substantive legal argument on the issue of the culpability of his client. It is a misconception of the criminal process to assume that a trial represents a choice to make a substantive defense and a guilty plea a choice not to do so. For the majority of street and violent crimes, a guilty plea does represent a choice to substantially limit the amount of resources put into a substantive defense, even though substantive legal argument is often part of the plea negotiation process. But in white-collar cases, often the choice not to go to trial is not intended to limit the resources put into or the vigor of a substantive defense. Rather, it is a choice to invest resources at an earlier stage in the process, into what I have called the precharge substantive defense. Where the substantive defense is first concentrated in the precharge period, the defense attorney will force the government to scrutinize legal questions before the charging decision is made. This examination sometimes results in the government's closing of the case or reducing potential charges. Substantive argumentation by the defense has an effect on the outcome of a case independent of information control.

The main concern of the substantive defense is to take a given set of facts and derive factual and legal conclusions favorable to one's client. The intellectual tools of this task are logical inference for drawing factual conclusions and comparison and differentiation for drawing legal conclusions. When making substantive legal argument, the defense attorney constructs the most favorable factual reality and then persuades an adversary or a judge what legal consequences that reality should have for the client. In a persuasive mode of presentation, the attorney may oscillate between factual and legal points, blurring the difference between the two; but logically, each constitutes a distinct objective of the substantive defense. In a substantive defense, the attorney uses the evidence known to him to have been obtained by the government, and any other evidence known to him to be beneficial to his client, to argue that an offense is not shown by that evidence. "These accusations," he argues, "cannot be proved beyond a reasonable doubt." In so doing, the attorney draws on all the sources that define the substantive boundaries of offenses: statutes, regulations, the Constitution, and court decisions interpreting them.

While the substantive defense can be pursued entirely independently, information control may play a significant part. As stated by one attorney, as he prepared to meet a prosecutor to present his legal arguments against the issuance of an indictment,

> At that point, by the time the case got to the U.S. Attorney's office, I knew more about the facts of the case than the investigators did. Because I got into the case early enough I was able to track what they were doing, and I also had the advantage of being an insider, of being able to go to sources that they didn't know to go to, to find out what had happened.

Knowing more than the prosecutor, the defense attorney was aware that he had a favorable evidentiary setting: the client's behavior could be made to appear, through substantive legal argument, closer to the boundary of the statutory definition of culpability than it would have appeared had the prosecutor had access to all relevant information. After handling the case successfully, the defense attorney commented that this was an instance of a strategy he often adopts, called "hiding the ball" in which the success of his substantive argument was dependent on preventing disclosure of certain damaging facts. The defense attorney's legal position was made possible as a result of prior information control maneuvers on his part. Subsequent to information control, the essence of the attorney's work in this case was traditional legal argument on the question of the fit of the law to the available evidence.

Substantive legal argument is, of course, not unique to the precharge stage of the criminal process. Indeed, it is the essence of the criminal trial. It is also commonly a part of plea negotiations, during which the defense attorney will argue to the prosecutor that the crime charged cannot be proved. And knowledge of substantive law is still more basic to the entire criminal process, for even when the defense attorney is engaging in information control, a strategy not based on making a substantive argument to an opponent, he must know well the substantive law in order to assess information and determine where control needs to be applied.

But the substantive defense in cases handled by the attorneys studied has a distinctive feature because it takes place at the precharge stage of the criminal process. One defense attorney opened his interview comments with the following statement, asserting that the cases that generate substantive legal argument at the precharge stage are white-collar cases and that the opportunity for precharge argument gives white-collar defense work a special character.

> Well, I think the major difference between white-collar and street crime, at least at the inception, is that it takes longer to investigate from the government's point of view in most white-collar situations. You take the average tax evasion case: the case starts at the investigative agency, in the tax division. The intelligence agents come in and they do a long investigation which may take somewhere between six months and a year, maybe even longer than that.

> It then goes through a series of reviews at the IRS, from the district director's level to the regional counsel, and from the regional counsel it finally goes down to the Department of Justice tax division. From the Department of Justice tax division it then goes to the U.S. Attorney's office that is going to prosecute the case. At each of these stages you [the attorney] get your opportunity to present your view of the matter. The same basic pattern, although it is not as extensive as it is in the IRS area, but the same basic pattern applies in the securities cases. It will take the SEC, working through the offices of their attorneys and their investigators, quite a period of time and they will generally take it through a civil complaint stage before they even think of sending it criminal. So again, a couple of years will go by with the government investigating it and thinking about it and so forth. You are essentially litigating all the issues even before the case becomes an official criminal prosecution.

This statement makes clear one of the reasons for precharge substantive argument: the now institutionalized opportunity provided by certain government agencies—administrative agencies with sanctioning powers and U.S. Attorney's offices—for precharge adversarial review of cases. These arrangements not only provide a forum for the proactive defense attorneys to address substantive legal issues, but their very presence invites otherwise passive attorneys to make substantive arguments before charging. And the large amount of resources now invested into precharge review by some attorneys has contributed to giving those procedures a quasi-judicial character. The more attorneys press the rights of their clients before administrative agencies, the more those agencies are forced to apply principles of due process.

Attorneys in the research group felt that there was a second reason for increased salience of legal argument in the cases they handle: ambiguity of definition in the statutory sections defining offenses. As examples, respondents often mentioned tax fraud, mail fraud, conspiracy to defraud the United States, and bribery. Whether ambiguity in statutory definition in fact results in greater substantive argument about criminal liability is an empirical issue not tested in this research. But attorneys studied here did believe that the cases they handle typically create a high degree of ambiguity about whether the substantive offense has been committed, and that this causes them to make substantive legal argument more frequently than they would if they were handling other types of cases in which they perceive less ambiguity.

Thus the review procedures of government agencies and high resources of clients are each factors that raise the likelihood of a precharge substantive defense. So is the high degree of ambiguity in typical white-collar cases. In what follows I detail how attorneys executed such defenses in cases having all three of these characteristics.

Precharge Litigation in an SEC Investigation

The SEC's division of enforcement and compliance carries out investigations of publicly owned companies and, where violations of statutory standards are found, imposes civil sanctions and makes recommendations for criminal prosecution.[1] A person or business that violates statutory standards is then exposed to a range of escalating sanctions. Though the SEC investigation is technically a civil process and the ultimate resolution of the matter may result in no sanctions or only civil sanctions, a serious violation is a potential criminal case, and attorneys are recruited during the agency investigation to provide protection from criminal prosecution as well as from civil sanctions.

Asked to give an example of a matter litigated before the SEC, one respondent discussed an alleged false financial reporting scheme. In this particular case, the attorney felt that there was a high probability of a recommendation for criminal prosecution, but not a certain one. The client in the investigation was a major building investment company then traded on the New York Stock Exchange. Five years prior to the investigation, building company executive officers had met with SEC personnel to obtain approval to sell certain land owned by the company. The sale had required SEC confirmation because the building company's audit firm wrote an opinion-letter stating that there was "some question" about whether the sale could be treated as a legitimate transaction by the seller company. The audit firm had doubts about whether the buyer was truly an independent business entity. After negotiations with the SEC and submission of documents, the sale was formally approved by the SEC as an independent transaction.

The approved sale of property resulted in a substantial increase in the liquid assets of the company. However, at the time of the sale the new assets on the books of the company represented only an obligation due to it by the purchaser. Payment had not yet been made. About a year after the sale, and as a result of a high-risk development on the land, the purchaser became insolvent and the debt was not paid. A year later the building company was unable to pay its own debts and was forced to stop trading on the Exchange. A declaration of bankruptcy was followed closely by an SEC investigation. The defense attorney described his initial contact with the clients, chief executive officers of the company:

> In this instance, I started by appearing with the president and vice-president before a hearing officer and then eventually got involved in a very large document submission. From the questions that SEC officers asked at our initial appearance, it was immediately evident that they thought there had been some monkey-business in the sale of land from our client, the building company, to the purchaser. They [SEC officers] learned from the bankruptcy trustee that the interest that our clients had in the purchaser—an interest that wasn't re-

vealed in the original negotiations with the SEC—made the purchase, or so they argued, something of an artificial transaction. To put it in a nutshell, it looked like the clients defrauded the building company by having its capital assets in the form of land sold to a nonpublic company where they could do with it what they couldn't do while it was owned by the building company, a public company. After the sale they would not have to stay within the restrictions on land use that appear in the articles of incorporation of the building company.

At that point in the case there had been no official indication from the SEC that a recommendation for criminal prosecution was being considered. The concern for potential criminal implications was a private matter known only to client and attorney. The evidence supplied to the government by the bankruptcy trustee showed that the president of the building company had an ownership interest in the purchaser. It was an interest that had been obtained after the sale of the land, but before a decision was made to use the purchased land for a high-risk development project. The question that faced the SEC was whether the acquiring of an ownership interest in the purchaser company by an officer of the building company constituted a fraud on the building company when the purchaser company caused it to go into bankruptcy as a result of a high-risk venture. This was the issue argued before the SEC, and here is an account of how the defense attorney viewed the matter.

> There were two approaches to this question. First we had to turn over all documents related to the sale. One issue was whether any of those documents would show that an agreement had been entered into before the sale between our client and the purchaser to make the high-risk investment after the sale. That would have strengthened greatly the SEC case, because they could have shown that our client knew that he was exposing the building company to a risk before he negotiated the sale. But the other question, and I don't think the SEC officers were really prepared for this, was whether the investment made by the purchaser was really a "high-risk" venture. Let's assume that there was an improper conflict of interest in which our client, as a director, violated his fiduciary duty to the building company. That couldn't be a criminal matter unless some palpable damage resulted directly from the actions on the director's part. So what we eventually argued, and to do this we devoted a great deal of time to financial analysis and legal research . . . we argued that the investment was not a high-risk investment.

In the course of handling this case the attorney reported that he had more than ten meetings with SEC officers, presented expert testimony from investment analysts, land experts, and market economists, and submitted three substantial legal briefs. After a twenty-four-month investigative period the case was closed by the SEC without any action. In commenting on the result in the case, the attorney reported:

> We were fortunate to keep the focus on the legal issue related to the question of whether the investment made by the purchaser was high-risk. We had a weak point in that negotiations had taken place prior to the land sale between my client and the purchaser company which could have been used to show that both of them intended to use the land for a high-risk investment. We probably would not have been able to prevail in the matter the way we did had the government been able to show that my client and the purchaser *thought* it was high risk. We won the case on the legal issue, and that was the only legal issue that they saw.

In his presentation of argument to SEC officers this attorney carried out tasks similar to those he would perform at a trial, were the matter to go that far. His arguments were factual and legal. The factual argument was aimed at disputing the government's definition of the nature of the capital investment. The question was, "What did the facts show?" While controlling the introduction of facts into the arena of argument was an a priori information control function, the task of the attorney at this stage was to take the facts introduced and convince the government that its inferences—that is, its overall factual conclusion—were incorrect. A second goal was to examine the substantive legal standards. If the facts showed that there was a high-risk investment, did the law apply criminal responsibility to this transaction? Did knowledge on the part of the potential defendant need to be shown? Did the sale occur between two independent legal entities such that the fate of the land after sale had no connection to the acts of the officers of the seller, the potential defendant? Did the officers of the building company violate a fiduciary duty to the company?

Precharge Litigation in an IRS Investigation

In any matter where criminal violations of the Internal Revenue Code are suspected, the criminal division of the IRS has sole authority for conducting a criminal investigation.[2] Within the criminal division, authority is stratified; the criminal investigator has exclusive responsibility over the field aspect of an investigation and makes the first decision on the question of sufficiency of evidence.* Subsequently, there are several appellate stages before a case reaches a U.S. Attorney's office. The defense attorney thus has various opportunities for

*Criminal investigators are called into a case in many instances by civil investigators who have uncovered evidence of fraud during an audit procedure designed not to search for criminal violations but rather for determining proper financial tax liability. When a criminal investigator is put on a case, the authority of the civil investigator is reduced substantially.

arguing substantive issues, with revenue agents, who are civil auditors, and with criminal investigators and appellate officers.

Several respondents described investigations of "questionable corporate payments" in which substantive defenses were used in the precharge stage. Cases known by this label involved both IRS and SEC investigations of bribe and bribelike payments by corporations to foreign and domestic government officials for the granting of influence and preference in business and political decision-making. Specialists in criminal tax work say that these investigations have brought into the criminal process, at least into its early stages, unprecedented numbers of highly placed executives of large corporations.

One questionable payments case in a firm that handled several executives and corporations as clients involved the following situation. The Aeroflight Corporation (a pseudonym), headquartered in Chicago, had for years sustained a slush fund from which payments were made to American government officials and foreign agents. Officially, however, the fund was identified as an entity for supporting the political campaigns of various U.S. national political candidates. As such, it was a legal fund, and any individual could make contributions to it. The SEC had become interested in the fund because it appeared to constitute a vehicle for facilitating illegal payments to government officials by the company. The IRS then became interested because the method of cash contribution to the fund appeared to constitute a tax fraud.

In its investigation, the SEC came to the conclusion that Aeroflight had created the fund by granting bonuses to top executives, specifically, an automobile that for all practical purposes became the private vehicle of the executive, though it was owned by the company. Simultaneously, certain key executives brought pressure to bear on the recipients of the automobiles to make cash contributions to the fund. The SEC report concluded by saying that the cash contributions to the fund were, in fact, the executives' compensation to the company, compelled by company pressure for the automobiles. The company had created the fund, argued the SEC, by giving a bonus with an implied condition.

The tax problem identified by the IRS was this: Aeroflight was taking a capital depreciation for the automobiles, thereby deducting from its annual tax liability the cost of creating the fund. Not only was there a trust violation by the company in its making of bribelike payments to government officials, but there was tax fraud in the scheme used to establish the fund.

For its part, Aeroflight argued that all the contributions to the fund were made by executives *voluntarily*, without company pressure, so that it was incorrect to view the contributions as a quid pro quo for the automobiles. It followed, so argued the company, that the capital depreciation on the automobiles had no connection to the cash contributions to the fund.

When the defense firm was retained by Aeroflight the IRS already had obtained most of the facts relevant to its case, from the SEC and from an independent audit committee that the SEC had required Aeroflight to establish to conduct an in-house investigation.[3] Together, the SEC findings and the audit committee report constituted the major factual base from which the IRS worked. Upon entering the case, the defense attorney first met with IRS field investigators. I asked the attorney how he handled this meeting. He responded:

> You can see that this tax case is just completely different than the junk in the street. When a guy commits a burglary there's just not a question that a crime has been committed. The question is ''Who done it?'' Here the question was whether there was a crime at all. If there was one, there's no question but that my client did it. So I started by saying to the special agent, ''There's no crime here; that's all there is to it, there's no crime here, no elements of fraud, no proof. What's the crime?'' I asked him. ''Well, the crime is taking a depreciation allowance to create a slush fund,'' the agent said. I said, ''I don't see any crime like that in the IRS Code.'' He said the whole automobile scheme was a sham, and we had a lot of argument about that.

In saying ''a lot of argument,'' the attorney was underplaying the amount of resources that went into developing legal positions argued to the IRS criminal investigator. Associates in the law firm spent many weeks researching legal questions and preparing memoranda for the senior attorney. Several meetings with the investigator were conducted in which oral argument was made. And later written memoranda were presented to the IRS.

When the chief field investigator decided not to accept the arguments made by defense counsel, and the case was referred with a recommendation for prosecution to the IRS district counsel's office, the defense attorney's goal was to seek a second substantive review in the IRS district counsel's office. It was crucial to the attorney that the field investigator who had carried out the investigation and made the prosecution recommendation should be kept out of the review forum. His preestablished view would disrupt the defense attorney's contrary argument when he would make it to the district counsel. Before meeting with the chief counsel at the IRS, the defense attorney wrote the following letter:

> In contemplation of the conference that is scheduled with you in the above-captioned matter, we want to bring to your attention our objection to the presence or participation of the special agent [investigator] who has handled this matter during its investigative stages. This conference has been requested in order that we have an opportunity to *independently* present and argue our views. Such opportunity will not have been properly granted to us should the conference be or have the appearance of being influenced by the special agent.
>
> Our objection to the inclusion of the special agent at a conference is consistent with, indeed dictated by, the currently applicable directives in the *Order*

[3040.1] of the office of the chief counsel, Internal Revenue Service, at p. 6, August 29, 1979. The Internal Revenue Service has recognized and made obligatory the rule that law enforcement officers of the government who handle a case at one stage in a proceeding should not be involved in the subsequent stages. The underlying principle is that a meaningful review by an officer of the government can only be achieved when that officer carries out his or her task independently of and without continuing communication with other officers whose decision has already been made and whose authority has terminated.

As stated in the above-cited *Order* of the office of chief counsel, entitled "Prosecution Considerations and Responsibilities,"

> *Conduct of the Conference*. It is normally undesirable to invite the attendance of investigating personnel at the conference since: (1) Counsel's involvement is basically an independent legal review of the case; and (2) the presence of such personnel may tend to inhibit the principal and/or his representative in a free discussion of all facts of the case. [Order 3040.1, p. 6]

A proper conference is carried out "in the absence of investigating personnel." This facilitates a free discussion of all facts of a case and ensures that the conferee is uninhibited in carrying out his independent review tasks.

For the foregoing reasons we object to the presence of the special agent at our conference with you and expect that you will respect our request.

The defense attorney obtained a meeting with chief counsel in the district alone and presented argument orally. Eventually he submitted an extensively documented brief in which he argued two main points: first, he argued that depreciation of the company automobiles was a well-established practice even where executives obtained a percentage of personal use; and second, he argued that the contributions of the executives to the fund were voluntary, so that the creation of the fund could not be interpreted as related directly to the providing of the automobiles or to the tax consequences. Presenting these arguments required analysis of the original interviews of the employees done by the SEC, analysis of subsequent interviews done by the audit committee, and reinterviewing of the executives in order to establish that the executives had contributed voluntarily.

The focus of the legal argument became the meaning of "voluntary" in the context of salaried officers' payment to a company fund. In meetings prior to the submission of the brief, the IRS investigator had argued that indirect collective pressure by senior executives and the implied threat of reprisals through corporate advancement delays or other limitations on favorable treatment created an "involuntary atmosphere." In response, the defense attorney argued that the executives may have contributed out of a feeling of loyalty to the corporation but that that could not make the corporation or any of its directors responsible for the payments to the fund. Though all the beneficiaries of the automobile program made contributions, the defense reported that a noncontributor would not have lost his car. The investigator responded by asking why executives who did not receive cars also did not make contributions.

Throughout the meeting between the chief counsel and the defense attorney, the facts available to the two adversary parties relevant to the question of criminal liability were the same. Defense advocacy required the skills of an attorney with knowledge of IRS administrative procedures used for determining questions of criminal responsibility and the applicable substantive law of the Internal Revenue Code that defines criminal responsibility. It also required the services of an attorney who had office resources for the large amount of legal and factual analysis required at the various stages of substantive review. And, as the attorney claimed, it required an experienced strategist. As he explained,

> What I mean by strategy here is locating the weak point in the agent's theory. This is the goal of any litigator in any case. Our ability to succeed in this matter can be attributed, at least in part, to the fact that we created in the mind of the agent a substantial doubt about the service's likelihood of succeeding with a jury on this issue. We showed him that he would find himself in deep waters trying to prove that the desire for career advancement and the behavior it results in is a criminal act. It was the way we characterized the situation and the anxiety we planted in the district counsel that the case would be turned back up above. And they knew we had a carte blanche budget behind us.

In the early spring of 1978 the district counsel notified the defense firm that the investigation was closed and that a recommendation for criminal prosecution would not be made against the company or its officers.

Precharge Litigation with a Prosecutor

Prosecutors in the federal courts—the U.S. Attorneys and their assistants—carry out two distinguishable functions in preparing a case for disposition. They do original investigation, handling a case from its inception as a matter with criminal potential, and they prepare cases for trial or for the receipt of a guilty plea after the investigation has been completed. The inflow of cases from federal agencies—the IRS, SEC, and FBI, for instance—requires only the latter function if the investigation has been carried forward far enough. But many of the cases that originate in the agencies require further investigation. When the prosecutor is acting as an investigator, defense attorneys often are able to obtain hearing opportunities for substantive review of the merits of a case as it evolves in the precharge stage, much as they are at an independent agency like the IRS or the SEC. There is a less formal and less institutionalized review structure. Sometimes obtaining a review meeting with the chief prosecutor depends on who the defense attorney is, but in most of the cases examined here review meetings at the U.S. Attorney's office were relatively easy to obtain.

From the defense perspective, it is important to initiate the adversary contact at the earliest possible stage in the investigation and to continue it at later stages before the charging decision is made. When a case starts in the prosecutor's office or when it arrives there after agency referral, the defense attorney immediately will attempt to meet with the assistant in charge. As indicated earlier, this is part of the defense investigative role, for prosecutors may supply significant information about the nature of the investigation—the issue being examined, the identity of targets, the nature of the evidence already located. Now, however, the defense attorney is concerned with opportunities for adversarial argument on substantive issues.

As in the context of SEC and IRS precharge review, the main thrust of the defense attorney's argument is that the prosecutor is mistaken in his proposed factual conclusion and his application of law to facts. The defense attorney may even be willing to admit the existence of the alleged fact-pattern—that is, the client did what the prosecutor alleges—but he argues that what was done does not fall within the ambit of a criminal statute. One attorney makes this point in the following story:

> The case I am about to describe to you never had an indictment. I want to describe a process of preindictment intervention which was successful. In doing so, I am going to be very vague about the facts so that I don't even identify remotely the client because that is confidential. There was a particular person who was the subject of a federal indictment, and I won't tell you whether it was the Eastern District of New York, Southern District of New York, or the District of New Jersey, because I have dealt with all three of them a lot. It was a case in which the subject of the investigation was mail fraud. The defendants were thought to have engaged in a scheme by which they caused businesses to buy advertising in a publication by pretending that they [the businesses] had bought advertisements in the publication before. Thus, they would call up a company and say, "Do you want to renew your advertising?"
>
> The theory of the defense, the substantive argument, was that the victims, or the alleged victims—because I don't believe that there were victims—who gave up money got exactly what they were offered, namely, their advertisements were circulated as promised. The government argued that deception had been used. But I argued that even if that were true, the answer to that was the case would be vulnerable to dismissal at the end of the prosecution's presentation on the theory that there was no crime committed. There may have been this and there may have been that, but there was no fraud because what was bargained for was provided.

What I did was to argue my legal theory and gather up a massive amount of evidence that sustained my contentions that every promise made was delivered on in terms of printing and distributing the magazine. I had printing bills and copies of the magazine and indications of all of the attempts made to circulate, so that anybody who bought the advertisement got the benefit as a bargain. There is a leading Second Circuit case on this point of it not being fraudulent, if you get what you were promised.

This case was a good example of being apprised early on by the issuance of grand jury subpoenas that an investigation was going on—a lot of witnesses were being called before the grand jury and documents were being subpoenaed. I was fully aware that there was an investigation going on. I must tell you the prosecutor was not 100 percent in agreement with my legal positions but my arguments were strong enough so that the doubt was resolved in my favor.

This case was successfully handled by the defense attorney in the precharge stage solely on the basis of oral legal argument made to the assistant U.S. Attorney handling the matter.

It is customary for attorneys to have long meetings at the prosecutor's office when making substantive argument to a prosecutor who is conducting an investigation. Some attorneys also submit written briefs of their arguments, very much like the briefs they would present to a court if the issue were decided there. In making their substantive argument, attorneys treat the prosecutors as if they were judges bound by the legal standards that control ultimate decisions about a defendant's criminal liability. Attorneys take this approach in spite of the fact that prosecutors need only a prima facie case, and not a case beyond reasonable doubt, to ask for the issuance of an indictment.

The next example of a substantive defense shows just how similar the precharge adversarial process can be to a trial. Here, the investigaton by the U.S. Attorney's office in the Southern District of New York focused on a real estate project carried out by the AMREP corporation through a subsidiary, Rio Rancho Estates, who sold land located in New Mexico to purchasers in all parts of the United States.[4] According to the assistant U.S. Attorneys investigating the matter, Rio Rancho had acquired more than 86,000 lots near Albuquerque for an estimated $170 million. The government contended that Rio Rancho fraudulently misrepresented the nature of the land by claiming that it would be a "good investment," in particular by implying that it was an area to which the population of Albuquerque had to expand. To substantiate its claim, the government expected to be able to show that most of the lots, sold to unwary purchasers, were located on unpaved roads and were without utilities. Rather than being developed land, the Rio Rancho property was mainly rolling hills with sparse growths of sagebrush and native grass in sandy soil. And the sales were carried out, the government argued, through slickly organized and carefully scripted promotional dinners and tours. In short, the government argued that the land was unfit for development, the company unable to develop it, and that representations that water was available, that the land lay in a path of rapid development, and that there was a substantial resale market were false, and that AMREP, through Rio Rancho, had perpetrated a carefully planned scheme of fraudulent misrepresentations and deceived hundreds of purchasers.[5]

Examination of the eighty-page brief submitted to the U.S. Attorney's office in the precharge period demonstrates how an experienced defense attorney handled precharge substantive argument on a matter described by him as a case of complex white-collar crime.

In defining the purpose of the defense brief, the attorney first wanted to remind the chief prosecutor of the role he should take in considering the case for prosecution. He declared at the outset,

> This brief is addressed to the U.S. Attorney in his capacity as an "administrator of justice," or neutral magistrate, not an "advocate" (ABA Minimum Standards Paragraph 1.1(b)). The purpose of the brief is to demonstrate that despite an 18-month-long investigation, neither the company nor its principals are appropriate subjects for criminal prosecution and that the conduct being questioned is not criminal, or at least, there are substantial if not overwhelming doubts that criminal activities occurred.

Then, in summarizing the government's position, the attorney wrote:

> The core of the alleged fraud is a knowing misrepresentation that the purchase of the land is a "good investment." Such a representation, we submit, is a statement of opinion and cannot be a fraud unless that opinion is not honestly held.

The method of argument in the brief can be divided into three parts. First, the defense presented material to create a factual picture of the actual representations made by the company to the investors. This included an analysis of brochures distributed by the company, representations made in television commercials, and statements made directly to purchasers by sales representattives. For example, a brochure entitled "How to Live—Retire—Invest in the Sunny Southwest" was presented to show the modest manner in which the land was described to potential purchasers. Two versions of the brochure were compared in order to demonstrate that the company changed the original version several years prior to the investigation to comply with state regulations, the implication being that this demonstrated good faith and an intention to act lawfully. Among the many sections of the brochure quoted at length in the brief were the following, which were statements of the reasons why the purchase of the property was a good investment. From the original version:

> [There is the] chance of reaping future rewards with a relatively small speculative investment in an area where land values have shown a consistent tendency to steadily climb. It is a demonstrable fact that land prices in general in the Albuquerque area have increased 20, 30, even 50 times or more in the past 20 years. Now with Albuquerque's population predicted to almost double once again by 1990 or so—one does not have to be an expert to predict that land prices in our area should continue to reflect increasing population pressures . . . and perhaps at an even livelier pace as population pushes more and more into the growing Northwest Mesa neighborhood where Rio Rancho Estates is located!

The attorney then presented the revised version, which contained a watered-down description of the investment opportunity. The reasons why the purchase of the property was a good investment were now described this way:

> [Your opportunity is] to obtain land that has a *reasonable long-term potential. No one can predict the future* with any certainty, but because Albuquerque is surrounded on three sides by Federal, Reserved, or Canyon Lands, the Northwest Mesa where Rio Rancho Estates is located is in what *appears to us* to be in the logical path of progress.

By presenting these and other excerpts the defense attorney was first developing a picture of the behavior of the defendant. Since the charges involved misrepresentation, the facts he examined were the statement made by AMREP to purchasers.

The second part of the brief was also devoted to factual analysis. In this part the attorney aimed at showing that the statements made to purchasers about the land were accurate or reasonably accurate representations of truth. To do this, he focused on surrounding circumstantial facts. He asked whether it was "a fair representation that Albuquerque is expanding towards the Northwest Mesa and Rio Rancho." He supported this proposition with expert opinion and the implications he could draw from that opinion, citing in footnotes a large quantity of statistical reports. For example, he wrote,

> In 1963, Jose Luis Yguado and Associates, in a "Growth and Development Study, Northwest Mesa Area—Albuquerque, N. Mex.," stated:
>
> > It is reasonable to assume that any major expansion of the city to accommodate necessary growth and development in the ensuing years shall be on the Northwest Mesa Area. This is primarily because of its proximity to the present "center" of the community as well as the limitless development potential. This is especially evident when one looks at the recent development activity which is already taking place in the Northwest Mesa Area. [p. 10]

Other authorities, he said, have come to the same conclusion:

> The reasoning which supports the prediction that Albuquerque would grow to the northwest is based upon the physical nature of the city of Albuquerque and the growth and development potential of the Northwest Mesa Area.
>
> The physical character of the city of Albuquerque is unique; the city is bound by effective physical barriers preventing the expansion to the east by the Sandia Mountains, to the south by Kirtland Air Force Base, the Manzano Military Installations, and the Isleta Indian Reservations, to the north by the uncertainty of legal title created by the Elena Gallegos Grant and by the Sandia Pueblo Indian Reservation (*Albuquerque News*, June 19, 1975; column by Walter Kubilius entitled "Behind the News"). Development to the southwest is highly improbable because prolonged litigation over ownership of the 25,000-acre Atrisco Grant has made development virtually impossible. Accordingly there are traditional and physical growth barriers which shape, restrict, and influence the growth of the Albuquerque Metropolitan Area forcing expansion to occur in a westerly direction toward the West Mesa area in which Rio Rancho Estates is situated.
>
> Although some authorities would disagree, the burden of authority agrees and historical fact has shown that the Northwest Mesa Area was prepared to accommodate extensive growth and that any major expansion of the city of Albuquerque in the ensuing years subsequent to 1970 has been and will continue to be to the Northwest Mesa Area.

The objective of the defense brief in presenting this circumstantial evidence was to establish the truth of the representations made to the purchasers. The government would also have to address this issue through the use of expert witnesses. Government witnesses would have to determine that population was not spreading to the situs of the land and that demographic and other social and economic data would not support such a claim. In attempting to rebut prospective government testimony, the defense established early on its position with its own experts.

The first two parts of the brief were straightforward, aimed at representing the facts in a way that would minimize the problematic character attributed to them by the government: Rio Rancho had made representations about the land less extreme than the government maintained; the representations made by Rio Rancho were clearly based on fact, as supported by surrounding data; and even if the government's version of the Rio Rancho's factual representations was correct, that version was also reasonably based in the surrounding facts.

The third part of the brief addressed the more difficult question of how the law applied to the factual conclusions drawn by the government and the defense. First, the attorney argued, the defense's factual version clearly placed the defendant outside the ambit of criminal responsibility. But second, and more important, the defense argued that even if the government's version of the facts was accepted, there was no basis in law for making a criminal charge. In the section of the brief citing legal standards the attorney argued,

> Even if the prosecution premise that AMREP sells Rio Rancho land principally as a good investment were supported by the company's advertising material, such a representation cannot, under the undisputed circumstances of this case, form the basis of criminal fraud charges. . . .
>
> The representation the government claims was made by AMREP—that the purchase of Rio Rancho land is a ''good investment''—is clearly not an explicit representation of any existing fact which can be labled ''true'' or ''false,'' but rather a *statement of opinion* or prediction concerning the present and future value of Rio Rancho land, that is, that the present value of Rio Rancho land will increase in the future. Although it has been held that statements of opinion and suggestions and promises as to the future can form the basis of a criminal fraud charge [citations omitted], courts have uniformly stressed that criminal liability for such statements can only result when the opinion represented is not in fact held or honestly entertained [citations omitted]. This is so because the only representation of existing fact embodied in a statement of opinion or prediction is the implicit representation that such opinion is in fact held.

The defense attorney then went on to show that the government was not able to prove that the statements made by the defendant were not honestly held opinions. In fact, he argued, the contrary was true.

According to the existing legal standards that define culpable criminal behavior, there is at least reasonable doubt, wrote the defense attorney, that the potential defendant committed a crime. In addition, he argued that good faith is an absolute defense, that the company relied on the advice of attorneys, and that government regulators had approved the company's sales practices—all legal reasons not to prosecute the company. In concluding his precharge brief to the U.S. Attorney, he wrote:

> During the course of the July 24, 1975 conference with counsel, the U.S. Attorney rightly acknowledged that criminal charges should not be brought unless he was convinced beyond a reasonable doubt of the guilt of the parties (see ABA Minimum Standards Relating to the Administration of Criminal Justice, The Prosecution Function, paragraphs 3.4, 3.9).
>
> Concededly, the mail fraud statute has broad application and nowhere is its embrace precisely limited. To be sure, virtually any business dealing with the public could, in the hands of an imaginative and possibly over-zealous prosecutor, be subjected to its sanctions. Toothpaste ads which suggest the en-

hancement of one's love life, cereal ads, the betterment of one's health, airlines' representations that their fares are "lowest," that "there is no better investment you can make than a fine piano—a Sohmer Piano," or even savings bank advertising proclaiming their accounts to be the only "safe and sure" investment may all be attacked on one basis or another.

To preserve the basic integrity of the justice system, therefore, only the decency and fairness of the prosecutor stands between an unjust charge of mail fraud and a just one. We submit that a qualitative evaluation of AMREP and its principals shows an overwhelming honest operation, beset only infrequently by aberrational conduct of some of its salesmen. There is not mere reasonable doubt as to falsity or scienter; if anything, we respectfully suggest that unless one blinds himself to patent fact and at the same time resolving any and all doubt *against* those being investigated, there can be *no doubt* of the fundamental lawfulness of AMREP's business.

We suggest, too, that there would be a quality of unfairness or even cruelty in an indictment. The company and the individuals operated throughout based on guidance from their lawyers and regulation by various agencies of the government. At its best, the prosecution theory is a strained one. *Indeed, during the entire course of this investigation neither defense counsel nor regular counsel were able to perceive just what it was that was the subject of complaint*. Only at the July 24 conference was the shade opened. This aside, there are other and substantial indicia that the company and its principals never considered or had reason to consider that their actions were fraudulent. Again, these persons should not be subjected to the anguish of prosecution based on an experiment in the criminal law.

As the Supreme Court wrote in *United States v. Mersky*, 361 U.S. 431, 441 (1960): "In the framework of criminal prosecution, unclarity alone is enough to resolve the doubts in favor of defendants."

Far from being condemned as frauds, AMREP and its principals should be (and, indeed, have been) praised for the creation of a viable and handsome community of thousands of people. Rio Rancho is not arid desert with cows grazing on the sagebrush. Factories, stores, 2,018 families, extraordinary recreational facilities, the most modern sewerage system in the southwest, roadways, a medical center, and religious facilities all form part of the community. AMREP's and others' moneys in the sum of nearly ninety million dollars have been plowed into Rio Rancho (with no dividends having been paid to AMREP shareholders of whom the principals are the largest).

An indictment would not only destroy the persons' names but have serious negative implications to almost 6,000 residents of Rio Rancho and, perhaps, endanger the continued sustenance and development of the community by the company. The blow to AMREP and the Rio Rancho community would not be the only consequence. Rio Rancho Estates, Inc. is one of the largest employers in the state of New Mexico and a major factor in the state's economy. Accordingly, many people are dependent upon the company for their very means of living.

It should also be considered that there are in excess of 20,000 people who own their Rio Rancho property outright and that if the company and its principals are destroyed to a significant extent these people too will be affected.

Simply put, frauds do not build Rio Rancho. Frauds take the money and run, leaving the cows and frogs to occupy their "development." If there are questions or problems with Rio Rancho, we suggest they best be resolved in the confines of the presently pending FTC action.

This defense attorney attempted to demonstrate what every attorney attempts in a case argued on grounds of inadequacy of evidence of substantive liability: the opponent is going beyond legal standards in framing its case. The distinctiveness of this argument in the white-collar cases is that the attorney presents it before issuance of a formal criminal charge. The early intervention puts the government to the test of legal standards in an adversarial setting as if a trial of the facts were taking place. If the defendant wins, he avoids indictment and public exposure. When the street-crime defendant wins after presentation of substantive argument by an attorney, he will be acquitted, but he will have suffered already the opprobrium of public accusation and all the collateral sanctions that follow in the workplace and family.

When Precharge Litigation Fails

When the information control defense and the substantive defense have failed at the precharge stage, the defense attorney will have to choose between plea or trial. At this point, there will be strong incentives to make a plea agreement, if there is still any willingness on the part of the government. The defense attorney is then facing a government case that has been tested by much adversarial argument. This is not a case in which the government makes its decision isolated from the critical faculties of a probing opposition. Adversarial procedures have already been used for reviewing the facts and assessing the legal prospects of the case. When the precharge information control and substantive defense are unsuccessful in bringing a case to a close, the defense attorney is likely to believe that the government will be successful at trial.

There are, of course, cases that still go to trial, even after failed defense efforts of the type described here. Some cases are on the margin. The government thinks it can win. The defense attorney thinks that the case is close enough to the margin to justify going to trial. Continuing with the research assumption that the clients in this study are objectively guilty of a crime, the factors that explain the perception of marginality after the precharge stage are the same that create marginality and the potential for a successful defense during the precharge stage: all the facts have not been discovered by the government; the charging statute is so ambiguous that it is difficult to determine, at the margin, what is and what is not prohibited; the client's behavior is directly on the margin of illegality. While in some cases the persistence of these factors lead to a defense decision to go to trial, more often it leads to a decision to continue to pursue the substantive defense at the sentencing stage. The perceived likelihood of losing at trial and the aggravated penalty that is assumed to follow when defendants are convicted after trial, as compared to after a guilty plea, motivate a high rate of guilty pleas, but they do not similarly motivate a routine sentencing hearing. A very special kind of sentencing hearing takes place in white-collar cases, in which the attorney again executes a substantive defense while trying to profit from any previous information control.

10 *The Postconviction Substantive Defense*

When the defense attorney arrives at the sentencing stage, he is handling a case in which the guilt of the client has already been determined. He may have been successful in excluding certain information from the adjudicative process, and he may have persuaded his opponent that certain substantive charges were unjustified. But he has not excluded enough information nor has he been sufficiently successful in presenting substantive argument to have prevented the issuance of indictment and the rendering of conviction, either through a plea or after a trial. Now that guilt has been determined, the question is what sentence should be meted out.

The judge of course makes this decision, and in so doing he has a large amount of discretion. The typical federal criminal statute provides a maximum prison penalty and maximum fines but does not give the judge any guidance about where to set a sentence within the broad range between the minimum and the maximum, that is, between a suspended sentence, probation, or small fine, on the one hand, and a maximum term of imprisonment and maximum fine, on the other. Tax fraud, for instance, carries a maximum five-year prison term. But not all persons who attempt to evade paying their proper taxes should be given the maximum sentence. If this were the rule, there would be no need for a discretionary system of sentencing.

Judges are supposed to individualize the punishment according to their best evaluation of each case. There are two dominant themes in the conventional understanding of the judge's use of discretion in sentencing decisions that are significant to this study. The first is that the sentencing process is primarily an administrative procedure, in which the judge receives the principal input of information from a probation department that conducts a professional study of the defendant and submits a presentence investigation report.[1] Using this report and their own sense of the seriousness of the offense, judges make decisions about sentences. As compared to other stages in the criminal process, the sentencing hearing, according to the conventional understanding, is not primarily an adversarial procedure.

The second theme is individualization, which means that the judge focuses on the "character of the defendant."[2] In the earlier stages of the process, guilt for committing a particular offense has been determined, so that the sentencing stage is used for evaluating the characteristics of the defendant that have not already been disclosed by the charges brought before the judge. Is he a recidivist? Is he a "bad person"? What is the likelihood of rehabilitation? Has he shown by other conduct that he is likely to continue to endanger society? The conventional understanding of the sentencing process focuses on the court's evaluation of the defendant's personal background as a significant factor in determining whether an otherwise deserved sentence should be mitigated.

The findings of this study show that these two themes— the administrative character of the process and the focus on the history of the defendant—do not portray accurately the sentencing process in cases of white-collar crime. The sentencing process in the cases studied here was intensely adversarial in style, rather than administrative, and put substantial focus on the nature of the offense and the role of the defendant in the offense, in addition to the defendant's background. For the white-collar crime defense attorneys, sentencing is a more open process than it is for the defense attorney in the typical street crime. Basic issues about the charcteristics of the offense committed and the blameworthiness of the defendant for the crime are argued, much as if a trial were taking place at the sentencing stage and no previous determination of guilt had been made. The defense attorney and the prosecutor submit memoranda and make oral argument on these issues, after significant periods of study and preparation. Sentencing is elevated to a major period of adversarial conflict in which redetermination of substantive criminal responsibility is of main concern. This is how one defense attorney described the importance of his role at sentencing:

> I think sentencing is the most underdone area in all of criminal defense work. Attorneys just don't realize how important their input at sentencing can be in the white-collar case. In a case that we take a guilty plea on, much of our defense work may be centered on putting together a sentencing memorandum. The fact that we lose at trial does not mean that the judge is not open to considering all the issues of our client's responsibility. You may be talking about a massive fraud or about the use of a welfare check obtained with a false statement. So your client has pleaded guilty to fraud. Now at sentencing the judge is going to want to find out what he is really dealing with. That's where our role comes in.

Another defense attorney stated that he sometimes spends as much as a hundred hours preparing sentencing memoranda in a complex case, and he sees the sentencing "litigation" as being determinative for the outcome of the case.

There are several reasons why sentencing is handled with an adversarial approach. First, defense attorneys cite the ambiguity in the typical white-collar crime statutes. This allows the attorney to create doubt about whether a client's actions fall within the area of proscribed behavior. Coupled with the difficulty that prosecutors have in obtaining all the evidence about a defendant's action, the ambiguities in white-collar statutes often lead judges to feel that they have inadequate information about "what really happened" in the case. This is why judges say that their sentencing task is made easier when a trial has occurred, an event that brings out many facts that would not be disclosed through a guilty plea. Thus ambiguity, which was previously identified as resulting in the high salience of substantive statutory argument at the precharge stage, is also a reason for increased substantive argument at sentencing.[3] Defense attorneys stated that judges make known to them that they are looking for guidance in clarifying the true nature of the underlying crime. Understanding that judges are bothered by ambiguity, defense attorneys often attempt through adversarial arguments to accentuate ambiguity as a way of making it difficult to mete out a heavy sanction.

The second reason why sentencing has become more of an adversarial procedure in white-collar cases is the frequent concurrence of highly relevant sanction-mitigation factors and highly relevant sanction-aggravation factors. The former factors include all or some of the following: the defendant is an exemplary parent and spouse whose family will suffer immeasurably if the defendant is incarcerated; the defendant has made continuous valuable contributions to the community, which indicate that he is worthy of being given understanding and "credit against which to balance off this mistake"; the defendant has already suffered great shame and numerous professional disabilities as a result of indictment and conviction and will be handicapped by this for the rest of his life; and, since his involvement in the matter for which he has been convicted, the defendant has shown outstanding behavior in his work, community, and family. Against these factors is one critically important counterfactor: judges believe that visible and stiff sanctions have an effective deterrent impact on high-status and affluent persons, the typical defendant in these cases. There are strong incentives to mete out heavy penalties where they are likely to have a deterrent effect. Weighing the multiple mitigating factors against this strong punishment-aggravating factor, judges find themselves in a decisional bind, which creates opportunities for attorneys to have an impact. The defense and the prosecution arguments at the sentencing hearing are often perceived to be the key to tipping the balance.

Even after a defendant's behavior is satisfactorily understood and the relative merits of deterrence and mitigation are weighed, judges experience considerable difficulty in determining what standards should be used in setting length and type of sentence. This is the third reason why the sentencing hearing has come to take on an adversarial style. Unlike the situation in street and violent crimes, here the judges do not have a reservoir of cases of similar fact patterns to draw on as a measure of the appropriate sentence. This gives the defense attorney the opportunity to raise fundamental questions about basic sentencing standards; in so doing, he strives to influence the measure created for his client in the case at hand. In turn, this has led to arguments supporting the meting out of alternative sentences as a compromise: court-imposed free professional service, volunteer community work, public speeches, or a weekend sentence that will allow the client to continue to fulfill his family and occupational roles. Because judges make new sentencing policy when they handle first-impression cases, the defense attorneys feel that they are participating in a legislative process shaping new standards and new sentencing alternatives.

Litigation of Substantive Liability at Sentencing

In this section I will present excerpts from actual sentencing arguments made by attorneys handling cases they define as white-collar crimes. My goal is to show how deeply attorneys are able to enter into questions of substantive criminal responsibility at the sentencing stage, despite the fact that it might have been assumed that a prior plea to an indictment or a conviction already would have resolved the issues being raised.

The Arctic Natural Resources Fraud

In 1975, the U.S. Attorney's office in the Southern District of New York prosecuted a large New York–based investment company for making false representations to buyers about its stock. The company, Resources Investment, Inc. (RII), marketed interests in oil, gas, and other natural resources, including property in the Canadian Arctic region. The indictment alleged that gross overvaluations had been made for customers and that as part of a scheme to defraud RII obtained fraudulent expert opinions. RII was also charged with artificially raising the price of its shares by arranging bogus sales to third parties at inflated prices.

In its sentencing argument, the government stated that it was RII's practice to purchase resource interests on one day and sell them to innocent buyers the next at a "markup ten to twenty times their worth." Shares were sold at a price as high as $15 per acre on the basis of false valuation; the government alleged that their value was $2. RII grossed $44 million in profit from sales of $68 million of shares to its victims, the government argued in its sentencing memorandum.

After the conviction for securities fraud, facing the serious characterization of the crime by the prosecutor in his sentencing memorandum, the defense attorney's task was to develop an argument that would lead the judge to conclude that the "crime" was substantially less serious than it appeared, or, in the words of the attorney, de minimis. Even though a formal determination of guilt had already been made, the attorney raised again, at the sentencing hearing, the central issue of criminal responsibility.

In opening his argument on the question of culpability, the defense attorney declared: "We believe that it is fair to state that the securities fraud for which the defendant has been convicted is lacking in the characteristics that normally cause an SEC case to be prosecuted as a criminal matter." He attacked directly the very determination that a crime had been committed, enumerating different types of securities fraud that this case was not, all of which he implied were clearly criminal violations, and distinguishable from this case. The factors that distinguished this case, he continued, included the absence of an intent on the part of the defendant to harm and the obvious good faith demonstrated by facts that supported the defendant's belief in the high value of the property. The attorney then set out the evidence demonstrating the reasonableness of the defendant's views. The attorney wrote:

> The evidence fairly supports the view that if Mr. Jones withheld certain material information about alleged side agreement, he did not do so with intention of harming anyone thereby. In fact, it appears basically uncontradicted that Mr. Jones sincerely believed that no one would be hurt as a result of the Arctic revaluation.
>
> Although this court ruled that evidence of Mr. Jones's personal belief in the value of the Arctic properties was not relevant to the question of whether or not there had been a material misrepresentation or omission, we respectfully submit that his belief is surely relevant to the seriousness of any such fraud. Despite numerous witnesses called by the government, the introduction of a myriad of documents in support of the prosecution's case, and the opportunity to examine Mr. Jones extensively at trial, none of the evidence and none of the testimony seriously challenged Mr. Jones's sincere enthusiasm about the potential [value] . . . of the interest in the Canadian Arctic [property]. Indeed, his confidence appears to have been shared at every level with the Jones's complex, to say nothing of the industry as a whole, and exists today even among the principal actors in this tragedy, including many of the alleged victims. Even Dr. Armand Frederickson, who compiled dossiers of accusations against both of the defendants and launched what amounted to a personal crusade against them, testified that he believed strongly in the tremendous potential of [the] Canadian Arctic property.
>
> In other words, this is not the more typical securities fraud case in which the defendant has misrepresented the value of worthless goods. Instead, it is a case in which the mechanics of the transactions, and not the value of the underlying asset, were at issue.

The principal argument made by the attorney was that the client genuinely believed in the high value of the resources and that this belief was supported by others around him. Because intent to defraud was an element of the crime, the defense attorney aimed at negating circumstantial evidence of intent that the prosecution had presented. A person's mental state, argued the attorney, is formed by the information available to him. Thus, if the information about the property that the client received supported the client's view, it would be erroneous to conclude that the client intended to misrepresent the value of the property.

The defense attorney then presented a detailed account of what others had said about the value of the property.

> The experts consulted by the purchasers shared the view that as of 1970 the shares were worth no less than 4 times what they paid for shares in 1968. For instance, in July 1970, the research organization estimated that the purchasers' interest was then worth approximately $4 per acre. Shortly thereafter, an interest in a small portion of this property was sold to a major international oil company at a price of approximately $64 an acre. Had the small portion of acreage (.003 percent of the whole) which was the subject of that sale been valued by ———, evaluation would have been increased to more than $5.50 per acre, as compared with the $8.01 per acre valuation placed on the property by the defendant's company. Given the recent strikes in the area and the proven potential of the particular property at issue, who is to say that the $8.01 figure was unreasonable in 1969? . . .
>
> In short, we submit that the [experts] confirm that Mr. Jones's enthusiasm for the Canadian Arctic was reasonably based. Otherwise the [experts] would not have believed that in early 1971 it was perfectly appropriate to postulate the economics of exploration in the Canadian Arctic by comparing the area to the Prudhoe Bay acreage, which was what Mr. Jones had been suggesting in 1968 and 1969.

In an eighteen-page factual memorandum the defense attorney presented detailed evidence on the method of resource valuation, arguing that the client's state of mind accurately reflected independent, valid facts. The client's interpretation of the facts as they were known to him at the time of the events in question was a reasonable interpretation. The government's post hoc interpretation misconstrued the factual picture as it was actually known to the defendant at the time encompassed by the indictment.

The defense attorney argued, in concluding the factual presentation, that absence of concealment on the part of the client was consistent with the absence of criminal intent. In sum, the attorney concluded that there was no proof of criminal fraud and that the facts of this case were outside the margin of criminal liability:

> For allegedly sophisticated criminal conspirators, these defendants were remarkably open and guileless with respect to covering up their actions. No government witness testified that either defendant ever told him not to discuss the transactions in which he was involved. Although practically everyone in the case was represented by the same auditor, Arthur Andersen, no attempt was made to insulate witnesses from inquiries which the defendants obviously must have anticipated. Whatever actions the defendants took, they could not have hoped that such actions would go undetected when people like [various

government witnesses] knew all about them. The fact is that the defendants took no steps to cover their tracks because they were not conscious of the need to do so.

The SEC's decision to pursue Mr. Jones as tenaciously as it has was obviously affected by the exaggerated and speculative accounts of his fall which appeared in books, magazines, and newspapers. Jones was a natural target for civil litigants intent upon fixing blame, and their conjectures fed newsmen and writers intent upon sensation. However, the major investigations of Jones's activities have come to nothing. The original Denver investigations had so little substance that a grand jury failed to find enough even to initiate prosecutions. The major thrust of the investigation leading to this case has been stated by the government to have been the defrauding of [a company] but the evidence adduced at trial shows that alleged fraud to have been—at its very worst—normal sales puffery. What is left is an antiseptic, hypertechnical "fraud" which would have been left to the civil courts were it not for the surrounding coloration provided by allegations for which there is no proof. It is respectfully submitted that the facts of *this* case do not warrant serious criminal penalties.

In the Arctic Land fraud the issues that the defense attorney focused on at the sentencing hearing had already been briefed and argued at the SEC, in precharge and pretrial discussions with the government, and at a trial in district court. The sentencing hearing was a forum for repeating what had already been done several times in the life of this criminal case. The main defense strategy at sentencing was to argue that the defendant was simply not guilty of a criminal offense. The attorney could have argued that extenuating circumstances in the defendant's personal background or in the immediate personal context of the offense should lead the court to sentencing lightly for an offense that was otherwise serious. Using that approach, the attorney would have had to address his client's mental health, showing that the client had had a long history of psychiatric problems that culminated in this unusual and uncharacteristic behavior, or that pressures in the company had become unbearable and forced him to act without his usual care.

Rather than focusing on factors that would tend to excuse the client's admittedly deviant actions, thus lowering the penalty imposed by the court, the defense attorney argued that there was no deviant action. What the defendant actually knew about land values from the circumstances in which he worked and what he actually believed about land values should lead the court, the attorney argued, to conclude that at most his client had committed a civil wrong. But because it was too late to undo the conviction, this form of argument was aimed at reducing the defendant's culpability to the minimum consistent with conviction, thereby influencing the judge to give the minimum available sanction.

A Stock Sales Fraud

Another securities fraud case in which the attorney litigated basic issues of culpability at the sentencing stage related to a securities selling scheme with characteristics similar to those of the RII case. Again, innocent purchasers of securities were misled by an artificially hyped market price created through the device of false sales. This time, however, the defendants pleaded guilty. The judge's understanding of the case prior to the sentencing stage was limited by what was described in the indictment.

The indictment stated that nine defendants conspired to offer and sell securities in several companies "employing a device, scheme, and artifice to defraud" and engaged in a course of transactions that operated "as a fraud and deceit upon purchasers of said companies." It stated further that the defendants executed purchases for friends and relatives at preferred prices, discouraged and prevented customers from selling the companies, purchased the companies for their own accounts in the names of nominees, encouraged other broker-dealers to "make a market by guaranteeing such broker-dealers that they could be protected from loss," made sales conditional on future purchase, "parked" shares of the companies with other broker-dealers, and made "swap" deals with other broker-dealers.* And a separate indictment naming five of the nine defendants charged also that a fraud was carried out on the Securities Investors Protection Corporation (SIPC), insurer for stock purchasers, by "turning back the clock on the time stamping machine used at Security-Broker, Inc., to make it appear that trades had been executed prior to the time that the company had been compelled to stop doing business." All the defendants in the first indictment were named as officers of Security-Broker, Inc. and as conspirators in carrying out the fraudulent stock sales. All the defendants in the second indictment were named as perpetrators of backdated sales. Thus, according to the charges in the indictment, each defendant was equally responsible for the crimes charged. Each defendant pleaded guilty.

The sentencing litigation presented here in summary form related to one of the vice-presidents of Security-Broker. This defendant pleaded guilty after a long period of precharge defense efforts had failed. After the plea of guilty, the defense attorney focused on the sentencing hearing. He devoted a large portion of his argument to demonstrating that the defendant, Smith, did not in fact commit the offense to which he had pleaded guilty because he lacked the requisite intent. His first aim was to show that Smith had not been with the company long enough to be part of the stock plan at its origin:

*"Parked" means selling a stock to another broker for a short period in order to inflate sales activity in a particular company. "Swapping" is when two brokers concurrently park with each other and then trade back.

> Of the nine new issues underwritten by Security-Broker, six were completed before Smith became a principal, and the three which were completed thereafter were commenced prior to the time he became a principal. At no time was Smith engaged in activities relating to the marketing of these securities. The prosecution in its sentencing memorandum stated, on the other hand, that Smith was aware, when he became a partner, that Black [another partner] was barred from the securities industry . . . . He was also aware that false and misleading statements were being made to customers about the Security-Broker stocks and that statements were being made to salesmen to the effect that customers should be discouraged from selling stock.

From the government's perspective, Smith's acting as a principal in the company with knowledge of wrongdoing by other principals was enough to justify a conviction and a heavy sanction. But in addition to attributing to Smith criminal liability for the actions of his associates, the government pointed to specific actions on his part.

The specific charges relating to Smith, and to which he pleaded guilty at arraignment, alleged that he committed fraud on stockholders of Security-Broker by making backdated sales for a select group of stockholders after the company was ordered by the SEC to stop selling. Through the plea of guilt, Smith's attorney had had his client agree to the factual allegations of the indictment, a statement equivalent to a declaration not to contest the legal conclusions. At the sentencing hearing, the attorney argued to the contrary. He wrote in his sentencing memorandum:

> With respect to Smith's activities on the evening of February 2, 1972, dealing with the backdated order tickets, the facts are as follows: commencing at the beginning of that day, Smith received numerous calls from customers whom he had introduced, advising that there were rumors on Wall Street that Security-Broker was in serious difficulty and would soon be out of business. These customers insisted upon the immediate liquidation of their positions. Smith, in fact, executed sell orders for these customers as rapidly as possible after speaking with them. Of the approximate twenty (20) trades for accounts of Smith's customers, approximately fifteen (15) were accomplished *before* Security-Broker discontinued operations. The balance were executed after the close of operations only because there was not enough time to execute them prior thereto. The government had indicated that it is dubious about Smith's contention because, since Security-Broker itself was struggling desperately to sell stock, it is unlikely that Smith would have sold customers' stock. The government's position presupposes that Smith was a participant in the activities of Security-Broker's principals to manipulate the price of the stocks. In fact, by this time, Smith was sufficiently disillusioned with Security-Broker so

that he had refused, as early as the previous month, to pay for his stock. Smith's only concern was the protection of his customers.

Any question with reference to this fact can be resolved by a hearing at which the testimony of these customers can be adduced.

In fact, although Smith was tempted to backdate tickets for customers who had not directed that their securities be sold, he changed his mind when he realized the wrongfulness of his conduct and destroyed the few tickets he had improperly written.

On the second of the two charges alleged against his client, the attorney argued that the violation was technical only. In essence, all the transactions should have been executed before the closing of the company; Smith was performing a proper duty, even though he should have accomplished it in another manner.

A major part of the government's case having been called into question, the prosecutor had to make rebuttal argument. At the sentencing hearing, he provided his version of the backdating incident:

We indicated that Mr. Smith had written a number of backdated tickets on Feburary 2nd, quite a number of backdated tickets on that day. Indeed over 20. Smith has said that all of the customers had called in on that day and they were written on that day for those who wanted to sell Security-Broker stocks. There are a few backdated and in those instances he said he didn't have time to get to those orders until Security-Broker was put out of the business and he felt a moral obligation to trade the stock for those people.

We don't fully agree with that. We have four tickets written on Feburary 2nd for nominee accounts for Collins in the handwriting of Smith and I don't think Abel [the attorney] really contests that those are in the handwriting of Smith. Now, with respect to the others, Mr. Smith has indicated that some of them are in fact backdated but he says he had a moral obligation to write them. We don't fully credit Smith's response to that. And for this reason: as of February 2nd, 1972, Security-Broker, Inc. was in dire financial strains. The NASD [National Association of Securities Dealers] had indicated to Security-Broker that they needed one million dollars in additional capital to get back into proper net capital position. On February 2nd, in the early afternoon, the Security-Broker principals had been negotiating with the NASD. Mr. Smith remained in his office and a number of other principals did, but some were with the NASD. They were so desperate on February 2nd, 1972, that the partners went through a list of customers and wrote buy orders for the customers. In other words, they created false buy orders so that Security-Broker could have a better credit position. In other words, customers would own Security-Broker stock and the partners would appear to have money even though the trades had not been called in by the customers. Now, Mr. Smith is contending that at the very time Mr. Black was running around creating these false buy orders so that Security-Broker could get into a proper credit position, Mr. Smith, because of a moral obligation, was writing sell orders for his customers. I described what I think Mr. Black would have done to Mr. Smith if that in fact had happened. I told him I think Mr. Black would have committed murder because he was not about to see his firm go under because partners in the firm were in essence selling Security-Broker stocks at the same time Black was running around creating false buy orders. For that reason I do not credit Mr. Smith's statements that in fact this was all part of a moral obligation. In fact the government believes that based upon the pattern of the trades on that particular day and the fact that Mr. Smith admits to having sat down with the partners with the clock sitting there and they are all agreeing to do backdated trades that he in fact did quite a number of them and that they were not all called in during that day.

Now, he may very well have felt a moral obligation to get some of his customers out of the Security-Broker stocks, but we do not believe that that was a result of phone calls and that he had been trading the stocks earlier in the day for those customers.

In his sentencing memorandum the defense attorney attempted to undercut the prosecution's version. In effect, he said that his client was pleading guilty to having backdated, but that backdating in the particular circumstances of this case did not constitute a fraud. It was a corrective action to prevent wrong from being perpetrated on Security-Broker customers, rather than a wrongful action against the federal insurer. If the judge were to accept this interpretation there could be no prison sentence, for the offense charged required an intent to defraud. Faced with this possibility, the prosecutor had to protect his own interpretation of events. What had occurred up to that point—investigation, negotiation between prosecutor and defense attorney, and the guilty plea—had not resulted in the adversary parties concluding that the central issue of culpability had been resolved. The sentencing hearing became the forum for substantive argument about the defendant's culpability.

A Tax Fraud

The third example is a tax fraud prosecution of a top executive in a large New York entertainment company that I will call IRT. As the indictment read, the defendant subscribed to a false and fraudulent personal income tax return in that he failed to include as income payments made to him by IRT for personal travel, accommodations and vacations for himself and his family, for the renovation of his apartment, and for a bar mitzvah. He also failed to report the value of a Mercedes Benz automobile given to him by the company. During a three-year period, Mr. Cohen was charged with failing to pay $47,000 in tax liability.

The first issue addressed by the defense attorney was directed at the relationship between the charges and the plea made. Recognizing that judges often sentence not on the charge in the indictment but on the underlying behavior reported by the prosecutor and the probation officer, the defense attorney sought to restrict the judge from considering any tax liability or any act beyond the narrow plea made by his client:

> As the court is well aware, Mr. Cohen's admissions of guilt in this matter are far narrower than the charges contained in the indictment. He has admitted only the charges contained in a *portion* of one count of the six-count indictment and continues to assert his innocence on *all* other charges contained in the indictment.
>
> It should also be noted that this case was not the typical plea bargaining situation where the defendant admits one charge in a series of crimes in an effort to insulate himself from a high maximum possible sentence, but fully expects the court to consider all charges. In the instant case, Mr. Cohen pleaded guilty to an aspect of this case different and easily separable from the other charges in the indictment. At the time of the guilty plea, Mr. Cohen's position that he believed that he should be sentenced only on the admitted facts was made explicit on the record. Mr. Cohen has admitted tax evasion with regard to the omission of $8,800 of income in 1972—a year in which he reported $340,000. All other charges remain in dispute and Mr. Cohen is, by law, *presumed innocent* as to these matters. If the court were to consider the other charges in the indictment in reaching its decision on a proper sentence for Mr. Cohen, the only way it could do so would be somehow to resolve the untested allegations. It is respectfully submitted, however, that such a resolution is virtually impossible in this case.

The defense attorney felt that if he did not press the judge to consider only the facts relevant to the limited scope of the plea, the judge might consider more. He approached the sentencing hearing with the assumption that there is no clearly recognized rule for what would appear to be a basic issue of criminal procedure. His legal argument required first litigation of an evidentiary question: what facts can the judge consider in meting out sentence?

Following this procedural issue, the defense attorney addressed the substantive allegations presented in the indictment. His intention was not to negate the accusation of wrongdoing, as the attorneys in the previous examples had, but it was to show that the wrongful actions of his client were close to the margin of legality. Establishing that the wrongs were close to the margin would reduce the seriousness of the client's culpability. The attorney's description of the two trips taken by the client and paid for by IRT, which allegedly should have been reported as personal income, demonstrates how the defense shapes a substantive legal argument at sentencing:

JAMAICA

In December of 1971, Mr. and Mrs. Cohen and their children went to Jamaica. The airfare and accommodations (paid for in 1972 by IRT) according to records supplied to us by the government amounted to $2,230.20.

It is clear that this trip was paid for by IRT with the knowledge of Mr. Cohen. In his mind, Mr. Cohen justified this expense because he spent a great amount of his time in Jamaica working. The work Mr. Cohen performed consisted in large part of planning and budgeting the following year's operations for the entire company and this, of necessity, had to be done outside of the office with its distractions of meetings, phone calls, and attention to staff problems. In addition, Jamaica had become a world center for a new form of music called reggae music which was, at that time, becoming a sweeping new musical taste in England. Mr. Cohen spent a good portion of his time visiting music studios and night spots looking for talent and seeking to learn about this new music form, which has since become very popular in the United States. Finally, a newspaper man writing an article for the *New York Times* magazine section about Mr. Cohen accompanied him on his trip, consuming much of his time.

CALIFORNIA

California is one of the two business centers in the industry (New York being the other). The majority of artists' representatives, agents, and lawyers in the industry reside in this area. Several of IRT's major competitors had transferred their company headquarters to California. In addition, two of the industry's trade papers (*Cashbox* and *Billboard*) had also moved to California. IRT, unlike many of its competitors, did not have a major executive presence in California. In each year that he headed the company, Mr. Cohen had found it necessary to allocate a substantial portion of his time to business in California. Thus, in 1972, Mr. Cohen decided to move to California for the entire summer. He rented a home there which he quickly converted into an office. Naturally, for such an extended period of time, Mr. Cohen took his family.

With Mr. Cohen's knowledge the airfare for his family (including a nurse, a housekeeper, and pet) for this trip was paid for by IRT for a total of $1,419. In addition, a trip back to New York for Mr. Cohen's children, Fred and Lauren (to visit their mother), and for his wife was also paid for by IRT for $921.

While Mr. Cohen did obtain approval to rent the California house from a superior, he neglected to obtain specific approval for the airfares. None of these trips were reported as income as they should have been, and all constitute a part of the $8,800 of omitted income.

The defense attorney presented a large number of supporting facts to characterize his client's trips as related to work. While admitting that they were technically improper, he was arguing that the circumstances of the wrong called for a light or merely token sentence. The basis for the argument was that the so-called crime was almost not a crime because of its factual characteristics. The factual picture showed that the situation for which the defendant was convicted was very similar to situations admittedly legitimate. The defense attorney exploited whatever ambiguity could be found in the tax law and the facts of the case. The gist of his argument was this: there being no clear demarcation in the law between what constitutes tax fraud and what does not, and there being no definitive conclusion about what the defendant knew and believed about his tax deductions, only light sanctions were warranted. It is as if a compromise was reached. The lack of certainty in the law and facts entitled the defendant to a mitigated sentence, in spite of the decision of guilt rendered at an earlier stage in the process.

Another issue related to culpability, on which the prosecutor and defense attorney presented argument, was raised by the judge at the hearing. Thus, adversarial postures on issues of substantive culpability were not only pressed by the parties but invited by the judge. The judge stated:

> The question in my mind is whether there was not some form of misappropriation of funds of IRT so that it is not just culpable tax evasion but involves tax evasion where the source of funds was misappropriated. That is my question and I want you and Mr. Cohen to consider that. It is not the only question but it is a serious question in my mind. I want you and Mr. Cohen to consider it because I would like to have more information on this. How did Mr. Cohen believe that these things [payment vouchers] were processed at IRT? Did he or did he not believe there was misrepresentation or concealment of these transactions vis-à-vis IRT?
>
> I raise those questions. I feel that they are questions that relate very directly to what has been pleaded and I realize that I am not conducting a trial but I think that to the extent I can be satisfied on those questions, it is necessary for me to intelligently impose sentence . . . . [In regard to] Mr. Cohen, as with any person who ever appeared before me, those would be my questions.

Though the judge may have been convinced by the defense attorney's argument that only the one year of tax evasion and $8,800 in unreporting be taken into account at sentencing, even though three years and $47,000 in liability had been charged, he wanted to know if another separate wrong was involved— misappropriation of funds from the company. The judge was going to sentence on this issue whether or not there was a statutory charge in the indictment. The defense attorney was then required to argue this issue on short notice. Here is how the interchange between them proceeded:

> ATTY: Now, with regard to Your Honor's question, what I understand is,

did Mr. Cohen at the time that these trips were taking place intend at that time to be defrauding IRT? The answer to that is no and I think that is why we have submitted to Your Honor and we have carefully . . . researched the context of each trip. When Mr. Cohen took these trips, he knew that in each instance there was going to be a colorable claim of business activity. And at that point he had the option of doing one of two things. He could even have made a colorable claim that these were legitimate business expenses; he could have put it on the tax return or instructed his accountant to claim them and at least the IRS would have had that information in front of it to assess his claim.

JUDGE: You say he had the choice of putting these things down as business deductions on his own tax return?

ATTY: Certainly.

JUDGE: He hadn't paid IRT. How could he do that?

ATTY: That is why he didn't do that. He could have reimbursed IRT and put them down as deductions but he chose not to do that and that is what the crime is. The crime is not paying taxes with regard to those monies.

JUDGE: And his other choice would have been to . . .

ATTY: To try to get corporate approval, which he did not do. But there was no intention at the time these trips took place, Your Honor, to in any way put them in through phony bills or invoices and really defraud IRT. At the time that he actually took these trips—

JUDGE: How did he expect those to be carried on IRT records? Frankly, Mr. ———, I don't understand how he could think that they could be—I am putting it too strongly—I won't go that far. I just don't know, but my question is whether . . . when you have several hundred dollars or maybe a thousand dollars or more, there has to be some paperwork. IRT just doesn't pay money out—TWA or the Gary Travel just doesn't send invoices to IRT without explanation and have them paid. So there has to be some paperwork.

ATTY: There was paperwork.

JUDGE: . . . I think Mr. Cohen would have to state the reason for the expenditure. I don't think I have to know every detail but let's just say paperwork. The paperwork would have to either state the facts or state something else. If the facts were stated and the paperwork said that the airfares were for members of his family, and if they went through the proper channels, did Mr. Cohen think that that would get through or did he think it wouldn't get through?

ATTY: He had to think it would get through because it was a fact nobody ever challenged it and the reason it got through, at least the reason he thought it got through, number one, he was the head of the company so that the junior officer was not about to come to him and challenge his travel expenses. And number two, if they had been legitimately submitted, on the face of them, each of them indicated what the purpose of the trip was for, still nobody would have challenged him. When you look at the trips one by one, there is nothing so extraordinary that would have shown on the face of the voucher to say . . .

JUDGE: Who was the paperwork submitted to?

ATTY: To the controller's office.

JUDGE: In other words, somebody subordinate to him?

ATTY: That is correct.

JUDGE: And you are saying he would assume that his subordinate would approve this even though he had not gotten approval? From the person who really had the right to approve it? But as far as processing payment the subordinate would not challenge it?

ATTY: That's right. You take the European trip, for instance. There must have been five hundred people from IRT who traveled to Europe so when two other names showed up of individuals who went to Europe with Mr. Cohen, including his children in that instance, because Mr. Cohen had been taking his children to conventions for years, nobody would challenge that, with regard to that. The same thing with regard to California. It was no secret in the company that Mr. Cohen was going to live in California for three months. He got explicit approval with regard to the housing and the expenditure of the $13,000 in housing. So when the tickets came out showing Mr. Cohen and his family had gone to California, nobody would challenge that.

In the cross-examinaton by the judge, the defense attorney attempted to show that his client had not concealed his activities from the company and that, therefore, no additional wrong had been committed. The issue was the defendant's culpability, the judge addressing himself to a crime that had not been charged in the indictment. As the sentencing hearing continued, the attorney presented evidence on company expense reporting procedures. Even though the defendant had already been convicted of tax fraud, the judge wanted to know if the actual behavior of the defendant indicated that another crime had been committed.

The issues put before the judge at sentencing in each of the three preceding cases addressed the substantive culpability of the convicted offender. The essential question was whether the requisite intent had been formed by the defendant, or what was the true dimension of the intent. For this purpose, the adversaries presented argument on one or all of the following questions:

1. What information did the defendant receive about matters relevant to the offense, for example, did he receive a memorandum that would have informed him of facts essential to his having formed criminal intent?

2. Was there information in the environment of the defendant that he should have received had he taken reasonable actions or paid reasonable attention, for

instance, were there generally available reports that someone in his position should have perused?

3. What was the actual belief of the defendant in regard to the facts constituting the offense? For instance, did he actually believe that nonreporting of income in the circumstances was permissible?

When the defense attorney presents argument on these issues, his objective is to characterize the defendant as having behaved in a normal manner, given the particular circumstances in which he acted. It follows that he says to the judge: the prosecution's understanding of the circumstances is incorrect. This argument does not fit the street-crime situation. There, the defense attorney must admit that his client's behavior was deviant. Any attempt to reduce the level of culpability attributed to the defendant must focus on the defendant's personality. The attorney argues: the defendant is so abnormal that he—rather than a prosecutor—was incapable of appreciating the meaning of the circumstances in which he acted.

I have already maintained that substantive legal argument at sentencing is one of the distinctive characteristics of the white-collar crime defense practice. The question is whether the white-collar crime defense attorney is able to make this kind of substantive argument—that is, persuade the judge that the defendant was not fully culpable—any more than the street-crime defense attorney is able to make his argument about the client's mental capacity. The tentative answer to this question seems to be yes. Though I did not conduct a systematic study of sentencing in street-crime cases, there are convincing indicators that this hypothesis is correct. First, in the considerable study of defense practice in the environment of the lower criminal court, no one has pointed to the centrality of substantive legal argument at sentencing.[4] The major input into sentencing in the street-crime case has been seen as the plea agreement made between the parties. Second, there is deeply rooted in the criminal law the idea that abnormal personality does not exculpate a defendant for otherwise criminal conduct except in the most extreme cases, where the insanity defense can be proved, or in the narrow category of murder, where the diminished capacity defenses are law.[5] This means that judges tend to be unreceptive to arguments about a defendant's inability to form criminal intent. In spite of such unreceptiveness, however, attorneys do make these arguments, in part no doubt because they cannot raise them at earlier stages in the process. But there seems to be a narrower area open for substantive argument about criminal responsibility when the issue is the offender's individual capacity to form criminal intent.

In the white-collar case, the situation is quite different. The defenses identified above, which address the question of the knowledge possessed by the defendant at the time of the offense, are well-recognized defenses in the substantive criminal law. It is easier to bring them into the sentencing stage because there is no doctrine of law instructing the judge to disregard those factors. And if there is ambiguity in the statute defining the prohibited behavior, the judge is likely to have his own questions about substantive responsibility after the formal conviction.

The third factor influencing the frequency of substantive argument at sentencing is defendant resources. It is obvious that affluent defendants are able to support well-prepared and more active defenses at all stages of the criminal process. There is no reason why this factor would not affect the way that defense attorneys handle advocacy at sentencing, increasing the likelihood of an intense adversarial disposition.

Accepting these tentative hypotheses, we can generalize about the criminal process: at arraignment or trial a preliminary decision is made that determines whether the defendant had the minimal level of intent necessary to convict him of the crime defined by the statute and entered into the indictment. Following this decision, a second, more finely tuned decision about intent is made. There the defense attorney can argue that there was a low level of the particular kind of intent required by the statute, and the prosecutor can argue that there was a high level. The judge may be looking at aspects of the behavior not identified in the indictment, and the defense attorney then will also have to make substantive argument about issues raised by the judge. One must conclude either that the question of substantive criminal responsibility is moved from the arraignment/trial stage to the sentencing stage, or that in both stages of the process the same question is asked, the first time using a rudimentary test, the second time a finely gauged test.

Factors Favoring Sentence Mitigation

Part of the defense function at sentencing is directed to litigating the appropriateness of the sentence rather than the culpability of the defendant. Independent of the question of whether the defendant formed the intent required by the offense, defense attorneys present detailed memoranda and oral argument aimed at demonstrating that a light sentence is appropriate for other reasons. Three issues appear systematically in defense sentencing memoranda in white-collar cases. They relate to (1) the defendant's personal background (a traditional sentencing issue), (2) the infliction of presentence sanctions, and (3) the general ineffectiveness of prison sentences. Judges tend to pay close attention to the first two arguments but disagree fundamentally with attorneys in regard to the third.[6] The conflict that judges experience in determining appropriate sentencing in white-collar cases results in part from their difficulty in balancing the effect of the first two and the opposite effect of the third. In what follows, I present excerpts from attorneys' sentencing arguments to demonstrate how they approach these issues with judges.

Defendant's Exemplary Background

Defense attorneys believe that by emphasizing the positive characteristics in their client's personal history, judges can be influenced to mitigate sentences. The message of the defense attorney's argument is that the defendant is essentially a good person, the wrongful behavior was an exceptional mistake, and "good deed" credits that the defendant has earned prior to his "mistake" should result in forgiveness. This argument was made by the attorney in the IRT tax fraud case discussed above. First, the attorney described his client's modest background and family hardship:

> Mr. Cohen was born in Brooklyn in 1932, into a family of lower-middle income status. Mr. Cohen's father was a plumber and a traveling salesman; his mother was a housewife.
>
> At the end of his freshman year in college, [when he was] 18 years old, his mother died suddenly at the age of 47, and eleven months later, his father died at the age of 57. Thereafter, Mr. Cohen went to live in Queens with his older sister and her family, commuting to school in Manhattan.

Then the attorney focused on Mr. Cohen's academic and professional achievements:

> Mr. Cohen graduated magna cum laude from New York University and was a member of Phi Beta Kappa. Since he had no financial resources, he was able to attend Harvard Law School only because his outstanding college record earned him a full scholarship. Once again, he applied himself diligently and graduated in the top 10 percent of his class. Shortly after graduation, he joined a law firm, where he once again excelled and was hired by [a large corporation] for its legal department. The letters the court has received from partners at the law firm bear witness to Mr. Cohen's tremendous ability and dedication to his work, but even more importantly, to his integrity and his decency.

Following the picture of family hardship and academic and professional achievements, the client's humanitarian works were highlighted:

> The court has received letters from three of Mr. Cohen's college classmates which describe with sincerity the academic tutoring, counseling, and encouragement they received from Mr. Cohen. In addition, each of these men referred to the high standard of integrity which Mr. Cohen maintained as a young man. This character trait remains with him, as attested to by the scores of letter writers who have dealt with Mr. Cohen as an adult in the highly competitive world of business.
>
> It is significant that so many leaders of this industry count Mr. Cohen among their close friends. It indicates that he has touched their lives in some special way and it demonstrates that the compassion and concern for others

> which he exhibited as an unknown, parentless student remained a central part of his character after he rose with spectacular swiftness to a position of singular preeminence in the industry, leading the company he made the major producer in the world, and personally earning up to $300,000 a year. For example, in his letter to the court, Mr. Taylor describes the severe reading disability from which his son suffers. Mr. Taylor goes on to say that Mr. Cohen organized and hosted a week of shows to raise money for a school which treats these youngsters. In addition, he contributed personally to the school. As a result, the school (which is called Park Century School and which also sent a letter citing Mr. Cohen's help) survived a severe financial crisis and is one of the most successful schools of its kind today. Another impressive testament to Mr. Cohen's compassion is the little known fact that for thirteen years he was a Big Brother for a disadvantaged young man named Jerry White. Mr. Cohen made this boy part of his family—he was a constant visitor to the White home and went to sporting events and other activities with Jerry as if he was one of Mr. Cohen's own sons. Mr. Cohen provided guidance and emotional security to the youngster for years, and today Jerry White, 31 years old, has made a success of his life. In addition, Mr. Cohen has been honored as MAN OF THE YEAR for his charitable work by the Parkinson Disease Foundation and the Anti-Defamation League of B'Nai Brith.

The defense attorney then retrained the focus of his memorandum on the hardships suffered by his client:

> Mr. Cohen's personal life has been exemplary, but not without travail. During the early stages of his career Mr. Cohen faced a severe domestic crisis. His first wife became increasingly depressed after the birth of their second child, and insisted on moving out of the country. Mr. Cohen tried to convince her of the impracticality of this rash change, but she was adamant, and eventually the marriage ended in an amicable divorce. Mrs. Cohen was unable to meet her responsibility toward their two children and Mr. Cohen willingly accepted custody of them. At this critical time in the lives of these children, Mr. Cohen was there and sensitively led them through this family tragedy. He regularly came home early in the evening to have dinner with the children and/or to visit with them and put them to bed before rushing off to a business engagement. It is a tribute to Mr. Cohen's strength of character that he met this responsibility to his children so well, while at the same time supporting his former wife both financially and emotionally far beyond any legal obligations. A most convincing testament to Mr. Cohen's character is to be found in the letters to the court from his former wife, and from his former mother-in-law. Both speak of his tremendous strength of character and his devotion to his children.

What relevance do these arguments have for sentence? The difficult background and the distinguished performance in adulthood are presented by the attorney for the purpose of having the judge grant the defendant credit for overcoming past handicaps and doing good deeds. These arguments are not presented as part of an effort to negate culpability. The attorney is not saying, "A person like this could not have done that." What he is saying is that the defendant did so much good in such difficult circumstances that society must now grant a measure of forgiving dispensation. Or, society should not treat harshly a person who is essentially an exemplary citizen because he has made one mistake. As stated by the defense attorney in his concluding paragraph:

> In short, the court must pass sentence upon a man with an unblemished record, whose character is one of the highest and whose achievements have been truly outstanding. It is submitted that nothing in this record suggests that Mr. Cohen needs prison rehabilitation or that he is ever likely again to break the law. In considering only this man as a human being, it is submitted that a prison sentence is unwarranted. The record of total good during a life span of 44 years weighs heavily against the isolated transgression of the evasion of taxes . . . .

Presentence Sanction

The arguments about the defendant's exemplary background are used most effectively in conjunction with another argument: the defendant has suffered a serious sanction prior to sentencing. In fact, an indictment can result in a series of sanctions that inflict great harm. A convicted person may lose his job and reputation in his community, be rejected by friends, and be alienated from immediate family and relatives. Sometimes a convicted person will be formally sanctioned by an administrative body, losing a professional license and/or paying a monetary penalty. Shame and opprobrium are suffered. At the postconviction stage of the criminal process, defense attorneys often argue that this presentence sanction makes additional sanctions unneeded and unjustified. One attorney argued this in a securities fraud matter:

> During the five years which have passed since the SRC matter was first exposed, Mr. Street has endured punishment administered by various agencies of government and the securities industry as well as the lifetime stigma which attaches to everyone assoicated with the SRC fraud. As a result of these matters, he and his family have also suffered financial hardship; he has been able to support his family and to shelter his children from the harmful fallout of his involvement in this crime only through hard work, the close support of his wife, and a willingness to accept work lacking any of the prestige of his prior employment.
>
> The failure [of his company], of course, left Mr. Street without employment in the securities business; it also saddled him with certain personal debts

arising from his business, in the amount of approximately $10,000, which he has continued to carry, and to gradually pay off. The failure of his business also led to the following official actions. In December 1972, pursuant to a complaint by the SEC charging various violations of bookkeeping rules and the net capital rule, Mr. Street consented to the appointment of a trustee under the Securities Investor Protection Act of 1970. He also consented in December 1972 to a permanent injunction enjoining [him] from engaging in acts and practices in violation of various antifraud and other provisions of the Securities Act of 1933 and the Securities Exchange Act of 1934.

Most significantly, in January 1975, Mr. Street in settlement of an SEC administrative proceeding, consented to a lifetime bar from association with any broker or dealer, registered investment company, or investment advisor. And in February 1975, Mr. Street settled a complaint brought by the National Association of Securities Dealers, Inc. in connection with the failure by agreeing to a permanent bar from association with any NASD member as a principal, or in any other supervisory or managerial capacity. Thus, Mr. Street has surrendered his rights to practice his chosen profession and has thereby saved the SEC and NASD the considerable expense and delay of contesting his personal registrations with the SEC and NASD. We must say to this court that when Mr. Street consented to the lifetime bar and to the permanent injunction, he believed that his consent would put an end to further government prosecution, administrative or otherwise, of him. . . .

Following the failure of his business, Mr. Street and his family, who had enjoyed a modest but by no means extravagant standard of living, and who had very little accumulated savings, were thrown into total financial disarray. In order to meet the mortgage and to avoid the dislocation of his two young children which a forced move would entail, Mr. Street and his wife went to work as waiter and waitress in a family restaurant owned by Mr. Street's younger brother. During this period, in 1974 and 1975, Mr. Street was unable to find work in the financial world and the only supplement to his family's earnings was approximately $3,000 to $4,000 a year from the life insurance business which he had continued to maintain. The recommencement of government action against Mr. Street by this indictment, just as he had been recovering from this most difficult financial period, has presented a further obstacle to the family's recovery. Moreover, by coming at this late date, the indictment has exposed his children to the adverse publicity associated with indictment and a guilty plea by their father, at a time when they are now old enough to comprehend the awful significance of a criminal matter.

A recurrent theme in sentencing arguments of this type is that the criminal process has an impact on defendants of high status that it does not on defendants of lower status. This approach may also have been taken by the attorney at the precharge stage. To the investigator and prosecutor, the attorney argues that the charging decision may be completely determinative of the case from his client's perspective because the charge imposes deprivations no less damaging in the long term than a prison sentence. To the judge, the attorney wants to demonstrate that such sanctions actually have occurred or are about to occur. As defense attorneys repeatedly present this argument it raises a fundamental question for judges: should the indictment-spawned sanctions imposed on a high-status person be taken into account in determining sentence, providing a sentence discount to high-status persons, compared to lower-status persons who have no such position from which to fall?

Some judges clearly believe that the high-status person is entitled to such a discount. This was borne out in research in which judges were interviewed about their sentencing practices.[7] The judges were asked specifically whether they sentence differently in white-collar cases because of the different impact the system has on the defendant. One typical response is the following:

> There is no doubt that in most white-collar crimes as such, the return of the indictment is much more traumatic than even the sentence. Pronouncing of the sentence is not as injurious to the person, his relationship to the community, to his family, as the return of the indictment. A loss of credit, a loss of bank credit, a loss of friends, social status, occasionally loss of wife, members of family, children around the father. They react to this more when they hear that an indictment has been returned and he has been charged than they do after they have gotten used to the idea and he is sentenced for it. There is no question about the fact that that is much more severe on the white-collar criminal than it is on the blue-collar defendant.

Ineffectiveness of Prison Sentences

In the framework of the sentencing hearing, defense attorneys also approach basic sentencing policy as an issue open for adversarial contention. Many pages of sentencing memoranda are devoted to citing treatises on sentencing policy and research reports that demonstrate the ineffectiveness of imprisonment. Some attorneys use conventional textbooks in their sentencing memoranda, but others have made special efforts to collect research findings and solicit expert assistance where the client's budget permitted. One attorney, as shown in the following excerpt, presented expert testimony to the court at the sentencing hearing. The case involved a stock fraud in which the president of the fraud-perpetrating company had falsified books. In his sentencing memorandum, the defense attorney focused on issues related to the defendant's culpability. At the hearing, he addressed the question of sentence effectiveness and introduced his expert witness, a professor from a university department of criminal justice. The professor testified:

> The most recent major national effort, Your Honor, to examine the question of

general deterrence was before a presidential task force on offender rehabilitation, 1969–1970. The task force was encouraged by the new Chief Justice, Justice Burger, who in his first State of the Judiciary message addressed himself entirely to the question of deterrence in offender rehabilitation. At this national task force fifteen permanent members of the national community, many of whom are specialists in research concerned with various kinds of deterrence, including myself, whose life work has been in this area, introduced testimony, introduced scientific evidence from the various human sciences, from the growing body of judicial opinion, nearly two thousand opinions in the last twenty years, specifically raising this question of the effectiveness of general deterrence. We heard witnesses, we entertained testimony, and the conclusion of the group in general was that we should rely less and less on incarceration and more and more on alternatives to incarceration because of a changing philosophy, and in the light of very persuasive evidence from the social sciences.

Several years ago, for example, as a research scientist of the then Governor Rockefeller's special committee on criminal offenders, I examined close to 259 research documents, many involving experimental controlled researches on many of the questions inherent to the question before you, Your Honor, and the evidence from the hearings of this task force on offender rehabilitation and from the body of studies that was reviewed and from studies that had been generated in the last few years, and I can recite them, I have them all here to recite, and the conclusion is that with respect to the deterrent effect of general incarceration, that produces no general deterrent effect. In respect to specific categories of offender, there is no general deterrent effect by incarceration. The growing body of evidence also points out with respect to specific categories of offense that nonincarceration, the use of alternatives, not only produces demonstrably measurable deterrent effects, but also does an awful lot in the public interest in protecting society and in making a positive contribution. The most recent studies, to be specific, dealing with what I prefer to call cavalier offenses, rather than white-collar offenses, since very few people wear white collars any more anyhow, is that the use of nonincarceration, the use of alternatives to incarceration, produces a beneficial effect of a magnitude which cannot be controverted, the most recent having been produced by a study by Professor Olin at Harvard University who has served four presidents in these very areas, in which he measured deterrent effects by various kinds of legal measures, administrative measures, and human measures throughout the state of Massachusetts, where it was clearly indicated that alternatives to incarceration are in the public interest, producing the deterrent so often sought by judicial decisions and by judicial sentences.

This statement is representative of the arguments being made to judges about sentencing alternatives. Defense attorneys contend that because prisons are clearly not rehabilitative institutions, a prison disposition cannot be expected to have any salutary effect on the defendant. And it is manifest, attorneys argue, that white-collar defendants are not such a danger that prison sentences are necessary in order to protect a community. This leaves general deterrence as the only remaining acceptable justification. In cases that are judged serious enough to warrant a heavy penalty, defense attorneys have thus gone to academic literature and private research organizations to obtain material for adversarial demonstrations of the ineffectiveness of the prison sanction as a general deterrent.

An Adversary Model of Sentencing

Traditonal theory of criminal procedure defines the period from arraignment through trial as the stage in the criminal process for substantive legal determinations about the correctness of the allegations made in a charging instrument. Subsequent to this determination of legal responsibility, the judge evaluates other factors that tell him or her where within the range of sentences applicable to the substantive offense the particular sentence in the case at hand should be set. Traditional Anglo-American criminal procedure is a system that bifurcates the decision about substantive legal responsibility and the decision about sanction.[8]

Corresponding to this bifurcation of decision is a difference in decisionmaking styles. The arraignment and trial have been defined as an adversary process; strict procedural and evidentiary rules are applied and the parties have the function of presenting the best case in their own favor. The judge is passive.[9] In distinction, the sentencing process has been defined as an administrative procedure. Evidentiary and procedural rules are substantially loosened; the court as well as the parties investigates the facts and has a role in their presentation.[10]

In contrast to this traditional model, the literature on plea negotiation emphasizes the great extent to which decisions about sanction take place at the arraignment or during pretrial contacts.[11] There, the defendant is informed that cooperation with the government can bear substantially on or determine the sentence. A promise of mitigated sentence is given by a judge. Or a plea bargain includes a change in offense charge that lowers the sentence ceiling. In the plea-bargain literature the arraignment and pretrial is a period for sanction setting, as well as for determining substantive criminal responsibility. The style of decisionmaking is correspondingly different from what is found in a traditional model of the criminal process. The arraignment period is administrative in many of its characteristics. The judge is active; the parties are more like negotiators motivated by a multiplicity of interests.

The findings presented here demonstrate that a reverse dynamic has also occurred in the criminal justice process. Whereas the plea-bargain literature showed that sentencing issues had moved into an earlier stage, the findings here show that arraignment and trial issues have moved into a later stage. In many of the cases studied here, defense attorneys and prosecutors adjudicated basic issues of substantive criminal liability at the sentence hearing. They argued or reargued the factual issues defining what the defendant did and the legal issues defining whether an offense was thereby committed, or what offense was committed. In general, these cases show that litigation of substantive liability occurs in the sentencing forum in spite of the fact that prior adjudication of substantive liability occurs at arraignment or trial.

A difference in decisionmaking style corresponds to this difference in issues decided. The sentencing hearing in the cases studied here seem more like full-blown adversary confrontations than administrative hearings conducted by judges. The parties present facts in an adversarial style, both orally and through the submission of memoranda. The judges put heavy reliance on the parties' presentations of facts and their descriptions of the legal implications that should follow. In so doing the judge makes a new, more finely tuned decision about the seriousness of the crime and the blameworthiness of the defendant. In the guilt-determining stage of the process—precharge, pretrial, and trial—a decision was made that the defendant was guilty of something described generally as, for instance, tax fraud or securities fraud. At the sentencing stage, the adversaries will be trying to convince the judge of their version of the true nature of the crime—what the defendant really did. It should not be forgotten that in carrying out these sentencing tasks, the defense attorney may benefit from prior information control success. If he has kept damaging facts out of the arena of legal argument, he has already reduced the seriousness of the crime and the blame that can be attributed to his client.

The parties will also face the task of showing the judge what sentence fits in the particular case. Here judges appear to be substantially influenced by the adversaries' discussion of general sentencing standards: by the defense's focus on the sanctions already meted out to his client and the client's exemplary background, and by the prosecutor's focus on the deterrent effectiveness of stiff sanctions in white-collar cases. Typically, the judge faces a concurrence of strong leniency factors and strong severity factors.

In attempting to integrate the conflicting factors into a discrete sentence, judges look for and attorneys often propose compromise solutions. One kind of compromise solution is what has come to be called an alternative sentence—one which applies a traditional punishment in a newly mitigated fashion, for instance, weekend prison terms, or an entirely novel sanction that imposes obligations on the defendant that are greater than traditional probation but less than prison. The latter category includes public service and individual restitution of many types.

To the extent that judges apply compromise sentences, the sentencing hearing has received something of the air of a legislative body; defense attorneys and prosecutors have taken on the task at individual sentencing hearings of discussing basic sentencing policy and judges of deciding the efficacy of different forms of punishment. Rather than arguing that a particular punishment is inappropriate in a particular case, defense attorneys implicitly ask judges to declare a court policy against prison sentences and to institute the use of entirely new sentencing dispositions in their place. Prosecutors, in their turn, rebut defense attorneys and argue for a general policy of prison sentences in cases of white-collar crime. In the absence of legislative guidance, the adversaries and judges are making new sentencing law.

11 *White-Collar Crime Defense and the Adversary Process*

The attorneys observed and interviewed for this study are almost all recognized specialists in white-collar crime defense practice. Most are former federal prosecutors who prosecuted white-collar cases, and those who are not had other prosecutorial training or worked with experienced defense attorneys handling white-collar cases. The study group is an elite group of attorneys not only because they are specialists, but also because its members studied at top law schools, received the finest training available in criminal practice, and serve the highest paying clientele of the legal profession—corporations, corporate executives, and other persons of high socioeconomic status.

The cases are not a representative sample of all white-collar cases, nor do they constitute a representative sample of all the white-collar cases handled by the particular attorneys studied. Many white-collar cases do not receive such large amounts of time and resources. And others simply provide no opportunity for defense because of the overwhelming strength of the government's evidence and the simplicity of issues. But this study of a select group of cases has provided a setting for identifying and evaluating the general nature of defense tasks precisely because of the special character of the cases. Without the setting of the complex white-collar case and the client who brings substantial resources to a defense attorney, it is difficult to conceptualize and appreciate the full range of defense strategies and the potential nature of defense leverage.

These white-collar cases present a system of defense advocacy that is highly adversarial. This is not our customary picture of the criminal justice process, shaped primarily by what we know about the handling of street crime and the cases of defendants with no or only modest means to mount a defense. Deriving its study material almost exclusively from street crime, existing literature has focused primarily on how that process fails to provide the defendant with the rights set out in appellate cases and fails to comport with normative adversary standards identified in models of how the system should operate, such as the due process model.[1] Researchers have concentrated on the defense practice in which the legally available procedures and rights are replaced by alternative modes of case resolution, based for the most part on negotiation, compromise, and expediency. They have emphasized the absence of combative advocacy and the dominance of shortcutting of procedural rules. To describe the concept common to this research, Malcolm Feeley uses the term *plea bargain model*: "The plea bargain model is the realist's revision of the system of due process . . . and in recent years it has come to be recognized as the model of how the system actually operates."[2]

An integral part of that model is the dominant view of the criminal defense attorney as a person who substantially compromises zealous advocacy of his client's interest to attend to other independent or conflicting interests. The defense attorney in the plea bargain model is not a Perry Mason craftily guiding a case through a dramatic criminal trial. Rather, he is an "operator" concerned with currying the favor of the prosecutor and the judge, restraining adversariness in order to finish cases efficiently. This defense attorney puts high premium on helping the court organization run smoothly because it helps him to maintain an economically viable practice in which a sufficient number of cases are handled at a low enough cost. In a well-known essay, Abraham Blumberg emphasized the extent to which the criminal defense attorney downplays his role as an advocate in order to contend with the exigencies of the system:

> Organizational goals and discipline impose a set of demands and conditions of practice on the respective professions in the criminal court, to which they respond by abandoning their ideological and professional commitments to the accused client, in the service of these higher claims of the court's organization. All court personnel, including the accused's own lawyer, tend to be coopted to become agent-mediators who help the accused redefine his situation and restructure his perceptions concomitant with a plea of guilty. . . .
>
> The defense attorneys, therefore, whether of the legal-aid, public defender variety, or privately retained . . . ultimately are concerned with strategies which tend to lead to a plea. . . . Indeed, the adversary features which are manifest are for the most part muted and exist even in their attenuated form largely for external consumption.[3]

Blumberg's picture of the criminal justice system in operation and the work of the defense attorney contrasts starkly with the picture I have drawn here. The defense attorneys studied here are intensively adversarial in their approach to their opponents, and they provide clients with adversarial advantages that most defense attorneys handling street crime have no access to.

There is, then, a paradox in the existing literature on the criminal process: intensively litigated cases handled with high resource input, such as those examined here, have been analyzed as appellate cases only, for the purpose of extrapolating the principles of law that emerge at that point. Characteristics of the criminal process that cannot be gleaned through the decisions of appellate judges have been subordinated, if not excluded. When the criminal process has been studied at its earlier stages—by examining the work of trial judges, prosecutors, and defense attorneys—the subject of research has been almost exclusively cases handled with low resource input and not intensively litigated. The net result is that adversariness in the criminal process and the strengths of defense are undervalued and insufficiently regarded.[4]

The findings of this research suggest that the criminal justice system is improperly characterized by the plea bargaining literature, to the extent that the literature claims to provide a whole picture. In part of the system plea bargaining dominates, and adminstrative efficiency and organizational equilibrium are preferred values. But there is another part, one which is not as open to public view, characterized by a carefully planned clash of positions and contest of sophisticated tactics and strategies; there, adversariness is the preferred value. Thus, any model of the criminal justice system that has a particular fixed structure of process will not adequately describe the system; not all cases are handled with the same procedure, and the actors in the system have different ways of behaving, depending on the cases they handle and the resources at their disposal.

Throughout, I have tried to give a detailed picture of what defense attorneys can do in white-collar cases to protect guilty persons from the criminal sanction. A central theme emerging from this description is that white-collar cases, independent of the size of the fee paid, provide attorneys with distinctive defense opportunities: to assist clients in keeping inculpatory information out of government reach, to make substantive legal argument so early in the criminal process that many clients are saved from the public disgrace of indictment, and to make substantive legal argument in the very latest stage of the criminal process, stretching the guilt-determining decision into the sentencing stage. When the funds are available to pay high fees, defense attorneys exploit these opportunities.

Defining the Conditions of the Defense Strategies

The long period over which I made observations and the large number of interviews I conducted with attorneys who are regarded as specialists suggests that the distinctive defense strategies of white-collar crime are empirically valid phenomena. One still wants to ask when and where they will be found. What is it about these so-called white-collar cases that facilitates the distinctive defense strategies?

In analyzing the cases with this question in mind, I identified eleven primary characteristics that most directly facilitate the use of the distinctive defense strategies. I derived these characteristics, specified below, by inductively analyzing the common dimensions of the defense tasks. These characteristics are organized on the dimensions of what practitioners call a "case"—the offense, the offender, and the criminal process—in order to emphasize the way in which each affects opportunities for successful defense.

Dimension I: The Offense

1. Influence over Information Sources

This is a measure of the extent to which the client and the defense attorney have influence over sources holding inculpatory information.[5] Certain sources of information are subject to the influence of the client and, through the client, of the attorney; other sources are not, and still others lie somewhere in a midrange—providing influence but not certain influence. An artifact (for example, a document) held by a client can be destroyed. The client can influence the behavior of close associates and confidants. In contrast, the client is likely to experience great difficulty influencing an individual aware that he was victimized by the offense being investigated. The important question is whether the client has sufficient influence over the sources of inculpatory information to keep the government from detecting them.

Any assessment of the extent to which information is subject to the client's influence must take into account the considerable factors that create influence over persons and objects. An exhaustive theory of information control would examine all the dynamics of social structure that create interpersonal influence and influence over disposition of objects.

Information control as a result of influence is closely associated with the theory of organizations. The type of crimes that create information control defense strategies often occur in organizational contexts because organizations create multifaceted structures of influence. A president of a company is more likely to be able to influence information inside the company than outside, unless the outside holder of information is part of a different social network that also provides influence, for instance, a common family or friendship network. A company, a family, and a group created for the purpose of committing crime are examples of social organizations that provide control through influence.[6]

Influence over information may also be achieved in the absence of social networks or legal relationships. Violence or the threat of violence and payoff can be used to influence persons completely outside a social network. Some targets of criminal investigations employ these measures to control sources of information, and these do constitute strategies of defense. They are not, however, included in this analysis as defense strategies because the subject of inquiry is distinctively legal defense strategies, that is, strategies systematically employed by attorneys. The question addressed here is what factors facilitate the use of distinctively legal skills to protect a client from criminal prosecution. Control provided by social structure is frequently used by attorneys. Control provided by violence is not, and it is in no sense a skill distinctive to the legal profession.

2. *Dispersion of Potential Evidence*

A constant feature of crime is that information sufficient to make the government's case is always located in the target, when the target is in fact guilty. An essential goal of the information control defense is therefore to control the client. But information control also is likely to require control of third-party sources of inculpatory information. Thus a critical question for an attorney considering an information control defense is how the inculpatory information is dispersed among third-party sources, if at all.

The information needed by the government can be dispersed among many third-party sources, none of which independently holds enough information to incriminate the client. For instance, if document 1 is held by source A, document 2 by source B, document 3 by source C, all of which are essential to the government, and oral statements are needed from sources D, E, and F, the government will have to obtain access to many sources in order to make its case. Another form of information dispersion produces a significantly different access potential: when one third-party source holds enough inculpatory information to incriminate the client, government access to that one source will be sufficient. In a third situation, many third-party sources each hold enough inculpatory information to incriminate the client. Access to one party is sufficient, and there are many opportunities for the government to locate one party.

The manner of dispersion of information among third-party sources directly affects what the defense attorney, as well as the government, must do in order to locate and control information. But the effect of this factor on the potential for executing a successful information control defense cannot be measured without taking into account the degree of influence the client has over the source or sources. When taken together, influence and dispersion create a number of different evidence-location situations that can be ranked in order of the potential for defense control, and its inverse, prosecution access.

The evidence-location situation most favoring the defense is dispersion of inculpatory information among many sources, none of which holds evidence sufficient to incriminate the client, with the client having a high degree of influence over all sources. The situation least favoring the defense is concentration of inculpatory information among many sources, each one of which holds information sufficient to incriminate the client, with the client having no or only weak influence over the sources. Full elaboration of the evidence-location possibilities would lead to a continuum ranging from high potential for defense control, correlated with high likelihood of defense success, to low potential for control, correlated with low likelihood of defense success. Again, my continuing assumption is that the government has chosen, as it usually does, an objectively guilty target.

3. *Exposure of Evidence*

Certain crimes create sources of information—witnesses and artifacts—which are exposed as potential evidence or sources of evidence.[7] One example is the victim of crime who knows that he has been victimized and complains to law enforcement authorities. The complainant actively exposes information, forcing the government to take notice of potential evidence. Other crimes do not expose information as evidence to the same extent. Some crimes do not alert the victim; a complainant is not created and the government is not mobilized by a complaint. The artifacts used for the commission of some crimes are not readily identifiable as evidence, for instance, individual documents in a complex filing system. And witnesses in some crimes are not readily exposed because the location of the occurrence of the crime is not apparent, as in a bankruptcy of a multistate company. Sometimes potential sources of evidence are not readily distinguishable from other artifacts and persons that are not potential inculpatory information.

The exposure of evidence is an important factor related to control, and it affects the likelihood of executing an information control defense, independent of the disperson of evidence and the influence held over sources. When inculpatory information is embedded in normal social life, that is, when it is not easily identifiable as potential evidence, there is a higher probability that the government will not identify it. Thus even where the client has no influence over the source and the information is concentrated in one third-party source (not dispersed)—conditions that work against the success of an information control defense—the defense attorney may conclude that he can rely on the government not discovering the information because it is embedded. Making this conclusion is part of the expertise of the defense attorney. For instance, attorneys studied here were able to counsel clients that underreporting of income from bank interest was unlikely to be discovered by the government in spite of the fact that the IRS held bank reports of interest paid. This is because the IRS was largely unable for technical reasons to identify and match bank reports with income reported by taxpayers. An attorney who knew this could counsel a client to assert innocence. An attorney who did not would counsel the client to start plea negotiations.

4. Ambiguity of Crime Definition

The manner in which a crime is defined in statutes and case law affects the extent to which the substantive defense can be an effective strategy. It is a fundamental assumption of the legislative process that clear and precise definitions reduce the need for court interpretation of the meaning of statutes. The more ambiguity in statutes, the more there will be adversary litigation. In the area of criminal law, ambiguity of definition leads to increased substantive legal argument about the scope of prohibited behavior. A statute defining as a criminal offense "failure to file a tax return" has less ambiguity in it than a statute defining as a crime "defrauding the United States Government."

Other factors being equal—for instance, the resources of the client available to pay his attorney and the competency of the attorney—ambiguity of definition raises the potential effectiveness of substantive legal argument at all stages of the criminal process. However, early substantive argument may reduce the likelihood of later substantive argument. If a defense attorney wins his argument at the precharge stage, there is obviously no need for a trial or substantive argument at sentencing.

5. *Objective Nature of the Client's Behavior*

It has been assumed throughout that the clients are objectively guilty of an offense. What was also assumed, but must be made more explicit, is that the objective nature of the client's behavior directly affects the extent to which any defense will be available. Certain behavior falls clearly within the prohibitions defined by the criminal law; other behavior falls clearly outside the statutory definition and therefore is permissible; and still other behavior falls close to the margins. To evaluate the extent to which substantive legal argument or information control will be available as defense strategies the objective nature of the behavior must be a consideration. It is not a determining factor, because even the most clearly prohibited behavior may be immune from prosecution when the right information control conditions are present.

Excluding the objectively innocent from consideration, the question is whether the defendant's behavior is clearly prohibited or lies close to the margin of statutory definition, where differing views may be persuasively asserted about criminal responsibility. Because marginal behavior is a factor associated with increased probability of success of any defense, it must also be seen as a factor increasing the usefulness of the precharge information control strategy and the precharge and postconviction substantive legal defense. This factor is not dependent on the nature of the statutory definition but interacts with it. The more ambiguity there is in a statutory definition, the more room for behavior to appear on the margin of the prohibition.

Dimension II: The Offender

6. *Client Resources*

Any legal defense requires resources. The amount of financial resources available to the client to support the activities of an attorney is integral to the particular defense strategies described here, as it is to any other defense strategy. Even when defense-facilitating conditions are present—for instance, information is controlled and precharge review is offered by the government—neither substantive legal argument nor attorney-conducted information control can take place without the attorney being paid. Scarce resources greatly reduce the probability of the occurrence of the defense strategies described here, or if they do occur, the lack of resources inevitably will reduce their intensity. In criminal defense work, as in most other areas of law, money is time. When time spent is reduced, all the activities that a defense attorney carries out are reduced—fewer meetings take place, less research is done, fewer memoranda are written, fewer personnel are assigned to the case, outside expertise is limited, and so on.

Although high client resources is one condition strongly associated with the defense strategies defined here, it is not a sufficient condition. For instance, where many parties each hold information sufficient to make the government's case, and where there is little ambiguity in the statute and the client's behavior is not on the margin, and where the government does not provide precharge review procedures, high client resources will not have the same effect as they will when these conditions facilitate defense opportunities. It would thus be an egregious error to say that the defense advocacy described in these pages is essentially a reflection of wealth of the clients of the attorneys studied. Client wealth always can be translated into a vigorous defense, when defense opportunities are available. The interesting question is where, when, and how the resources can be applied.

7. Client Sophistication

The use of the defense strategies at the precharge stage of the process requires early recruitment of an attorney. Even where the client has high resources and all other conditions facilitate precharge defense strategies, some persons simply do not recruit an attorney until late in the government investigative process or until an indictment has been issued. There are two primary reasons for this. The first is lack of knowledge; the second, lack of client sophistication.

One government investigative technique is to keep the fact of the investigation unknown to the ultimate target as long as possible. This is done because government investigators know that targets and the target's defense attorneys can be disruptive of the investigative process in many ways. One measure the government takes to prevent the execution of defense strategies is to keep the investigation secret.

But even where a person becomes aware of the fact of an investigation, for example, because an associate reported that he was interviewed by a government investigator, recruitment of a defense attorney does not always follow. Some persons think that bringing an attorney into a case will make matters worse, the attorney's presence communicating a sign of guilt. Other persons apparently hope that their problem will simply disappear. And still others do not believe that they have done anything wrong and so do not act on the first signs of an investigation. Thus even when all the other factors facilitate early defense strategies, some clients are so unsophisticated about the import to their interests of early involvement of an attorney that they forgo certain defense opportunities.

Client sophistication also has an impact on the effectiveness of further defense strategies. Many of the actions taken by the attorney to control information require the participation or cooperation of the client. When an attorney is attempting to learn the facts of the case, the client has to be smart enough to understand all ways that he might have created evidence about the crime. And when the attorney wants the client not to disclose certain information, the client must be savvy enough to understand hinting and communicating by implication. Sophistication is also an important element in the client's own efforts to resist talking to third parties and government agents who may attempt to trap him into damaging admissions.

Dimension III: The Criminal Process

8. Method of Agency Precharge Review

Where the government carries out its investigation and considers the potential pool of evidence without allowing for communication with an attorney representing the target of the investigation, there is by definition no opportunity for the attorney to present any kind of substantive argument. Conversely, the more opportunity there is for communication between the attorney representing the target and the government prior to the making of a prosecution decision, the more likely is substantive argument about criminal responsibility.

Certain kinds of potential criminal cases are investigated and considered for prosecution independent of any institutionalized procedure for precharge meetings with defense attorneys. These cases move through the investigative unit, usually a police department or the FBI, and are referred to prosecutorial offices for consideration usually without notice or opportunity for a precharge hearing being given to the target of the investigation. This does not mean that there is no precharge communication between defense attorney and government agent or prosecutor. It means that the defense attorney may have to persuade the government agent or prosecutor to agree to a meeting. The very nature of that meeting, if it takes place, will, however, be shaped by customary institutional practices. Where the agency or prosecutorial office is not accustomed to allowing attorneys to make substantive legal presentations in the precharge period, even the attorney who presses the government agency for a meeting will find any opportunity limited in time and scope by government resistance.

In contrast, other kinds of cases routinely are investigated and considered for prosecution by agencies that have institutionalized precharge adversary hearings in which defense attorneys are permitted to make extensive presentation on the substantive merits of the potential criminal case. The IRS and SEC procedures of investigation are most typical of this situation.[8] In these agencies meetings can be held with field investigators, and internal review procedures are provided for making substantive legal argument to agency counsel. In the federal districts to which these cases are referred for ultimate exercise of prosecutorial discretion, review meetings with defense attorney participation are now customary. Antitrust investigations that originate in the Department of Justice and investigations that start in other federal regulatory agencies often entail similar multilevel review procedures in which there is defense attorney participation. It is obvious that where attorney review procedures exist, there is more opportunity for and a greater likelihood of the defense presenting precharge substantive legal argument on the merits of the case.

9. Method of Government Investigation

The extent of potential information control is also a function of the rules regarding government methods of information access. Where the government conducts physical searches with no forewarning provided, the likelihood of the defendant or attorney controlling information is lower than when the government makes written requests and allows a period of time for compliance. Thus where subpoenas and summonses are the typical method of government information gathering, the opportunity for the exercise of control by the target and the defense attorney is relatively great. Similarly, rules related to permissible procedures of interrogation will have substantial impact on defense information control. Clients who are interrogated while held in police custody are more difficult to control than clients who are summoned to interviews and appear voluntarily. The particular content of the rules governing permissible investigative procedure at any given time is a function of statutory and Constitutional law.

The practices of attorneys studied here included almost exclusively cases in which the government used unintrusive methods of information collection. There were no physical searches conducted in the cases studied and no arrests made. Documents were either subpoenaed or summoned, and information from clients was sought either in a noncustodial interview in which the client was accompanied by his attorney or through the use of a grand jury subpoena providing substantial lead time for compliance. As far as could be determined, information gathering from witnesses took similar form.[9]

It appears that in many of the cases there would not have been a legal base for conducting a physical search because of the absence of probable cause or the absence of specificity of identification needed to obtain a search warrant for documents. Probable cause is unlikely to exist during the investigative period for crimes in which inculpatory information is widely dispersed in the sense described above, unexposed, and whose disposition is highly influenced by the target. Constitutional and statutory rules are shaped such that crimes less likely to create probable cause are also less subject to intrusive government investigatory methods. Thus the rules of law defining government authority in searches have an independent effect in creating opportunities for information control defense, facilitating or limiting the availability of the information control and substantive defenses.

10. Indictment Standard

The government's decision to ask for an indictment or issue a charging information is not only controlled by the legal standard requiring a finding of probable cause; it also is a function of institutional customs and pressures. Assuming that probable cause is the minimal standard for charging, there remains a great deal of variation for timing the issuance of a criminal charge. The government can ask a grand jury to issue indictment just as soon as it decides that the bare minimum quantity of evidence has been located, or it can delay request for indictment until the investigation has been exhaustively completed and the case is ready to be tried.

Full investigation and full trial preparation before issuance of indictment has the obvious effect of lengthening the precharge period. The variability of the length of the precharge period is clear from a recent proclaimed change in federal prosecution policy. As a result of the enactment of the Speedy Trial Act of 1974,[10] federal prosecutors have said that they delay asking for issuance of indictments so that relatively little preparatory work remains to be done in the period after indictment, a period for which the new act establishes a time limit with a dismissal sanction.[11] The fact that federal prosecutors can delay asking for indictment in order to move case work from the period after indictment to the period before indictment demonstrates that indictment timing is determined by the exercise of prosecutorial discretion, as well as by government response to the legal standard requiring a minimum quantity of evidence. It also suggests that there is variation among districts in indictment timing and probably in other factors as well, such as backlog and resources. The impact of this variation on precharge defense strategies is simply this: the more indictment is delayed, the more time there is for precharge defense actions.

11. Quality of Defense Counsel

Quality of defense counsel is a characteristic of the criminal justice process that affects the use of defense strategies. The significance of this effect is suggested in the study group interviews, particularly where the attorneys speak of the bad advice received by some of their clients, who have arrived after a prior attorney made the mistake of allowing the client or other persons to make damaging statements.

The systemic relationship between quality of defense counsel and defense strategy is found in the overall quality of the bar of practitioners available for work on criminal cases. While the senior attorneys in the research group might disagree, there are indications that the move of highly qualified former prosecutors into specialization in white-collar defense has raised the level of defense practice. Today, it may be said that the government is facing a more experienced and better-trained defense bar, on the whole, than it was twenty years ago. This does not mean that a particular defense attorney practicing twenty years ago was less competent than the most competent one practicing today. What it means is that today there is a better-trained group of criminal practitioners, and the likelihood of the government prosecuting against an outstanding defense attorney may be greater. Whether this has any effect on the outcome of cases is a separate question. The quality of government practice may have risen also, counteracting any relative advantages to the defense in criminal cases.

It must be said that what is learned about defense strategy goes beyond the white-collar crime defense practice. The characteristics specified here as conditions facilitating the distinctive defense strategies are not exclusive to white-collar cases. Other cases bear some of the specified characteristics, or all of the characteristics in weak proportions, so that they too can facilitate the distinctive defense strategies, though less strongly. High resources and marginal behavior are conditions sufficient to support a precharge substantive defense. But the potential for this defense grows where, for instance, the charging statute is ambiguous and the government agency provides a forum for precharge review. Control over some sources of evidence may support an information control defense; control over all supports it better. Cases are multidimensional phenomena whose characteristics can vary widely in intensity and in combination. Some will bear a sufficient quantity and combination of factors facilitating the information control and substantive defense strategies in limited ways but would not be called white-collar crime. In crimes involving domestic violence, an attorney may aid a client to influence members of a family to remain silent. And in drug smuggling cases, an attorney may be able, for instance, to assist a client in covering up telltale bank deposits of large numbers of small bills. The relevance of the distinctive defense strategies thus goes beyond what is ordinarily defined as white-collar crime.

What is unique about the cases I have described is the dovetailing and concurrent strong effect of all or many of the specified characteristics. Inasmuch as these are cases we traditionally call white-collar crime, the above specification of characteristics would seem to expand our understanding of the phenomenon. It increases our awareness of the import of law enforcement and defense dynamics, emphasizing the way in which cases can provide defense attorneys with opportunities to prevent imposition of sanctions and create adversarial difficulties for investigators and prosecutors. This expanded concept of white-collar crime speaks directly to dynamics of the adversary process. It adds a process element to offender-and-offense-oriented definitions.[12]

Information Control and Professional Ethics

Principles of the Adversary System

When the defense attorney acts to keep information out of his adversary's reach, he is dealing with a factual issue the significance of which is not captured by the conventional bifurcation of issues in the litigation process between questions of fact and questions of law. That division discerns questions that must be resolved by making inferences about facts presented to the court by the parties from decisions about legal rights based on statutes and legal precedent. Information control is a different adversary instrument: it affects what factual conclusions are drawn, not because the attorney is better able to argue what factual inferences are appropriate in a given situation, or what legal conclusion must be drawn, but because he has kept the facts entirely from consideration.

Controlling which facts get into the arena of argument is the very objective of the rules of evidence; these rules are meant to control what is communicated to the decisionmaker about the events in dispute. The rules of evidence, with the exception of secondary prophylactic bars to admissibility such as the exclusionary rule, are shaped for the purpose of keeping *irrelevant* evidence out of the decisionmaking forum. The rules of information control are designed to achieve the opposite result: to keep *relevant* evidence out of the decisionmaking forum.[13]

Information control lies at the core of the adversary process in white-collar cases because here and not in street crime the defense attorney has a key role in manipulating sources of information. This is not a study of what clients do to control information unassisted by attorneys, which would lead to different conclusions about the relationship between crime and information control. If information control is the hiding of a crime weapon, the killing of a potential witness, the wiping away of fingerprints on a pane of glass, the threatening of victims to enforce silence—and these certainly fit any generic concept of information control—then street crime and violent crime may be just as much or more affected by the potential for information control. After all, it is not known how much undetected street crime there is or whether more street crime or white-collar crime goes undetected.

But this is not a study of detection per se. It is a study of the role of attorneys in preventing detection and proof of crime. The centrality of the rules of the adversary system to the relationship between white-collar crime and information control can be made clear by framing the issue this way: if a person seeks legal services in respect to a potential or ongoing criminal investigation, when will an attorney be able to use information control strategies? That is, when will distinctively legal skills be effective in advancing the information control objective? In the typical street-crime case, the guilt-determinative evidence is already in the government's hands by the time the defense attorney is called in. But even if it is not, the street-crime attorney is not likely to have much to do in the way of managing information, unless he is ready to hide the gun in his office or bury the drugs. It is the white-collar defense attorney who is in the business of managing information.

Information control is fundamental to the adversary system. This system starts by allowing each side in a legal controversy to take a passive role in respect to the other side, neither side bearing an obligation to give the other facts without first being asked. Starting from this minimalist notion, the adversary process is in great part constituted of rules that permit each side to resist the request for information presented by the other, unless preconditions are met.[14] Without proper specificity and without sufficient time for compliance, an information request need not be responded to by the opposing party.[15]

The fundamental rule of relevancy provides additional broad protection to the party to a legal dispute. It requires as a condition to obtaining information that an adversary show that a real legal dispute exists and that the information sought is sufficiently relevant to the dispute. In the field of criminal law, this principle requires the showing of probable cause that a crime has been committed before the government can intrude on the privacy of an individual and search and seize documents and physical evidence. And the probable cause showing is also required before the government can arrest a person for interrogation. Rules of relevancy in many ways make information control a basic part of the adversary system.

The formal role of information control is nowhere more keenly expressed than in the self-incrimination privilege, which states that a person need not provide information that may tend to incriminate him. It is a rule of the adversary system that openly affirms the right of the party to conceal information from an opponent. It makes information control an even more integral part of the adversary system: the lone citizen, it is said in the best tradition of American Constitutional law, deserves to be protected from the massive power of the government to call persons before its representatives and demand, on penalty of imprisonment, that true and full explanations be given to questions asked. Only when that citizen is protected from incriminating himself can the government be allowed to apply its full force to interrogate, to search, and to seize.

The legal profession is central to the operation of information control aspects of the adversary system. Without legal representation and counsel, the parties to a dispute are adrift before the law, unable to take advantage of its rights and trapped by its obligations. The attorney stands, for the most part, in his client's shoes, bearing no more and often less of an obligation to disclose information relevant to the client's actions. When information acquisition is an issue, the attorney exercises for the client his right to specificity and proper timing of a request, his right to application of the rule of relevancy, and his right to be protected by the privilege against self-incrimination. In other ways, the defense attorney educates his client about legal protection of information sources and the penalties of the law for behavior constituting a breach of information control limits. The adversary system thus creates a broad range of information control rights and opportunities, as well as obligations. The defense attorney is an expert in their use and is therefore formally attributed a key role in how information is managed.

Information management is not, of course, a task limited to the defense of white-collar crime. While important procedural rules are different, information control is a recognized feature of civil litigation. If the question is who committed civil fraud, or who was negligent, the defense attorney's adversary may not have the power to collect information that is exercised by a prosecutor in a criminal case, but the defense process relies heavily on keeping out of the adversary's reach the information needed to prove civil liability. An attorney who practices civil litigation is likely to say that what is described here is not unique to white-collar crime. He is familiar with the same strategies in his own practice, for instance, when he prepares a client to give testimony at a deposition hearing, or when he prepares a response to a discovery request for documents. The defense attorney in a civil case manages his client's disclosure to him, his client's disclosures to third parties, and he attempts to influence the behavior of third parties who might hurt his client's case. Indeed, many of the attorneys who participated in this research do a substantial amount of civil litigation. Though the substantive law defining legal rights is different, many of the processes of defense are identical, and this includes the information control and the substantive defenses. Much of white-collar crime legal work for private practitioners is more like civil litigation than it is like street-crime work.

The Ethical Rules

If the adversary system explicitly provides an information control role for the attorney, how far can the attorney go to control information that would be detrimental to his client's interest? No system would allow an attorney boundless leeway to conceal information. The ABA *Code of Professional Responsibility* aims at defining the proper role of the attorney, and it is to this that we turn to provide a perspective on the information control strategies used by attorneys in white-collar cases.[16]

Here is it useful to recall three paradigmatic situations from the cases in the study that focus on the attorney's role in information control and guide us to the relevant rules in the ABA *Code*. The first situation occurs when in the course of handling a client's case the defense attorney becomes aware that the client is continuing to commit the crime for which he is being investigated or is beginning or planning to commit a new crime. Attorneys do not like being given this kind of information because it brings them in close touch with the distasteful implications of their work. They often find themselves helping persons who are at the same time hurting others. As I described in chapter 6, attorneys have ways of avoiding this kind of information.

The avoidance is a function of moral distaste, not a necessity of legal representation. The ABA rule that applies to the above situation states that an attorney shall not reveal a confidence or secret of his client and that he may but is not required to reveal the intention of his client to commit a crime.[17] Even though an attorney may feel moral compunctions about representing a client who is currently committing a crime, the structure of the adversary system does not require that he abstain from representation or take other remedial measures.

Attorneys in the study group said that this rule is strongly justified in the context of white-collar cases. Given the ambiguous nature of many white-collar statutes, some persons simply do not understand that they are committing a crime, and others do not understand that what they think is a mere violation constitutes a felony. If an attorney was required to report a client's behavior learned about in a professional meeting, clearly the advisory role of the attorney and the self-incrimination privilege would be vitiated.

The second situation is logically subsumed in the first but is addressed separately in the ABA *Code*, presumably because it puts the attorney a step closer toward assisting the client in committing a crime and thus might seem to require a different ethical rule. It occurs when the attorney becomes aware that the client, in the course of his counsel and representation, has made a false statement to an adversary or court. When an attorney becomes aware of this, the relevant rule requires disclosure of the fraud to the affected person or court but includes a major exception, excusing the attorney from disclosing such information when it was obtained in a privileged communication.[18] When an attorney learns that a client to whom he has given legal counsel has intentionally not turned over documents in violation of a subpoena, he is not required to take remedial action unless he learns of this from a third party. In relation to the client, the attorney's information control capacity remains in full force, meaning that the attorney's obligation is governed by the former rule that allows but does not require the attorney to take remedial action. The ABA *Code* permits the attorney to collaborate in the client's design, in the sense that the attorney has no obligation to rectify a fraud committed on an adversary or court when the client has "used" expertise provided to him by the attorney.[19]

If information control is permitted in these two situations, it is prohibited in a third, and that is when the attorney would actively take part in concealment for which there is no affirmative privilege or actively take part in misrepresentation. This prohibition is set out specifically in the ABA rule that requires the attorney to refrain from *knowingly* engaging in conduct that would assist his client in defrauding an adversary or court, which includes a prohibition on knowing participation in misrepresentation and illegal concealment.[20] On one level, these rules express the obvious: an attorney cannot advise the client to engage in illegal behavior, such as advising a client not to turn over documents properly requested or advising a client to change a document or misstate a factual situation when he knows that this will misrepresent the truth.

The Problem of Knowing Participation in Illegal Information Control

We can now focus on the major ethical problem presented by the cases and defense strategies reported here: at what point does the attorney cross the line between the second situation above, that in which the attorney becomes aware after the fact that the client has misused his expertise, and the third situation, that in which the attorney knowingly causes the client's misrepresentation or illegal concealment? In other words, when does an attorney representing a client *know* that he is assisting his client in committing fraud on an adversary or court?

These typical attorney-client scenarios bring the question into sharper focus:

(1) the attorney questions his client about hidden income in an IRS investigation of unreported wage income, controlling his questions in order not to learn about secret bank accounts because such accounts are not implicated in the investigation, and the attorney wants to be able to assert to the investigator that "one unreported wage check is the only unreported income of the client" (having avoided knowledge of the unreported interest income); (2) the attorney tells his client not to describe to him the documents he has (requested in a subpoena) until the attorney explains what documents will be harmful to his interest and what documents are benign, and then he tells the client to take a week to conduct a search and report back; (3) the attorney tells the client that the client's employees are likely to be invited for interviews and that their statements will be seriously damaging to him.

Legal counsel of this type has a significant common pattern and demonstrates the ambiguity in the ABA *Code* and the difficulty an attorney has in knowing what behavior is formally permitted. In each instance the attorney communicates with the client on two levels. On one level, the attorney takes neutral actions, asking questions or describing the legal implications of likely events. Here, the attorney avoids acknowledging his client's intentions or readiness to engage in illegal behavior to conceal evidence. On the second level, the attorney is taking into account the likely impact of what he does. The form of his questions and his legal counsel is expected to have a beneficial result on the defense effort. The savvy client will withhold information detrimental to the defense position. Has the attorney knowingly assisted the client in misrepresenting or illegally concealing information? Judge Frankel described the attorney's actions this way: the "sharp eye of the cynical lawyer becomes at strategic moments a demurely averted and filmy gaze," so that he is "unfettered by clear prohibitions that actual 'knowledge of the truth' might expose."[21] Is he right?

The answer to this question depends on how attorneys are supposed to interpret the term *knowing*. The ABA *Code* is ambiguous. It states that an attorney must *know* that he is causing a client to act illegally before he will be held responsible, but there are few authoritative decisions on what constitutes knowing participation by an attorney. If the standard stated by the following case correctly interprets the law, then attorneys would be held responsible for a large range of illegal acts of concealment carried out by their clients.

> The effort to distinguish between a suggestion of a possible course of action . . . and advice or counsel . . . is without force or basis. The precise form of the words in which the advice is couched is immaterial. The question is: has the lawyer conveyed to the client the idea that by adopting a particular course of action he may successfully defraud someone or impede the administration of justice? If a bank official, who had . . . robbed his bank, should call upon a lawyer . . . and ask for his suggestion as to what he should do, could that lawyer escape responsibility by saying to his client, "Have you thought about . . .

going to . . . Argentina, where you are not likely to be traced for a long time?'' instead of saying directly ''I advise you to . . . run away?''[22]

This statement of the governing standard of conduct was *obiter dictum* in the context of the case decided because the attorney/defendant had openly advised a fraudulent course of action. Nonetheless, the statement is quoted in the commentary to the Proposed Model Rules of Professional Conduct of the ABA to support an interpretation of the ABA *Code* that would mandate counsel to avoid indirectly facilitating a client's illegal behavior.[23] In the same commentary, however, competing propositions are also set out. They state that the ''standard does not impose a general duty to investigate the client's purposes''[24] and that ''a lawyer does not violate this standard by giving advice on a doubtful question concerning conduct later found to be criminal.''[25] Taken together, the existing rule and the cases interpreting it give an attorney little concrete sense of what is meant by *knowing* facilitation and what behavior is meant to be prohibited.

The question can be stated in another way: Is the attorney to be held responsible only for words and actions that explicitly constitute advice or assistance in illegal conduct, or must the attorney be held to a standard that imputes to him knowledge of the reasonably foreseeable actions of a client? Or, as a third possibility, is some intermediate standard—what is called in the criminal law willful blindness or conscious avoidance—to apply to the attorney? The third standard attributes to the attorney only consequences that are more than *reasonably* foreseeable but not merely those that are explicitly advised.[26]

This question is open to debate on the part of the legal profession.[27] What is not open to debate, and this must be one of the major conclusions of this research, is that defense attorneys have adopted a role in representing clients that excuses them from knowledge of the causal connection between what they say and what their clients do, where the clients' actions are not more than a reasonable possibility. While the attorney often knows that his client, after meeting with him, is going to illegally alter or conceal a document, he does not have ''legal knowledge'' of a causal connection between the counsel provided and the client's action. The attorney is morally knowledgeable, which may disturb him, but he is instrumentally ignorant.

Very rarely did clients of attorneys studied make explicit disclosure of a fraud committed on an adversary or court in order to conceal evidence of the crime being investigated. This is information the attorneys tried not to receive because knowledge of it inevitably would complicate their defense. Even though they could make reasonable conclusions about a client's illegal concealment, they rarely were called upon to respond directly to the situation of illegal conduct because either their clients were intelligent enough not to disclose it or they had been skillful enough to control the client's disclosures. The reasonable conclusions about clients were sometimes talked about by attorneys in jest—''After what we have said, he's savvy enough to get rid of his diary''—but never did they entertain the notion that they could be held legally responsible for the client's actions: ''What the client does is the client's business.''

The high value placed by attorneys on their freedom to act in support of their clients' cause and their ambivalence about restrictions by ethical prohibitions accounts for the high degree of ambiguity in the current rules. Ambiguity serves many purposes in many contexts. It allows a person to take a position or make a statement which can be interpreted differently by different audiences. As such it neutralizes conflict. It also allows a person to cover his true motives, such as in a social setting where ambiguous statements protect the hearer from insult or embarrassment. The ambiguity in the legal profession's ethical rules relating to information control serves the purpose of allowing simultaneous pursuit of conflicting goals, putting some restrictive sanctions on attorneys while allowing them to fulfill a mandate to act zealously in the interest of their clients.

But this ambiguity must also be interpreted in the light of a companion rule of the ABA *Code*: the attorney is told to resolve doubt in favor of his client. Practically what this means is that when a statute or a rule creates an ambiguous standard of conduct, the attorney is mandated to strain toward maximizing his client's position in regard to that rule. If there is a question about whether an ambiguous tax law works for or against a client, the attorney is mandated to resolve that doubt, within the margin of ambiguity, on the side that supports the client. And if there is a question about whether defense strategy constitutes obstruction of justice, the attorney is similarly mandated to resolve doubt on the side of what works best for the client.[28]

One response to what I have described could be a rule requiring that attorneys take responsibility for all the *reasonably foreseeable* actions of their clients. Such a rule would make an attorney responsible for the client's fraudulent actions that followed on counsel received from the attorney, when the attorney could have concluded that the client was reasonably likely to act in that way. But there are major problems in such a rule. One can ask whether every client would not fall within this category. Is it not always reasonably foreseeable that a person who learns that a document he holds will result in his going to prison may destroy it rather than turn it over to a government prosecutor? If it is not always reasonably foreseeable, how is an attorney to distinguish the clients to whom this does apply from those to whom it does not? Can an attorney be saddled with this responsibility and still give legitimate and effective advice?

If the answers to these questions lead one to the conclusion that a standard of reasonable foreseeability is inappropriate, there is a much stronger argument for promulgating an intermediate standard of responsibility, which would define ''advising the client to do an illegal act'' as applying in situations where the client has made obvious to the attorney (that is, more than reasonably foreseeable) the likelihood of illegal action. This rule removes much of the stultifying effect on legal counsel associated with the stricter rule, while mandating the attorney to evaluate his client's intentions and to prevent, on proper forewarning, the client's misuse of legal counsel.

If an intermediate standard does or should apply, then this standard must be spelled out by specific legislation. The existing ambiguity in the ABA *Code* promotes a situation in which even the well-intentioned attorney falters in pursuing effective self-regulation. On the one hand, he properly feels compelled to provide every legitimate advantage to his client. That, after all, is what the client is paying for. On the other hand, he also feels compelled not to exceed the margin of proscribed conduct. In attempting to find the proper dividing line, the well-intentioned attorney is ineffectively guided, the wavering attorney is ineffectively warned, and the cynical, devious attorney is provided with excuses. There is, then, a pressing need for greater rule specificity.

In prescribing this remedy, however, it must be recognized and emphasized that the organized bar is hostile to any upgrading of the attorney's responsibility of the kind I have described. It may be merely a pipe dream to conjure up various possible new rules. The opposition of the bar to this type of reform has been demonstrated repeatedly in recent years.[29] But even if a change of this type were possible, there lies as an obstacle to real change a more vexing problem. There really is no way of knowing what transpires when a client and attorney conduct secret meetings. The view that I have been able to offer of attorney-client meetings goes well beyond that which is provided to any official body that might be able to mete out disciplinary sanctions. We are forced to accept that although we may be able to draft a disciplinary rule, and its effect may be significant on certain sectors of the bar, it is likely not to change the ingrained behavior of another large sector of the bar. Members of that sector will continue with conduct that will then be prohibited, not only because they have become accustomed to it, but because it is unlikely to be discovered.

The answer to the problem of inappropriate information control in white-collar crime prosecutions may lie not in changing the role of the defense attorney in the adversary system, but in changing procedural advantages between prosecution and defense in white-collar cases.

Expanding Government Investigatory Authority

One of the main weaknesses of the government position in investigating and prosecuting white-collar crime is created by the attorney's effect on the pool of evidence. After the attorney gets involved, evidence that might have been easily accessible and even voluntarily or unknowingly turned over to the government becomes inaccessible. Disregarding the question of whether attorneys conduct themselves properly, what we see is that the result of legal counsel is often concealment of inculpatory evidence.

If in some imaginary system the effect of legal counsel could be eliminated, it might be found that white-collar crime is more easily detectable and provable than street crime. White-collar crime may create evidence sources that are more difficult to control than evidence sources created by street crime, for example, documents in a standard file that simply cannot be destroyed because their destruction would be too obvious. Information may also be more difficult to control in the context of middle-class and elite social values, where witnesses cannot be threatened or killed. But this comparative hypothesis is speculative and, moreover, less important than the independently valid proposition that the defense attorney has a critical effect on information availability in white-collar cases. It is this effect, and not the question of whether the attorney has an improper causal role, that concerns us here.

This leads to the second major policy question: are overbroad information control opportunities created by an inappropriate concept of acceptable government investigatory procedures in white-collar cases? The cases studied here were as much characterized by distinctive tools of government investigation as by distinctive tools of defense. Unlike street crime cases, the government used *unintrusive* methods of information acquisition: subpoenas, summonses, and interviews in noncustodial circumstances.[30] The critical feature of the first two devices is that they request the target to hand over information and allow for substantial time between the request and the requirement of response, rather than using search-and-seizure methods. The critical feature of noncustodial interview is that the information request is made in relatively uncompelling circumstances.

One must ask whether it is improper that investigations of white-collar crime be carried out almost exclusively with unintrusive methods of investigation. In cases of street crime, search and seizure and custodial interviewing is the norm. My findings suggest that government investigators sometimes refrain from using search warrants where they have a legal basis. This pattern can be changed administratively. But a larger part of the difference in investigation method is a reflection of Constitutional rules. The rules of probable cause make search and seizure dependent on prima facie evidence and prior close specification of the object searched for. Current Constitutional rules directly result in both the limited use of intrusive investigative methods in white-collar cases and their widespread use in street-crime cases.

Are these rules with all their restrictive implications for investigating and prosecuting the kinds of crimes described here necessary features of our criminal justice system? Even rules rooted in Constitutional doctrine do change, and the question is whether a change is not called for—expanding, in closely measured fashion, the opportunities to use search and seizure in the context of white-collar investigations. When the public interest is inexorably bound up in the affairs of corporations, should not the agencies mandated to protect the public be able to assert quick and complete access to the instruments of corporate actions?

The use of the subpoena for documents, the summons for documents, and the grand jury and administrative interview are expressions in the American legal system of the high value given to the individual's right to privacy and freedom from government oppression. These values are central to the large degree of autonomy granted to the individual and the great distrust of official power. Any change in these rules therefore touches on the very heart of the social structure and should be countenanced only with great caution. Notwithstanding this cautionary warning, more intrusiveness into the realm of the corporate entity and the workplace may be justified by the high cost to society of crime that is covered up in these places. Certainly an examination of the costs to privacy and the benefit to law enforcement should be undertaken, and due attention should be given to the investigative procedures of other countries where search and seizure play a greater role in white-collar crime law enforcement, apparently without undermining individual rights and the democratic character of the society.[31] In this way, a remedy may be found for the implications of extensive information control found in white-collar crime cases, without altering the high value of the counselor role held by the defense attorney in the American adversary process.

Appendix 1 Persons and Entities Prosecuted by Offense Type, Southern District of New York, 1974–78

All cases prosecuted in the Southern District of New York during the period 1974–78 were classified using the description of the offense on the court docket sheet, rather than the statute section (unless there was no offense description). Using this procedure, I was able to obtain a detailed breakdown of cases. This is presented in the table that follows.

Persons and Entities Prosecuted by Offense Type

Offense type	*(N)*	%
Common crime		
Violent crime	(824)	10.6
Theft crime	(812)	10.5
Forgery and counterfeiting	(912)	11.8
Illegal transport of property	(205)	2.6
Contraband	(2329)	30.1
Gambling	(43)	.6
Subtotal	(5125)	66.2
White-collar crime		
Securities fraud	(291)	3.8
Tax fraud	(293)	3.8
Embezzlement by officer	(14)	.2
Corruption	(243)	3.1
Conspiracy to defraud	(41)	.5
Criminal regulatory	(119)	1.5
Antitrust	(42)	.5
Bankruptcy fraud	(6)	.1
Subtotal	(1049)	13.5
Failure to file tax return	(70)	.9
Mail fraud	(248)	3.2
False statement	(472)	6.1
Embezzlement by employee	(471)	6.1
Other fraud	(25)	.3
Subtotal	(1286)	16.6
Total white-collar crime	(2335)	30.2
Immigration	(76)	1.0
Collateral	(123)	1.6
Miscellaneous	(80)	1.0
Total identified	(7739)	100
Total population	(8248)	
Missing information	(509)	6.2

Appendix 2 Attorneys Identified as Specialists in White-Collar Crime Defense

Attorneys Identified as Specialists
by Ten or More Respondents to Mail Survey

Stanley Arkin
Louis Bender
Roy Cohn
Harold Price Fahringer
Peter Fleming
Milton Gould
Robert Kasanoff
Boris Kostelanetz
James LaRossa
Andrew Lawler
John Martin
Robert Morvillo
Gary Naftalis
Gus Newman
Otto Obermaier
Norman Ostrow
Jules Ritholz
Marvin Segal
Charles Stillman
Pat Wall

Number of Times Specialists Were Identified by Survey Respondents

Number of respondents	*Number of specialists identified*
49	1
33	1
31	1
28	1
26	1
22	1
20	2
15	1
14	3
13	1
12	1
11	2
10	4
9	3
8	1
7	3
6	1
5	2
4	5
3	13
2	29
1	107
Total	184

Number of Specialists Identified per Questionnaire

Number of specialists identified	*Number of respondents*	
	(N)	*%*
1	(11)	8.7
2	(15)	11.8
3	(21)	16.5
4	(17)	16.5
5	(8)	6.3
6	(8)	6.8
7	(4)	3.1
8	(4)	3.1
9	(7)	5.5
10	(25)	19.7
11	(5)	4.0
12	(2)	1.6
Total	(127)	100

Appendix 3 Note on Attorneys Practicing Criminal Law in New York City

In 1979, the Martindale-Hubbell *Law Directory* listed roughly 35,000 attorneys practicing in Manhattan and the Bronx, with 838 listed law firms, of which 13 had more than 100 attorneys and 55 more than 50 attorneys. How many attorneys handle criminal cases in New York City is difficult to estimate, but it is clearly a small minority of the bar. Only 58 firms, all but 2 with fewer than 10 attorneys, were listed in 1978 as practicing in the field of criminal law. Of the approximately 11,000 attorneys who were listed as associated with firms in 1978, only 202 attorneys, or less than 4 percent, were associated with firms who advertised that they handled criminal work. This underestimates the number of attorneys practicing criminal law in a formally organized multiattorney context. Jerome Carlin estimated in 1960 that approximately 65 percent of the total licensed members of the bar in New York City were in private practice. That was about 17,000 attorneys, and he calculated on the basis of research findings that 1 percent were practitioners of criminal law, meaning that they derived their largest source of income from criminal cases. If the proportion of attorneys practicing criminal law is similar to what it was twenty years ago (the only available assumption due to the absence in the interim of any additional broad-based survey research), there were roughly 350 private practitioners in New York City during the research period who met Carlin's definition of "main area of practice." This number again underestimates the proportion of the bar handling criminal cases because many of the attorneys appearing on the criminal docket derive their largest portion of income from noncriminal cases. While the geographic setting of the research was New York City, the research population was attorneys handling cases of white-collar crime in the federal district court of the Southern District of New York. Thus the universe of research subjects was a subset of all attorneys in New York City doing criminal cases. My examination of court records shows that in the five-year sample period (1974–78) there were 686 attorneys who handled all *prosecuted* criminal cases of white-collar crime in the federal district court of the Southern District of New York. Since many of these attorneys handled only one case or a few cases, the number of practitioners who could be said to have a criminal practice in which white-collar cases constituted a significant portion was tiny relative to the total population of attorneys in New York City.

Appendix 4 Attorneys Identified as Specialists in White-Collar Crime Defense by Specialists in Snowball Reference Procedure, and Demographic Background Characteristics

Attorneys Identified as Specialists

Elkan Abramowitz
Irving Anolik
Stanley Arkin
Michael Armstrong
Harold Baer, Jr.
Louis Bender
David M. Brodsky
Edward Brodsky
Roy Cohn
Paul Curran
Doug Eaton
Maurice Edelbaum
Sheldon Elsen
Gerald A. Feffer
Lawrence S. Feld
Robert B. Fiske
Thomas J. Fitzpatrick
Peter Fleming, Jr.
Milton Gould
Paul R. Grand
John M. Gross
Rudolph W. Guiliani
Walter J. Higgins
Neal J. Hurwitz
Robert Kasanoff
Barry Kingham
Boris Kostelanetz
James LaRossa
Andrew Lawler
Peter K. Leisure
Arthur Liman
Jerome Londin
Martin London
Andrew Maloney
Joseph J. Marcheso
John S. Martin, Jr.
Andrew T. McEvoy
Robert G. Morvillo
Michael Mukasey
Gary Naftalis
Gus Newman
Otto G. Obermaier
Norman Ostrow
Henry M. Putzel, III
Simon H. Rifkind
Jules Ritholz
Paul K. Rooney
Jonathan I. Rosner
Marvin Segal
Gerald Shargel
Edward M. Shaw
John E. Sprizzo
Charles Stillman
John T. Tigue
Jay Topkis
Harold R. Tyler
Arthur Viviani
Pat Wall
Gerald Walpin
John R. Wing

Year Admitted to Bar

Year	*Number of attorneys*
1920–29	1
1930–39	4
1940–49	2
1950–59	19
1960–69	33
1970–79	1

Law School Attended

School	*Number of attorneys*
Harvard University	10
Columbia University	10
New York University	9
Yale University	8
Fordham University	6
St. John's University	4
University of Virginia	3
George Washington University	2
University of Chicago	2
Cornell University	1
Georgetown University	1
University of Michigan	1
Brooklyn Law School	1
Cambridge University	1
Notre Dame University	1

Number of Attorneys in Firm

Number of attorneys	*Number of firms*
80+	12
20–50	11
2–15	28
1	9

Appendix 5 Background Data on Total Interview Population

Career Experience Providing Training in Criminal Law for Interview Population

Former position	*Attorneys (N)*	*%*
Assistant U.S. Attorney	(18)	40.9
Assistant District Attorney	(3)	6.9
Legal aid or public defender	(1)	2.3
Private practice	(20)	45.5
Internal Revenue Service	(2)	4.6
Total	(44)	100

Size of Firm in Interview Population

Size of firm	*Attorneys (N)*	*%*
100+	(5)	11.4
50–99	(3)	6.8
20–49	(3)	6.8
10–19	(9)	20.5
5–9	(5)	11.4
2–4	(10)	22.7
1	(9)	20.5
Total	(44)	100

Law Schools Attended by Interview Population

School	*Attorneys (N)*	*%*
Brooklyn Law School	(5)	11.4
Columbia University	(3)	6.8
Cornell University	(2)	4.6
Fordham University	(3)	6.8
Harvard University	(6)	13.6
New York University	(10)	22.7
St. John's University	(2)	4.6
University of Chicago	(2)	4.6
Yale University	(5)	11.4
Other	(6)	13.6
Total	(44)	100

Notes

Chapter 1

1. See Peter J. Sheridan, ''White-Collar Crime Costs Business $40 Billion a Year.'' *Occupational Hazards* 38:41–44 (June 1978); Chamber of Commerce of the United States; *A Handbook on White Collar Crime: Everyone's Loss* (Washington, D.C., 1974); August Bequai, *White-Collar Crime: A 20th Century Crisis* (Lexington, Mass.: Lexington Books, 1978).

2. This statement requires that a broad concept of the criminal justice system be adopted. In the broad sense, a person enters the criminal justice system when he or she becomes the target of any government process in which consideration of criminal prosecution is a motivating factor in the government action. The initiation of an investigation by government field personnel—enforcement investigators of the IRS, SEC, FTC, and other similar officers—puts the target of the investigation into the criminal process. Criminal justice textbooks usually do not deal with this early investigative stage and thus exclude part of the criminal process.

When a target of an investigation recruits an attorney early in the government investigation, a full-blown adversary procedure commences. It was impossible to obtain an overall quantitative estimate of the percentage of criminal cases closed after defense attorney intervention but before indictment or information was issued. But a glimpse of how this might be measured was obtained through an FOIA request made to the Manhattan District Office of the criminal investigation division of the IRS (that district being the geographic location of this research). In that request, I asked, ''Of the number of criminal investigations opened in Manhattan, what percentage of cases led to the issuance of criminal charges by the Department of Justice or U.S. Attorneys' offices?'' The following data were received:

Fiscal year	*Cases initiated*	*Prosecution recommended*	*Percentage recommended of initiated (%)*	*Returned by counsel*
1974	347	184	53	not available
1975	419	161	38	not available
1976	410	215	52	not available
1977	271	212	78	17
1978	292	159	54	21

(Letter from Robert S. Carroll, Disclosure Officer, Internal Revenue Office, District Director, New York, April 16, 1980. On file, Yale Law School.) These data do not actually show on an annual basis what percentage of the cases initiated led to a recommendation for prosecution, because some cases are opened in one year and the decision to prosecute or close is made in another. Still, the large difference between the number of cases initiated and the number prosecuted is convincing evidence that a very substantial number of the cases opened are closed prior to the issuance of a criminal charge. During the five-year period reported here, the number of cases recommended for prosecution was 53 percent of the number of cases in which criminal investigations were initiated. Evidence supporting the assumption that in some of these cases defense attorneys were instrumental in a decision to close the case comes from the attorneys studied here. All of them practice in Manhattan and most claimed to have represented during those years clients in tax fraud investigations whose cases were closed prior to the issuance of a criminal charge. If one considers the criminal process as starting with investigation, then the number of criminal cases closed prior to charge may represent a greater proportion of the total caseload of the criminal process than has previously been recognized.

3. Studies of defense attorneys at work have focused almost exclusively on their handling of cases in the plea negotiation context. See Abraham S. Blumberg, *Criminal Justice* (Chicago: Quadrangle, 1967); Jonathan Casper, *American Criminal Justice: The Defendant's Perspective* (Englewood Cliffs, N.J.: Prentice-Hall, 1972); Albert W. Alschuler, "The Defense Attoney's Role in Plea Bargaining," *Yale Law Journal* 84 (1975): 1179; Milton Heumann, *Plea Bargaining: The Experiences of Prosecutors, Judges and Defense Attorneys* (Chicago: Univ. of Chicago Press, 1978); Arthur I. Rosett and Donald R. Cressey, *Justice by Consent: Plea Bargains in the American Courthouse*? (Philadelphia: Lippincott, 1976); Jackson B. Battle, "In Search of the Adversary System: The Cooperative Practices of Private Criminal Attorneys," *Texas Law Review* 50 (1971): 60; Jerome Skolnick, "Social Control in the Adversary System," *Journal of Conflict Resolution* 11 (1967): 52. Other studies of defense attorneys have reported mainly demographic data and questionnaire responses but none has concentrated on describing what defense attorneys actually do in handling a case other than plea bargain. See Paul Wice, *Criminal Lawyers: An Endangered Species* (Beverly Hills, Calif.: Sage, 1978); Arthur Louis Wood, *The Criminal Lawyer* (New Haven: College and University Press Services, 1967); Jerome Carlin, *Lawyers' Ethics: A Study of the New York City Bar* (New York: Russell Sage Foundation, 1966). These latter studies have presented statistical data on practice settings and opinions of attorneys about situations they meet in their practice. This is substantially different from the perspective adopted here, the aim of which is to describe what attorneys do as opposed to who they are and what they say they do.

4. In a slim but rich volume, M. A. P. Willmer developed a broad analytic scheme for describing the conflict between police and criminal in terms of information control. He writes, "With [the] concept in mind of the criminal as emitter [of a signal] and the police as receivers and interpreters of information, I shall show that, in the above situation, the conflict between the criminal and the police can be regarded as a battle over information" (*Crime and Information Theory* [Edinburgh: Edinburgh Univ. Press, 1970], p. 8). I look exclusively at the role of the attorney in preventing emission of signals.

The concept of information control is also found in the theory of organizations and is employed in a manner analogous to that used by Willmer. Managers of organizations conceal information in order to protect the interests of the organization. See Jeffrey Pfeffer and Gerald R. Salancik, *The External Control of Organizations: A Resource Dependence Perspective* (New York: Harper and Row, 1978). They write, "Information control, then, is an important mechanism for both the exercise and the avoidance of influence . . . . What information is available about organizational actions is the outcome of a political process in which social actors, each trying to advance his interests, attempt to acquire or withhold information as it serves their position in the political struggle. While the public interest, confidentiality, and other claims are asserted in the contest over information availability, it must be remembered that these are arguments and, like all arguments, are used selectively to enhance the interests of those raising the argument" (p. 106).

A parallel concept is found on the level of personal relations. See Erving Goffman, *Stigma* (Englewood Cliffs, N.J.: Prentice-Hall, 1963). About personal identity he writes, "[When the individual's] differentness is not immediately apparent, and is not known beforehand (or at least known by him to be known to others), when in fact his is a discreditable, not a discredited person, then the second main possibility in his life is to be found. The issue is not that of managing tension generated during social contacts, *but rather of managing information about his failings*" (p. 42, emphasis added).

5. The term *adversarial* is used in law in at least two different senses. In the first, it connotes a manner of behavior on the part of a person; a person's disposition may be said to be adversarial when he or she is uncompromising or argumentative or tends purposely to act in a way that collides with another person's interests. In the second sense, it connotes a particular form of argument in which two parties have more or less equal opportunity to present their differing views on a subject before a decision is made. Adversarial information control is meant to draw on the latter, though it is also true that the defense attorney will act with an adversarial disposition, in the former sense. But what is distinctive about *adversarial* information control, as that term is used here, is that the parties, in theory, participate more or less on equal footing in the process of determining whether the information in question can be withheld or whether it must be turned over to the government. This is in contrast to managerial information control.

6. The term *managerial* is used here to connote the idea of an administrator controlling an organization. From an internal perspective, organizations are controlled through an administrative hierarchy in which the managers communicate to rank-and-file members how to act in order to further the best interests of the organization. Within the organization there is normally no need to justify one's actions to parties who have interests external to the organization. See Phillip Selznick, *The Organizational Weapon* (Glencoe, Ill.: Free Press, 1960). The defense attorney operates in an analogous context when he represents a client who is able to exercise control over a formal organization which is the context of the crime or over an informal organization made up of persons involved in the transactions under investigation by the government.

7. See, e.g., the review by Geoffrey C. Hazard, Jr., "Reflections on Four Studies of the Legal Profession," *Law and Society*, supplement to *Social Problems* (Summer 1965). One of his many trenchant comments in that piece concerned access: "The great difficulty with finding out in any detail what the Wall Street lawyers do, or any other lawyers for that matter, in fact do in their professional capacity is that they won't tell. This is of course because what they know is committed to them by their clients upon the understanding that it is confidential. In view of this obstacle, survey research technique simply doesn't work, except as a means of ascertaining personal miscellanea about the lawyers themselves" (p. 53). Principal studies of the legal profession include Carlin, *Lawyers' Ethics*, who took a representative sample of the New York City bar and used the survey method and hypotheticals to assess pressures on practitioners that lead to deviant behavior; Douglas E. Rosenthal, *Lawyer and Client: Who's in Charge*? (New York: Russell Sage Foundation, 1974), who describes exchange of information between client and attorney in personal injury claims; and Erwin Smigel, *The Wall Street Lawyer: Professional Organization Man*? (Bloomington: Indiana Univ. Press, 1964), who includes a chapter reporting what attorneys in large firms told the author about the work they do. A second group of studies focuses on more general features of the legal profession. See, e.g., Quintin Johnstone and Dan Hopson, Jr., *Lawyers and Their Work: An Analysis of the Legal Profession in the United States and England* (Indianapolis: Bobbs-Merrill, 1967), providing a general classification of the nature of attorneys' work; and Edward O. Laumann and Joseph P. Heinz, "The Legal Profession: Client Interests, Professional Roles, and Social Hierarchies," *Michigan Law Review* 76 (1978): 1111; "The Organization of Lawyers' Work: Size, Intensity and Co-Practice of the Fields of Law," *American Bar Foundation Research Journal* (1979): 217; "Specialization and Prestige in the Legal Profession: The Structure of Deference," *American Bar Foundation Research Journal* (1977): 155; *Chicago Lawyers: The Social Structure of the Bar* (New York: Russell Sage Foundation, 1982). The work of Laumann and Heinz is the most comprehensive examination of structural and organizational features of the legal profession, assessing, among other

things, the way the total pool of legal work is divided up among practitioners.

8. See Stanton Wheeler, "Trends and Problems in the Sociological Study of Crime," *Social Problems* 23 (1976): 525.

9. For a description of defense practices in street-crime cases, see Alschuler, "The Defense Attorney's Role"; Heumann, *Plea Bargaining*, and Malcolm Feeley, *The Process is the Punishment* (New York: Russell Sage Foundation, 1979).

10. Some of the most vivid descriptions of this fact appear in Blumberg, *Criminal Justice*, and Rosett and Cressey, *Justice by Consent*.

11. Heumann, *Plea Bargaining*, pp. 35–36.

12. Feeley, *The Process*, p. 28.

13. A great deal has been written about sentencing, but very little about what defense attorneys do to influence the process, aside from the impact defense attorneys have on sentences as a result of plea bargaining. Most of the research has focused either on statistical analyses of sentencing outcomes or on the judges' role in setting sentence. It would not be unfair to say that the role of the prosecutor and the defense attorney at the sentencing hearing after a plea bargain or after a conviction at trial has been almost trivialized. Probation officers have been given more attention and assumed to have a greater role in the sentencing process than representatives of the adversarial parties. Literature on sentencing gives the defense attorney and the prosecutor a decidedly insubstantial role in the sentencing process after conviction. See Robert O. Dawson, *Sentencing: The Decision as to Type, Length, and Conditions of Sentence* (Boston: Little Brown, 1969); Marvin Frankel, *Criminal Sentences: Law without Order* (New York: Hill and Wang, 1973); John Hagan and Ilene Hagel Bernstein, "The Sentence Bargaining of Upperworld and Underworld Crime in the Ten Federal District Courts," *Law and Society Review* 13 (1979): 467; John Hogarth, *Sentencing as a Human Process* (Toronto: Univ. of Toronto Press, 1971).

14. It is characteristic in cases of street and violent crime that plea negotiations take place in the period just prior to a scheduled trial and often in the corridor or the courtroom on the day of the trial. See Alschuler, "The Defense Attorney's Role."

15. See Jack Katz, "Legality and Equality: Plea Bargaining in the Prosecution of White-Collar and Common Crimes," *Law and Society Review* 13 (1979): 431.

16. See Ethical Consideration EC 7–1, "The duty of a lawyer, both to his client and to the legal system, is to represent his client zealously within the bounds of the law" and Ethical Consideration 7–39, "In the final analysis, proper functioning of the adversary system depends upon cooperation between lawyers and tribunals in utilizing procedures which will preserve the impartiality of tribunals and make their decisional processes prompt and just, without impinging upon the obligation of lawyers to represent their clients zealously within the framework of the law" (*Annotated Code of Professional Responsibility* [Chicago: American Bar Foundation, 1979]; all references hereinafter to ethical rules are taken from this volume).

17. The comment in the *Annotated Code of Professional Responsibility* says, "Canon 7 espouses an adversarial stance for the lawyer within the legal system. The lawyer's ethical role is to serve as the zealous champion of the cause of his or her client (EC 7–1). Serving as the client's advocate, the attorney must resolve doubts about the bounds of the law in favor of the client (EC 7–3, EC 7–4). In any situation in which the lawyer must draw upon professional expertise, the primary consideration of the lawyer must be the best interests of the client (EC 7–9). In general, the duty of the attorney to the legal system is seen as being coextensive with his or her duty to the client (EC 7–19)" (p. 281).

18. Disciplinary Rule 7–102(A)(3).

19. Disciplinary Rule 7–102(A)(5).

20. Disciplinary Rule 7–102(A)(7).
21. Disciplinary Rule 4–101(B)(1).
22. Disciplinary Rule 4–101(C)(3).
23. Disciplinary Rule 7–104(A)(2).
24. A more general perspective on information control as central to the process of deciding disputed cases is implied in the literature on civil litigation. See, e.g., "Developments in the Law of Discovery," *Harvard Law Review* 74 (1961): 950. The author writes, "A second purpose served by discovery is to bring about the disclosure and presentation at trial of all the relevant evidence. Permitting the parties to use discovery devices tends to ensure that all evidence will be unearthed and that concealment of relevant information and materials will be minimized" (p. 945). See also Note, "The Emerging Deterrence Orientation in the Imposition of Discovery Sanctions," *Harvard Law Review* 91 (1978): 1033 and Charles B. Renfew, "Discovery Sanctions: A Judicial Perspective," *California Law Review* 67 (1979): 264.

Chapter 2

1. See Edwin H. Sutherland, "White-Collar Criminality," *American Sociological Review* 5 (1940): 1–12.
2. See Jack Katz, "The Social Movement against White-Collar Crime," *Criminology Review Yearbook*, vol. 2, ed. Egon Bittner and Sheldon Messinger (Beverly Hills, Calif.: Sage, 1980).
3. See "Fighting White-Collar Crime," U.S. Attorney's Office, Southern District of New York, December 1972. One indication of nationwide change in prosecution policy is reflected in the increased number of indictments of public officials. In a report compiled by the Criminal Division, Public Integrity Section, U.S. Department of Justice, May 1979, there had been a 75 percent increase in the number of prosecutions of public officials. This is shown in the table below:

Year	*Persons indicted*
1970	63
1971	160
1972	208
1973	244
1974	291
1975	255
1976	337
1977	507
1978	557
Total:	2,622

(Press release, Department of Justice, May 3, 1979)

The SEC also reported a dramatic increase in the number of cases referred to the Department of Justice for prosecution.

Year	*Cases referred*	*Year*	*Cases referred*
1969	37	1974	67
1970	35	1975	88
1971	22	1976	116
1972	38	1977	100
1973	49	1978	109

4. In the 1960s presidential commissions were established for studying and recommending methods for reducing violent crime. The traffic in illegal drugs and drug-related crime occupied the public attention and was given the highest priority by law enforcement agencies. In additon, civil disorder prompted by the civil rights struggle, the Vietnam War, and other social causes substantially tapped law enforcement resources. See *The Challenge of Crime in a Free Society*, a report by the President's Commission on Law Enforcement and Administration of Justice (Washington, D.C.: Government Printing Office, 1967).

5. See Katz, "The Social Movement."

6. This trend was reflected sharply in the Department of Justice. In 1964 primary emphasis at the Department of Justice was on racketeering and indigent defendants (address by Attorney General Robert F. Kennedy to the Criminal Law Section of the American Bar Association, Americana Hotel, New York City, August 10, 1967). In 1972 street crime, antitrust, and narcotics were declared to be the primary targets ("Two Stings to Our Bow," remarks of Attorney General Richard G. Kleindienst at the Washington Press Club, Washington, D.C., June 13, 1972). In 1976 the assistant attorney general was able to say, "We are presently engaged in a concentrated effort to divert and apply substantial federal investigative and prosecutive resources to [narcotics and] . . . the massive depredations of 'white-collar crime' which imposes a huge hidden tax on the American citizen" ("The Federal Role in Law Enforcement"; address by Assistant Attorney General Richard L. Thornburgh, to the Annual Jaycee Week Banquet of the Hanover Jaycees, The Hill Tavern, Hanover, Penn., January 22, 1976). See also Victor Navasky, "A Famous Prosecutor Talks about Crime," *New York Times Magazine*, February 15, 1970.

7. See "Panel to Study Organized Crime," *New York Times,* July 29, 1983.

8. See *Federal Offenders in the United States Courts*, Administrative Office of the United States Courts (1982).

9. Annual Report of the United States Attorney, Southern District of New York, 1971 (on file, Yale Law School).

10. Annual Report of the United States Attorney, Southern District of New York, 1975 (on file, Yale Law School).

11. Annual Report of the United States Attorney, Southern District of New York, 1976 (on file, Yale Law School).

12. See "Corrupt Politics Spawns a New Kind of Lawyer," *Washington Post*, October 16, 1977: "Providing a legal defense for politicians charged with corruption is a booming field as federal prosecutors step up their attack on white-collar crimes"; and "Company Lawyers in Shadows at Seminar on Crime," *Washington Post*, October 16, 1977: "When the American Bar Association held a seminar this spring on white-collar crime, a small group of lawyers sat quietly in the back of the room taking copious notes . . . . They were, in fact, attorneys for large corporations who didn't want anyone to know they had an interest in white-collar crimes."

13. Attorneys from many jurisdictions also come to New York to hear the New York specialists lecture on defense and prosecution of white-collar crime. See Norman S. Ostrow, *White-Collar Crime* (New York: Practicing Law Institute, 1978), for a report on one such seminar.

14. The registraton of public offerings and disclosure requirements are regulated by the Securities Act of 1933, 15 U.S.C. §77(a)–77(aa) (1976). Trading on the national securities exchanges and in the over-the-counter markets of securities previously issued, and the registration of brokers and dealers, are regulated under the Securities Exchange Act of 1934, 15 U.S.C. §78(a)–§78(jj) (1976). For a review of the enforcement proceedings of the SEC, see Note, "The Securities and Exchange Commission: An Introduction to the

Enforcement of the Criminal Provisions of the Federal Securities Laws,'' *American Criminal Law Review* 17 (1979): 121.

15. See Appendix 1 for classification of all cases prosecuted in the district court of the Southern District of New York in the period 1974–78.

16. See Appendix 2 for a list of the names of the twenty most frequently identified white-collar crime defense specialists, as reflected in the mail survey, and a report of the total distribution of responses among all respondents to the mail survey.

17. See Appendix 3 for a note on the number of criminal practitioners in the New York City bar.

18. See Frederick F. Stephan and Philip J. McCarthy, *Sampling Opinion: An Analysis of Sampling Procedure* (New York: John Wiley and Sons, 1958): ''The selection by a group of judges or experts of typical . . . individuals is still and will continue to be a common form of sample selection. It aims to use what is known by the best-qualified persons in putting together a better sample than can be obtained without that knowledge. Undoubtedly there are many instances in which neglect of expert knowledge . . . will seriously weaken the sampling operation. Expert judgment has limitations in selections of samples, however, and even some biasing tendencies.'' Lack of representativeness is the main bias in judgment sampling. I designed the research to counteract this by conducting inquiries using two additional samples–one drawn randomly and the other drawn to diversify the respondents.

19. See Appendix 4 for names of the attorneys identified as specialists in white-collar crime defense by specialists in the snowball reference procedure and demographic background characteristics.

20. See Appendix 5 for background data on total interview population.

Chapter 3

1. For an analysis of the attorney-client exchange of information in personal injury claims, see Rosenthal, *Lawyer and Client,* and ''Control and the Lawyer-Client Relationship,'' *Journal of the Legal Profession* 6 (1981): 7–38.

2. An indictment or other public accusation is felt by many clients to be no less severe in the long run than a prison term. It may bring to an end a person's professional career or significantly affect further advancement. In some cases, professional licenses are revoked, in others family peace is undermined. As reported in separate research undertaken by this author in collaboration with Stanton Wheeler and Austin Sarat, federal judges said that they take into account in making sentencing decisions such presentence sanctions.

3. See Carlin, *Lawyers' Ethics*. He describes pressures that lower-status clients bring to bear on attorneys that facilitate ethical transgressions (chapter 4). Here the inverse dynamic is observed. When one attorney receives a client from another client who has a higher status, or whenever the client has a higher status by his own right, pressures are created that result in distinctive conforming behavior. For instance, one recurrent problem in some firms is how closely confidentiality is guarded. When a high-status client is present all papers are removed from desks and doors are always closed in order to maximize the impression of confidentiality. When lower-status clients are present desks are often strewn with papers and secretaries move in and out freely.

4. The phrase ''therapeutic approach'' is taken from the comment of one attorney who stated that his approach to meetings with clients was changed as a result of reading the work of Carl Rogers. He mentioned this in a tone of cynicism and then complained that

"some of my clients want their psyche treated as well as their legal problems." See Carl Rogers, *Client-Centered Therapy* (Boston: Houghton Mifflin, 1951).

Chapter 4

1. See 18 U.S.C.A. §201.
2. *United States v. Kovel*, 296 F.2d 918 (2d Cir. 1961).
3. See Pfeffer and Salancik, *The External Control of Organizations*, and Deborah A. DeMott, "Reweaving the Corporate Veil: Management Structure and the Control of Corporate Information," *Law and Contemporary Problems* 41 (1977): 182.
4. See, e.g., Note, "Disclosure of Payments to Foreign Government Official under the Securities Act," *Harvard Law Review* 89 (1976): 1848.
5. See Foreign Corrupt Practices Act of 1977, 22 U.S.C.A. §78a, et seq. (FCPA). This statute established broad new accounting procedures. Every issuer of a security is subject to detailed reporting requirements specified in the Securities Exchange Act of 1934, 15 U.S.C.A. §78m(b)(2).

In a program held by the City Bar Association of New York on the accounting provisions of the FCPA, June 19, 1979, Roger W. Kapp, a member of the firm of Donovan, Leisure, Newton, and Irvine, stated that the FCPA was enacted as a result of disclosure occurring in the Watergate investigation that showed widespread misuse of corporate funds. Eugene J. Minahan, Chairman of Internal Accounting Control of the American Institute of Certified Public Accountants, stated at that program that the accounting provisions of FCPA cover approximately 8,000 corporations, 75 percent of which have annual sales under $1 billion and 50 percent of which have annual sales under $25 million.

Chapter 5

1. The stage at which the defense attorney enters the investigation is of paramount importance. If a revenue agent is handling the case, the attorney has a basis for assuming that a decision has not yet been made to define the case as a criminal investigation. Many tax practitioners will handle a case as long as it is on the civil side. As soon as the case is referred to the criminal division, many tax practitioners feel that it is appropriate that a specialist in fraud or criminal cases be retained. On IRS investigative procedures, see George D. Crowley, "The Tax Fraud Investigation," *Journal of Criminal Defense* 1 (1975): 155.
2. Meetings between defense attorneys and investigators or prosecutors handling a case in an investigative capacity have come to be called "conferences." At the first meeting between an attorney and an investigator, discussions are usually limited to each party's attempt to get information from the other. The justification for the investigator meeting with the attorney is his need for information. At later stages in the investigatory process, conferences are directed more toward allowing the defense attorney to present argument. The nature of the latter conference is outlined in the *Manual for Criminal Tax Trials*, Tax Division, U.S. Department of Justice, July 1973:

> In the course of consideration of a tax case in the Department, a conference may be requested by the taxpayer's representative. See United States Attorneys' Manual, Title 4:4. A conference in the Tax Division is granted, of course, as a matter of grace, not of right. The purpose is to permit proposed defendants to present any explanations and evidence which may be considered helpful to the Department in reaching a proper decision on prosecution.

Conversely, a conference is not held to afford taxpayer's counsel an opportunity to explore the Government's evidence. The Department's practice is to advise conferees of the charges recommended by the Internal Revenue Service and to give the income and tax figures suggested for prosecution purposes with the admonition that both the charges and the computations are subject to whatever changes the Department deems proper. Beyond this, the Criminal Section attorney holding a conference may choose to discuss particular evidence only when he feels it will be helpful to the Government.

Absent unusually compelling circumstances, not more than one conference will be granted in the Tax Division in a particular case. If the case has been forwarded to the United States Attorney before a conference request is received, the request will be denied and the suggestion made that the taxpayer or his representative seek his conference with the United States Attorney. Whether, in such case, or in any case, the United States Attorney will grant a conference is usually left to be determined under the policy of his office.

3. Interviewees who were former prosecutors said that the most frequent mistake made by attorneys is "overcooperation" without having first arranged proper protections. Several accounts were given of targets who attempted to explain their way out of a situation and instead "dug themselves a hole that was impossible to climb out of." As one respondent said, "If we don't get the person on a substantive charge, then we get him on perjury—heads we win, tails you lose." But the situation is different, the respondents continued, when a competent defense attorney "controls what the client says."

4. Prosecutors are well aware of this problem. In their review of procedures used in the Watergate investigations, two federal prosecutors wrote,

> The prosecutors worked with some witnesses . . . first having an FBI agent interview them, later interviewing them in WSPF's offices, then questioning them under oath before a grand jury. . . . Any such contacts, in any investigation, involve a danger of letting the witness, particularly a hostile one, learn what the prosecutors already know and what more they want to find out. Thus a witness may obtain more information in an interview or grand jury appearance than he provides. If he is a potential defendant or wants to protect one, such information can help him fashion a version of the facts which will sidetrack the prosecutors' investigation without being so implausible as to raise suspicions. For example, in an office interview the prosecutors might ask a witness what had happened at a particular meeting he had attended. Realizing that they knew of that meeting, the witness could feign forgetfulness and avoid telling them anything of value. After the interview, he would be able to consult his records, and perhaps also consult others who had attended the same meeting, and concoct an account that would work to his or their advantage. *Watergate Special Prosecution Force: Report* (Washington, D.C.: Government Printing Office, 1975), p. 30.

5. This chapter looks at information *sharing* only. Chapter 8 discusses strategy coordination, in which a cooperating attorney takes an adversary position that appears to be based on the interests of a client of another attorney. Information sharing does not necessarily raise the ethical problems created by strategy coordination. The independent ethical question here is whether information passes between attorneys with or without the client's consent. The issue of consent is discussed in chapter 7.

6. Lack of exposure of evidence as evidence is a key characteristic in making investigation and prosecution of crime difficult. It therefore facilitates defense. For a discussion of this characteristic, see chapter 11.

Chapter 6

1. For discussion of ethical problems related to this conduct see chapter 11.
2. For discussion of ethical problems related to this conduct see chapter 11.
3. My use of the term *neutralization* draws directly from application of the term to delinquent subcultures by Gresham M. Sykes and David Matza. Sykes and Matza found that delinquents use the norms of the criminal law that express conditions of inapplicability of the substantive law to negate responsibility for their acts. They suggested that the criminal law is particularly prone to neutralization because its principles of inapplicability are clearly stated, as compared to moral precepts, whose conditions of inapplicability are more ambiguous. The findings here suggest a counterdynamic. The more the legal line between prohibited and permitted behavior is ambiguous, the more the potential offender will tend to justify his behavior by extending common notions of inapplicability. See Gresham M. Sykes and David Matza, "Techniques of Neutralization," *American Sociological Review* 22 (1957): 644–70.

Chapter 7

1. As soon as a civil revenue auditor determines that there is evidence of fraud, he must cease his work and refer the matter to the criminal investigation division. Thus there is a bifurcation of function in the IRS. Legal doctrine prohibits the IRS from using civil investigative techniques in cases in which a prima facie decision has been made that the IRS examination is pointed at possible criminal violations. See Boris Kostelanetz and Louis Bender, *Criminal Aspects of Tax Fraud Cases* (New York: American Law Institute, 1980), pp. 59 and 73–95.
2. The basic rules are that natural persons may invoke the privilege against self-incrimination but that corporations have no such privilege, and that a corporate executive may not invoke the personal privilege to refuse to produce corporate documents. *Grant v. United States*, 227 U.S. 74 (1913); *Wilson v. United States*, 221 U.S. 361 (1911); *Curico v. U.S.*, 354 U.S. 118 (1957). Ambiguity lies in determining whether documents relate to personal matters or corporate matters.
3. The "eleven questions" were published as part of the IRS *Manual Supplement* and were designed to elicit responses from corporate executives regarding how their corporation handled funds. For instance, question 7 asked:

> During the period from ——— to ———, did the corporation make any loans, donations, or other disbursements, directly, to corporate officers or employees or others for the purpose of reimbursing such corporate officers, employees, or others for contributions made, directly or indirectly, for the use or benefit of, or for the purpose of opposing, any government or subdivision thereof, political party, candidate or committee, either domestic or foreign?

See *Manual Supplement* 42G–313, August 5, 1974, and the commentary in *Report on the Internal Revenue Service Slush Fund Investigation*, New York State Bar Association, Tax Section, June 22,1976.

4. This is consistent with Canon 7 of the *Code of Professional Responsiblity*: "While serving as an advocate, a lawyer should resolve in favor of his client doubts as to the bounds of the law" (EC7–3).
5. Attorneys in each field of law develop a unique vocabulary based in part on their common assumptions about well-recognized rules in their own field. Defense attorneys make assumptions about information accessibilty. See, for instance, the assumptions set

out by Bart Schwartz, "Corporate Executives and Fifth Amendment," *National Law Journal*, October 1, 1979.

6. The point here was that an employee of a corporation asked about a conversation that the employee had with a person acting in the capacity of an attorney. Anyone acting in the capacity of an attorney for the corporation could invoke the attorney-client privilege to avoid disclosing the contents of the conversation. The scope of this privilege has engendered substantial controversy. Recently the Supreme Court upheld a broad interpretation of the coverage of the attorney-client privilege in the context of corporate counsel's representation of corporate employees. See L. S. Feld, "Supreme Court in Upjohn (101 S. Ct. 677) Protects Attorney-Client Privilege—Upholds the Work-Product Doctrine," *Journal of Taxation* 54 (April 1981): 201–14.

7. Federal district court has power to issue and duty to enforce grand jury subpoenas (F.R. Crim., p. 17) and administrative subpoenas. For the latter grant of authority see, e.g., 15 U.S.C.A. §77(v) giving district courts power to enforce subpoenas issued by the SEC.

Chapter 8

1. The literature on organizational control contains extensive discussion of how large organizations can be used to control their members. See, e.g., Michael Crozier, *The Bureaucratic Phenomenon* (Chicago: Univ. of Chicago Press, 1964); Rosabeth Moss Kanter, *Men and Women of the Corporation* (New York: Basic Books, 1977); Selznick, *The Organizational Weapon*. See also chapter 1, note 4, and chapter 11, note 2.

2. See Harvey L. Pitt, "Procedure to Limit Third-Party Disclosures," *National Law Journal*, January 22, 1979 (discussing ways to prevent such disclosure).

3. See Jack Katz, "Cover-up and Collective Integrity: On the Natural Antagonism of Authority Internal and External to Organizations," *Social Problems* 25 (1977): 3.

4. See, e.g., John Alan Appelman, "Techniques of Questioning," in *Cross Examination* (Fairfax, Va.: Coiner Publications, Ltd., 1963), p. 12; Howard Hilton Spellman, "Depositions," in *Direct Examination of Witnesses* (Englewood Cliffs, N.J.: Prentice-Hall, 1968); Lloyd Paul Striker, *The Art of Advocacy: A Plea for the Renaissance of the Trial Lawyer* (New York: Simon and Schuster, 1954); and F. Lee Bailey and Henry B. Rothblatt, *Investigation and Preparation of Criminal Cases* (Rochester, N.Y.: Lawyers Cooperative, 1970), chapter 4.

5. See Stanley L. Payne, *The Art of Asking Questions* (Princeton: Princeton Univ. Press, 1951): "In answer to hypothetical questions all the way from 'What would you do with a million dollars?' to 'What things would be most important to you in buying a refrigerator?' respondents are prone to give what might be thought of as 'normal' answers. These normal answers, while they sound all right and look reasonable enough, may not tie in with actual facts or behavior at all" (p. 198).

6. See *United States v. Fayer*, 523 F.2d 661 (2d Cir. 1975). See *United States v. Cioffi*, 493 F.2d 1111 (2d Cir. 1974) *cert. denied*, 419 U.S. 917, 95 S. Ct. 195 (1974).

7. See Nancy J. Moore, "Disqualification of an Attorney Representing Multiple Witnesses before a Grand Jury: Legal Ethics and the Stonewall Defense," *UCLA Law Review* 27 (1979): 63. See also A. S. Joslyn, "Corporations and Employees: Conflicting Interests and Choice of Counsel," *ABA Antitrust Law Journal* 46 (1977): 676; Peter W. Tague, "Multiple Representation of Targets and Witnesses during a Grand Jury Investigation," *American Criminal Law Review* 17 (1980):301, who wrote, "But any group of clients might benefit from united opposition to the government. If none cooperates . . . the

government may be unable to indict any client because no other credible sources possess enough admissible information.'' Tague found only sixteen reported decisions of motions for disqualifications.

8. Disciplinary Rule 5–105(c).

9. See *United States v. Fayer*, 525 F.2d 661 (2d Cir. 1975) (motive is corrupt when attorney aims at having client conceal his crime). Cf. *McNeal v. Hollowell*, 481 F.2d 1145 (5th Cir. 1973).

10. See *In re Taylor*, 567 F.2d 1183 (2d Cir. 1977); *In re Grand Jury Empaneled Jan. 21, 1975*, 536 F.2d 1009 (3d Cir. 1976).

11. See *In re Gropman*, 531 F.2d 262 (5th Cir. 1976); *In re Grand Jury Proceedings*, 428 F. Supp. 273, 278 (E.D. Mich. 1976).

12. 567 F.2d 1183.

13. 567 F.2d 1187.

14. 567 F.2d 1191.

15. See *In re Coordinated Pretrial Proceedings*, ETC 502 F.Supp. 1092 (D.C.C.D. Calif. 1980).

16. 502 F.Supp. 1096.

17. 502 F.Supp. 1097–98.

18. See, e.g., *Matter of Grand Jury Proceedings*, 428 F.Supp. 273 (E.D. Mich. S.D., 1976) (investigation of teamster's union; multiple repesentation of four witnesses gives rise to actual conflict; the full testimony in grand jury proceedings of one witness may be damaging to another witness, creating a conflict of loyalty in representation).

19. See discussion of how attorneys represent this position at sentencing hearings in chapter 10.

20. Disciplinary Rule 4–101(c).

21. Moore, ''Disqualification of an Attorney,'' n. 305.

22. See Comment, ''The Attorney-Client Privilege in Multiple Party Situations,'' *Columbia Journal of Law and Social Policy* 8 (1972): 179, 192–94; Note, ''Waiver of Attorney-Client Privilege in Inter-Attorney Exchange of Information,'' *Yale Law Journal* 63 (1954):1030.

23. *Continental Oil Co. v. U.S.*, 330 F.2d 347 (9th Cir. 1964).

24. 330 F.2d 350.

25. *United States v. McPartlin*, 595 F.2d 1321 (7th Cir. 1979).

26. 595 F.2d 1336.

27. Comment, ''The Attorney-Client Privilege in Multiple Party Situations,'' pp. 180–81.

Chapter 9

1. See Roberta S. Karmel, *Regulation by Prosecution: The Securities and Exchange Commission versus Corporate America* (New York: Simon and Schuster, 1982).

2. See *Criminal Tax Investigations, Conferences, and Prosecutions*, conference report, Program Chairman Cono Namorato (New York: Law and Business, Inc., Harcourt Brace Jovanovich, 1980).

3. See Samuel H. Gruenbaum and Martin A. Oppenheimer, ''Special Investigative Counsel: Conflicts and Roles,'' *Rutgers Law Journal* 33 (1981): 865.

4. *United States v. Amrep*, 560 F.2d 539 (2d Cir. 1977).

5. The brief was filed by Stanley Arkin, whose cooperation in providing me with a photocopy is greatly appreciated.

Chapter 10

1. See Donald J. Newman, *Conviction: The Determination of Guilt or Innocence without Trial* (Boston: Little Brown, 1966), and Robert O. Dawson, *Sentencing: The Decision as to Type, Length and Conditions of Sentence* (Boston: Little Brown, 1969).

2. See Hogarth, *Sentencing as a Human Process*.

3. The importance of ambiguity in the statute defining the offense is discussed more generally in chapter 11.

4. Attorneys are generally not quick to admit that substantive legal argument is used at sentencing, because it contradicts a competing assumption that at sentencing it is better to be contrite. It is, of course, difficult to deny guilt and be contrite at the same time. One specialist who wrote on white-collar crime sentencing states that "the most important point to impress upon the court is the defendant's contriteness." In practice, however, attorneys spend more time and effort on relitigating substantive responsibility. See John H. Doyle, III, "Sentencing and Postsentencing Remedies," in *White-Collar Crimes* (Philadelphia: American Law Institute, 1980), ed. Gary P. Naftalis.

5. See Wayne R. LaFave and Austin W. Scott, *Criminal Law* (St. Paul: West, 1972), p. 325 (evidence of an abnormal mental condition limited cases of murder).

6. Research reporting this finding was presented in Kenneth Mann, Stanton Wheeler, and Austin Sarat, "Sentencing the White-Collar Offender," *American Criminal Law Review* 17 (1980):4. For additional research on the sentencing practices of federal judges in white-collar cases, see Stanton Wheeler, David Weisburd, and Nancy Bode, "Sentencing the White-Collar Offender: Rhetoric and Reality," *American Sociological Review* 47 (1982): 641; and John Hagan and Eileen Nagel, "White-Collar Crime—White-Collar Time: The Sentencing of White-Collar Offenders in the Southern District of New York," *American Criminal Law Review* 20 (1982): 259.

7. In the context of the Yale project on white-collar crime, a study of federal district judges' sentencing practices was conducted. For a preliminary report see Mann, Wheeler, and Sarat, "Sentencing the White-Collar Offender."

8. See Newman, *Conviction*, and Dawson, *Sentencing*.

9. See Abraham S. Goldstein, *The Passive Judiciary: Prosecutorial Discretion and the Guilty Plea* (Baton Rouge: Louisiana State Univ. Press, 1981). For a description of the traditional role of the American judge, see Judith Resnik, "Managerial Judges," *Harvard Law Review* 96 (1982): 2.

10. See Dawson, *Sentencing*, p. 51: "Whatever devices were used for obtaining information . . . it gives the sentencing judge an opportunity to discuss the case with the police, prosecutor, defense attorney, and the defendant and to integrate these views with recommendations contained in the presentence report and psychiatric examination."

11. See Albert W. Alschuler, "The Trial Judge's Role in Plea Bargaining, Part I," *Columbia Law Review* 76 (1976): 1059; Note, "Judicial Sentence Bargaining in the Federal Courts," *Fordham Law Review* 48 (1980): 586.

Chapter 11

1. The predominance of plea bargaining in the research agendas of the academy has had a profound influence on more general theorizing about the operation of the criminal

justice system. Findings from empirical research have emphasized the dynamics in the criminal justice process that move counter to due process, emphasizing the move toward cooperation, bureaucratization, and other values that counter true adversary procedures. See Jerome Skolnick, *Justice without Trial: Law Enforcement in Democratic Society* (New York: John Wiley, 1966); Kenneth Culp David, *Discretionary Justice: A Preliminary Examination* (Urbana, Ill.: Univ. of Illinois Press, 1971); Judith Lachman and William McLauchlan, "Models of Plea Bargaining," in *Modeling the Criminal Justice System* (Beverly Hills, Calif.: Sage, 1977), ed. Stuart Nagel; Pamela Utz, *Settling the Facts: Discretion and Negotiation in Criminal Court* (Lexington, Mass.: Lexington, 1978). For a criticism of the bureaucratic perspective see Malcolm Feeley, "Two Models of the Criminal Justice System: An Organizational Perspective," *Law and Society Review* 7 (1973): 407 and *The Process is the Punishment*.

2. See Feeley, *The Process is the Punishment*, p. 27.

3. See Abraham Blumberg, "The Practice of Law as Confidence Game," *Law and Society Review* 1 (1967): 19–23.

4. Research has often stressed the overwhelming advantages held by the government. See Abraham S. Goldstein, "The State and the Accused: Balance of Advantage in Criminal Procedure," *Yale Law Journal* 69 (1960): 1149 (recent developments in criminal procedure "reflect entirely too little concern about the inherent inequality of litigating position between the expanding state and even the most resourceful individual" [p. 1199]). See Mirjan Damaska, "Evidentiary Barriers to Conviction and Two Models of Criminal Procedure," *University of Pennsylvania Law Review* 121 (1973): 506; Eleanor J. Ostrow, "The Case for Preplea Disclosure," *Yale Law Journal* 90 (1981): 1581 ("in the American criminal justice, the prosecutor has much greater access to the information available for conviction than does the defendant" [p. 1583]).

5. Here the defense attorney's role can be thought of in terms of boundary maintenance. See E. J. Miller and A. K. Rice, "The Boundary Control Function" in *Systems of Organization: The Control of Task and Sentiment Boundaries* (London: Tavistock, 1967): "An enterprise relates to its environment through a variety of import–conversion–export processes. . . .The boundary of a system of activities therefore implies both a discontinuity and the interpolation of a region of control" (pp. 5–9). See also Howard Aldrich, "Organizational Boundaries and Interorganizational Conflict," in *Organizational Systems: General Systems Approaches to Complex Organizations* (Homewood, Ill.: Richard D. Irwin, 1973), ed. Frank Baker. Aldrich describes two strategies available to organizations at the time of conflict to heighten the value of member participation. The first is clearly relevant to the defense function: "Organizational strategy in a situation of conflict may take the form of constricting the boundaries of the organization by strengthening the requirements of participation, with more being asked of each member in the way of conformity in organizational rules and ideology" (p. 388). And see Dean Champion, *The Sociology of Organizations* (New York: McGraw-Hill, 1975), chapter 8, "Communication in Formal Organizations."

6. The power of modern corporations to control information is far-reaching and complex in its effects. In proposing new principles for sanctioning of corporate entities, one author provided the following description in Note, "Structural Crime and Institutional Rehabilitation: A New Approach to Corporate Sentencing," *Yale Law Journal* 89 (1979): 353:

> Large companies have an inherent organizational complexity that tends to diffuse and to obscure individual responsibility for corporate actions. . . . The occurrence of structural crime [instances in which a corporation commits a criminal offense but no crimi-

> nally culpable individual can be identified] may reflect either of two underlying patterns. In one class of cases, no individual can be convicted because no one has acted or failed to act in such a manner that personal criminal liability is warranted. . . . In the second class of cases, no individual officials can be convicted despite elements of bad faith or intentional misconduct by some. If after diligent investigation by prosecutorial authorities the guilt of such individuals cannot be demonstrated, it must be the case that structural elements in the company have permitted culpable parties to shield their guilt [pp. 357–59].

See also Diane Vaughan, *Controlling Unlawful Organizational Behavior* (Chicago: Univ. of Chicago Press, 1983).

7. This quality of evidence has previously been suggested by Jack Katz. See Katz, "Legality and Equality."

8. For an explanation and review of IRS procedures see Boris Kostelanetz and Louis Bender, *Criminal Aspects of Tax Fraud Cases*; George Crowley, *Criminal Tax Fraud* (New York: Practicing Law Institute, 1976). For an official description of how conferences are supposed to be conducted, see Order 3040.1, "Prosecution Considerations and Responsibilities," Office of the Chief Counsel, Internal Revenue Service, August 29, 1979 (on file, Yale Law School).

9. See Stephen V. Wilson and A. Howard Matz, "Obtaining Evidence for Federal Economic Crime Prosecutions: An Overview and Analysis of Investigative Methods," *American Criminal Law Review* 14 (1977): 651.

10. 18 U.S.C.A. 3165.

11. See Kenneth Mann, "The Speedy Trial Planning Process," *Harvard Legislative Journal* 17 (1980): 54.

12. See Susan Shapiro, "Thinking about White-Collar Crime: Matters of Conceptualization and Research" (Washington, D.C.: National Institute of Justice, U.S. Department of Justice, 1980).

13. See Mirjan Damaska, "Evidentiary Barriers to Convictions." For an analysis of where the law permits attorneys to destroy evidence, see Note, "Legal Ethics and Destruction of Evidence," *Yale Law Journal* 88 (1979):1665.

14. Charles P. Curtis, *It's Your Law* (Cambridge: Harvard Univ. Press, 1954), and Martin P. Golding, "On the Adversary System and Justice," in *Philosophical Law* (Westport, Conn.: Greenwood, 1978), ed. Richard Bronaugh.

15. An enforcement order from a district court is needed before compliance can be compelled. See chapter 7, note 7.

16. See, generally, *Annotated Code of Professional Responsibility*.

17. See Disciplinary Rule 4–101(C)(3).

18. See Disciplinary Rule 7–102(B)(1).

19. See discussion of attorney's duty to disclose in *Model Rules of Professional Conduct* (Chicago: American Bar Association, Commission on Evaluation of Professional Standards, 1981).

20. See Disciplinary Rule 7–102(A)(1–8).

21. Marvin Frankel, "The Search for Truth: An Umpireal View," *University of Pennsylvania Law Review* 123 (1977): 1039. See also Marvin Frankel, *Partisan Justice* (New York: Hill and Wang, 1978).

22. *In re Bullowa*, 223 A.D. 593, 229 N.Y.S. 145, 154 (1928) as quoted in *Model Rules of Professional Conduct* (p. 21).

23. Ibid.

24. Ibid., p. 22.
25. Ibid.
26. The Model Penal Code, Section 2.02(7), states: "When knowledge of the existence of a particular fact is an element of an offense, such knowledge is established if a person is aware of a high probability of its existence, unless he actually believes that it does not exist" (Proposed Official Draft, 1962). The commentary to this section refers to British authors and what they label "wilful blindness" or "connivance." On the basis of both American and British authorities, Glanville Williams states: "To the requirement of actual knowledge there is one strictly limited exception. . . .The rule is that if a party has his suspicion aroused but then deliberately omits to make further enquiries, because he wishes to remain in ignorance, he is deemed to have knowledge" (*Criminal Law: The General Part*, § 57 at 157 (2nd ed., 1961). The standard of reasonable foreseeability, in the criminal context, has been criticized by courts: "A minority of jurisdictions apply the so-called objective test as to knowedge, being impressed, perhaps, by the difficulties of proof as to the actual state of a defendant's mind. . . . It appears to us that the minority jurisdictions . . . are failing to stress sufficiently the distinction between civil and criminal responsibility. In civil cases the failure of the defendant to act with the degree of care which a person of ordinary prudence would have used may be the test of his responsibility without any determination that the defendant, himself, was a person of ordinary prudence or that he had any wrongful intent. On the other hand, the very essence of this criminal offense is the intentional wrongdoing of the defendant. . . . The true test is, did the *defendant* know . . ." (*State v. Beale*, 299 A.2d 921 [Me. 1973]).
27. In the context where this question has been raised—perjury on the witness stand—commentators have offered two sharply contrasting views. The first holds that the defense attorney is obligated to provide his client with all information about the law without regard to what he thinks or knows about how the client intends to use the information. This viewpoint holds further that it is not the attorney's role in the adversary system to police the client and that the responsibility for perjury or any other obstructive behavior rests entirely with the client, as long as the attorney is only giving the client information about the law. If a client tells an attorney an incriminating story, it is permissible for the attorney to give the client information from which the client can conclude how to change his story in order to protect himself from criminal prosecution, even when the attorney knows that the client will so use the information. "To decide otherwise would not only penalize the less well-educated defendant but would also prejudice the client because of his initial truthfulness in telling his story in confidence to his attorney" (Monroe Freedman, "The Three Hardest Questions," *Michigan Law Review* 64 [1966]: 1469, 1482). See also Monroe Freedman, *Lawyers' Ethics in the Adversary System*, and Trevor Roper, *Anatomy of a Murder*. In Roper's well-known account, the defense attorney explained to his client, "If the facts are as you have stated them so far, you have no defense, and you will probably be electrocuted. On the other hand, if you acted in blind rage, there is a possibility of saving your life. Think it over, and we will talk about it tomorrow." The contrasting view about perjury holds that the attorney has an obligation to take account of his client's intentions and not provide legal advice where he reasonably suspects that the client will act on it in a way to subvert the truth. Persons who hold this position argue further that where the attorney has become aware of such an occurrence, he has an obligation to reveal it to a court or law enforcement agency. When an attorney already knows that the client is guilty but provides the client with information that the client can use to misrepresent testimony to his own benefit, under this view, according to John Noonan, "it becomes brute rationalization to claim that the legal advice tendered to a client is meant to contribute to wise and informed decision-making" (Noonan, "The Purposes of Advocacy," *Michigan Law*

Review 64 [1966]: 1488. See also Charles Wolpam, "Client Perjury," *Southern California Law Review* 50 (1977): 809, 843. For another critical view see Frankel, *Partisan Justice*: "Lawyers, trained and commissioned to seek justice, are engaged very often in helping to obstruct and divert the search for truth. More simply stated, the fact is that lawyers not infrequently help clients to lie" (p. 75).

28. See chapter 1, note 17.

29. When the ABA's policymaking House of Delegates considered the new Proposed Model Rules of Professional Conduct in February 1983, a major reform was gutted by amendments. Proposed Rule 1.6 would allow a lawyer to reveal information given by a client in confidence to the extent that this was done to prevent or rectify a criminal or fraudulent act. The American College of Trial Lawyers sponsored an amendment to this proposal that eliminated much of the new discretion proposed under the new rule. See *Criminal Law Reporter* 32 (1983): 2431 and *Criminal Law Reporter* 33 (1983): 2404.

30. Two federal prosecutors described the search authority available to government investigators this way: "Search warrants are generally less attractive and have therefore been utilized less in economic crime investigations than summonses or subpoenas. One reason is that, unlike a summons or subpoena which can be issued on an ex parte basis, a search warrant may be issued only by a judicial officer on a showing of probable cause" (Wilson and Matz, "Obtaining Evidence," p. 690). They found a sign of change, however, in the decision of the U.S. Supreme Court in *Andersen v. Maryland*, 427 U.S. 463 (1976). There a criminal investigation had been carried out on an alleged real estate scheme in which an attorney defrauded investors by stating falsely that property purchased was free of liens. A search warrant was obtained for documents and records located in the files of the development corporation managed by the suspect and included authorization to "search for fruits, instrumentalities, and evidence of crime at this [time] unknown." The Supreme Court held that the warrant in question defined with a sufficient degree of specificity the documents to be seized, complying with Constitutional standards prohibiting general warrants. The importance of this decision is in its apparent holding that if the crime is properly defined and there is probable cause to believe that the crime has been committed, the government need not provide a detailed list of the documents sought to be seized.

31. In Israel, investigative procedure allows for searches for evidence in all places that are not homes without a showing of probable cause. This is spelled out clearly, for instance, in the Tax Ordinance, Section 135. Thus all places of business are subject to physical searches without warning and without warrants.

Index